"Lavinia Ṭânculescu-Popa has skillfully explored and captured the internal territories of prominent Jungian analysts allowing us to connect and open ourselves to experience how eternally connected we all are. With co-editor Mark Winborn, *Beyond Persona* illustrates Jung's timeless ideas which are desperately in need of reconsideration in the face of contemporary life today."

—**Audrey Punnett**, *PhD, Jungian Child,*
Adolescent & Adult Analyst (IAAP)

"The interviews of Dr. Ṭânculescu-Popa are like bright gems, each with their own colour and texture. This extraordinary collection of biographies illuminates the rich cultural diversity of her Jungian colleagues."

—**John Hill**, *MA, Training Analyst,*
International School of Analytical Psychology, Zurich (ISAP)

"This volume offers a novel portrayal of three generations of Jungian analysts, contributing to a history of contemporary Jungians grounded in the personal rather than the theoretical. Through these stories, Lavinia Ṭânculescu-Popa and Mark Winborn gift us with their extraordinary effort to refashion how we know our colleagues, our lineage, and even ourselves."

—**Jeffrey Moulton Benevedes**,
PhD, Editor-in-Chief, Jung Journal: Culture & Psyche

Beyond Persona

This book presents intimate interviews with senior Jungian analysts and scholars from all over the world, providing unique insight into their childhoods, life experiences, and long careers in analytical psychology.

Each interview also focuses on uncovering the person beyond the professional *persona*. The interviewees are compelling, significant figures in analytical psychology. Their stories interact with significant events and time periods in world history: stories which are interwoven with World War I, World War II, the Korean War, the Arab Israeli wars, Vietnam, the counterculture movements of the 1960s, women's rights, fascism, communism, immigration, spirituality, slavery, racism, trauma, sexual orientation, and poverty, as well as many other themes. The scope of the lives captured in this volume is moving and inspiring.

Beyond Persona provides unprecedented access to leaders of the field and will be an inspiring read for psychologists and students of depth psychology and Jungian analysis and those wishing to follow in their footsteps.

Lavinia Țânculescu-Popa, PhD, is one of the first six IAAP Jungian analysts in Romania. She was one of the three Romanian translators for the *Handbook of Analytical Psychology* (Renos Papadopoulos, ed.). She is the president of the Romanian Society of Jungian Analysis (SRAJ) and the translator for the Romanian edition of *Interpretation in Jungian Analysis: Art and Technique* by Mark Winborn. Her research interests are in psychological anthropology, psychology and religion, and the unfolding of the Self in both personal and organizational life.

Mark Winborn, PhD, is a Jungian psychoanalyst and psychologist. Dr. Winborn is a training/supervising analyst of the Inter-Regional Society of Jungian Analysts and the C.G. Jung Institute in Zurich, Switzerland. His publications include three books, *Deep Blues: Human Soundscapes for the Archetypal Journey*, *Shared Realities: Participation Mystique and Beyond*, and *Interpretation in Jungian Analysis: Art and Technique*, as well as numerous book chapters and articles.

Beyond Persona

On Individuation and Beginnings with Jungian Analysts

Interviews by Lavinia Țânculescu-Popa

Edited by Lavinia Țânculescu-Popa and Mark Winborn

Routledge
Taylor & Francis Group
LONDON AND NEW YORK

Designed cover image: Yuri Arcurs as rendered on Getty Images
as the user who created this image. Courtesy of Getty Images.

First published 2023
by Routledge
4 Park Square, Milton Park, Abingdon, Oxon OX14 4RN

and by Routledge
605 Third Avenue, New York, NY 10158

*Routledge is an imprint of the Taylor & Francis Group, an informa
business*

© 2023 Lavinia Ţânculescu-Popa and Mark Winborn

British Library Cataloguing-in-Publication Data
A catalogue record for this book is available from the British
Library

Library of Congress Cataloging-in-Publication Data
Names: Ţânculescu, Lavinia, author. | Winborn, Mark, author.
Title: Beyond persona : interviews with Jungian analysts on
   individuation and beginnings / Lavinia Ţânculescu, Mark Winborn.
Description: Milton Park, Abingdon, Oxon ; New York, NY :
   Routledge, 2023. | Includes bibliographical references and index.
Identifiers: LCCN 2022046986 (print) | LCCN 2022046987 (ebook) |
   ISBN 9780367710118 (hardback) | ISBN 9780367710101
   (trade paperback) | ISBN 9781003148937 (ebook)
Subjects: LCSH: Jungian psychology. | Psychoanalysis.
Classification: LCC BF173 .T287 2023 (print) | LCC BF173 (ebook) |
   DDC 150.19/54—dc23/eng/20221011
LC record available at https://lccn.loc.gov/2022046986
LC ebook record available at https://lccn.loc.gov/2022046987

ISBN: 978-0-367-71011-8 (hbk)
ISBN: 978-0-367-71010-1 (pbk)
ISBN: 978-1-003-14893-7 (ebk)

DOI: 10.4324/9781003148937

Typeset in Times New Roman
by Apex CoVantage, LLC

For the people who inspired our lives

Contents

Foreword

Analytical psychology has continuously been dynamic and evolving, expressing its own individuation process. With an interdisciplinary path that incorporates other psychological theories and disciplines, our reflections about the individual and the collective, with the vicissitudes of cultural and contemporary challenges, are encouraged and welcomed. It is not simply an introverted psychology that works to transmute shadow and expand ego consciousness through the use of dreams, active imagination, or other imaginal content; it is also a psychology that encourages us to move in an extraverted fashion, to engage with collective issues. This intermingling of the individual with the collective reminds us that Jung expressly said we do not individuate alone. He instinctively knew that the collective waters in which we swim impact our individual psyches. At the same time, he maintained a fidelity to the unconscious, a tending to the individual psyche, as one of the most profound approaches that eventually impacts the consciousness of the collective.

Jung impressed upon us that evolution is an ongoing biological process within nature, thus highlighting the presence of individuation as a psychological pattern inherent in everyday life. Over the years, the unfolding of analytical psychology has revealed significant junctures where Jungian thought has made departures; while holding the origins of Jung's model of the psyche as a solid touchstone, there has been a contiguous process of reflection and stretching, an evolution of consciousness, that can only emerge by actively engaging the tension of the original and foundational with the inevitable exploration of the newly discovered and imagined.

Analytical psychology was naturally shaped by its intersections with contemporary psychiatric and psychosocial issues. Those early beginnings in Zurich and Küsnacht led to the formation of a compelling crucible for creative philosophical, psychological, and spiritual incubation. Jung's innovative work, with the image, spirit and matter, synchronicity, and collective unconscious, among other things, had a tremendous influence on the kaleidoscopic shifts in consciousness during the 20th century. Those who circled around him during the early seminars took their lived experiences and carried Jung's psychology from Zurich around the globe, from place to place, landscape to landscape. There was a sharing of the material of Jung's work via study seminars and lectures. Institutes took on specific aspects of Jung's philosophy, struggling with blind spots and engaging in unavoidable conflicts that arose through differences of opinions and natural human curiosities at the edges and outer bounds of psychic life. Individuals such as Marie Louise von Franz, Michael Fordham, Irene Champernowne, Erich Neumann, Beatrice Hinkle, James Hillman, and Wolfgang Giegerich are but a few examples of those who stretched further afield with either slight variations or distinct adaptations of Jung's initial model of the psyche. We recognize that healthy explorations, confrontations, and debates on the variations of theory, application, and training eventually give birth to new perspectives; this larger lens reveals the underlying individuation of analytical psychology itself.

If Jung were alive today, he might disagree or refrain from embracing every single turn and twist, but he might also agree that such changes cannot be avoided, as they each provide a stone towards the larger enterprise. He most likely would celebrate the expansion and inclusion of new psychological paradigms and disciplines, and in particular, express how grateful he was Jung and would never be a Jungian. Yet individuals may at times circumambulate back to wondering: What constitutes a *true* Jungian analyst? Is there even such a need or possibility when individuation is at the core of analytical psychology?

For Jungian analysts, the personal story often begins around midlife, a reflection of Jung's emphasis that at a certain age the ego has a confrontation with the unconscious, often after a major setback, followed by a dramatic turn in one's life circumstances. We are called to leave behind what was securely known and adopt a conscious willingness to engage with the *unknown*; that which has yet to become known. Behind the persona there is a personal story and an archetypal symbolic narrative, with its mixture of the rational and irrational, the wounds, marks and healing, the driving energy of a *daemon*, an inner genius, all of which pushes us into an individuation process that demands the acceptance of failure and defeat as much as new creative possibilities. The path of the wounded healer is unsuitable, and even incomprehensible, for many who are identified with the persona and find comfort in the conscious collective worlds. Yet for those who are captivated by the underworld of emotions and the imagination of analytical psychology, a messy but purposeful unfolding of differentiation and discernment ensues, a rigorous engagement with the unconscious. Unbeknownst to some, this shift is not just life-changing but life-giving.

In this collection of interviews with eighteen Jungian analysts, Lavinia Țânculescu-Popa and Mark Winborn seek the archetypal and the personal beginnings of their stories, their original experiences or impressions that provide clues about the forming of a pattern that eventually led them to Jungian psychology. What beckoned them and others to respond to the call, to take this journey? What experiences create a Jungian analyst? Certainly, we are not all cut from the same cloth, as the idiom suggests. So, how is it we come to C.G. Jung, analytical psychology, analytic training, and living our life as Jungians?

As Lavinia asks each analyst to recount some of their earliest unfettered memories of childhood with their specific patterns of time and place, we learn how the colored spools of life's threads eventually create a Jungian life, a landscape that includes the symbolic. In each interview, Lavinia invites the analysts to consider the dark and hidden threads that hang in the underworld. Her questions cut away any hint of a beautifully stitched persona or shared commonality of what it means to be a quintessential "Jungian." The remaining underlayers are personal insights and disclosures that acquaint us with multifaceted individuals who have responded to this calling. Each interview is a unique moment in time that echoes the analytic hour. While some threads of the interviews are left hanging and other threads are left undisturbed, Lavinia and Mark gather the more textured threads of the moment to bring shape and meaning to early memories, woven or stitched together in dynamic conversations, that are at times a kind of active imagination between two people.

What becomes recognizable are how the interests of Jungian analysts intersect, not just with Jung's ideas but also incorporating interdisciplinary paths that constellate the transcendent function personally as much as collectively. While the original stone remains an essential ingredient for analytical psychology, Jung's ideas are both timeless and in need of reconsideration in the face of pressing contemporary concerns and questions. The fact that analytical psychology is adaptable and undergoing its own individuation process is a testament to not just its agility, essential vitality, and timelessness but also the archetypal nature of the psychology itself.

The interviews venture beyond the edges of polite social expectations to catch the elusive energy of the moment, or a fleeting memory, so the invisible or half-hidden life breathes true, image by image, into one distinct version of the imperfectly lived lives that have been transformed. I'm reminded of *Mysterium Coniunctionis* where Jung writes:

> The state of *imperfect transformation*, merely hoped for and waited for, does not seem to be one of torment only, but of positive, if hidden happiness. It is the state of someone who, in his wanderings among the mazes of his psychic transformation, comes upon a secret happiness which reconciles him to his apparent loneliness. In communing with himself he finds not deadly boredom and melancholy but an inner partner; more than that, a relationship that seems like the happiness of a secret love, or like a hidden springtime, when the green seed sprouts from the barren earth, holding out the promise of future harvests.
>
> (Jung CW14, para 623, my emphasis)

Indeed, the widely wandering conversations contained in this collection illustrate an active search for a "hidden springtime," a communing until the "green seed sprouts," and serve as witness to the psychic transformations that have occurred. As readers, we are reminded that there is no distinct definition of what it means to "be a Jungian," as it is not a commercial brand that fixes the life of the analyst or those who come to do the work. Such a narrow focus is too ego-oriented. In a model of the psyche, where multiplicity and irrationality are valued for providing the sparks that change consciousness, there is also respect for psyche's innate capacity for wisdom and healing, veiled within the great mystery by which we are all stitched in together.

Jung privileged and respected the autonomous nature of the psyche, with its dark, conflictual, ephemeral, and numinous qualities, basing his early explorations on William James's notion of the transpersonal. If we are fortunate, the first imaginal expressions, with their archetypal roots, offer us the fabric that shapes a lifetime, with continued sustenance by way of dreams, visions, words, and images. And yet, the dynamic personal complexes that both challenge and nourish our psyche/soma states do not offer us prescriptions or guarantees of life, as Jung clearly explained in a letter dated December 15, 1933:

> Your questions are unanswerable because you want to know how one *ought* to live. One lives as one *can*. There is no single, definite way for the individual which is prescribed for him or would be the proper one. . . . But if you want to go your individual way, it is the way you make for yourself, which is never prescribed, which you do not know in advance, and which simply comes into being of itself when you put one foot in front of the other. If you always do the next thing that needs to be done, you will go most safely and sure-footedly along the path prescribed by your unconscious . . . if you do with conviction the next and most necessary thing, you are always doing something meaningful and intended by fate.
>
> (Jung 1973, *Letters I*, p. 132)

The fabric of my life began when I was conceived, after my mother had traumatically lost a baby at five months and was suffering from an unrecognized postpartum grief and depression. It was an unresolved story she could recall her whole life. As a replacement child, I imagine I was permeable in utero to my mother's prenatal fear and anxiety, and this absorption of emotions paradoxically inoculated me with an immunity for when, later in life, I focused my professional work on feminine issues of transition associated with loss, trauma, and perinatal concerns. My mother always said my arrival had soothed her grief and, because I was born just before Christmas, I had also rescued her from the season of expectations. With her particular early traumatic wounds and narcissistic needs, my relationship with her was burdened and complicated. Sometimes she was interested and encouraging, while other times she was preoccupied and emotionally cold.

Raised in the upper Midwest in the 1960s and 1970s, the changing seasons and social justice eruptions in the collective had a profound impact on the development of my psyche. In those days winter could last six months – with no need to make snow or create ice rinks – so it was common to suit up and engage with the elements. My parents were both artists and architects, survivors of the Great Depression, then WWII, followed by jointly leaving the church and then becoming antiwar and civil rights advocates. They designed and built their own homes and lived on a shoestring. Much of the time I was embarrassed by their alternative ways and their political/artist friends. But along the way I learned the Bible was literature, God was in nature, and both the practical and numinous could be found through gardens, the arts, books, and music – all of which offered me ways of relating to the unspeakable. It wasn't until I left home that my parents bought a television. Although their lifestyle was not unusual for some parts of the country during the 1960s, very little in our way of life was common in the small religious farm communities where we lived, so I learned to navigate my desire to belong with finding confidence in being different. This significant early childhood challenge set the stage for me to unconsciously identify with analytical psychology and to search for some meaning that could provide warmth and comfort to my soul.

I have often thought that the landscape of seasonal changes visibly illustrated an inherent energy within nature that influenced my imagination. There was time spent paddling in the cold spring-fed waters of Christmas Lake until I was four years old and the distinct smell of the wet dock drying in the sun. I can still feel the burning cold winter winds that chapped my baby face and froze my eyelids shut when I cried, the sledding down the hill onto the frozen lake, and the much-welcomed muddy snow that dirtied my red boots as the sun turned ice to running streams. Many years later, these memories shaped the metaphors for my emotional world, alchemical experiences that became part of my subtle body and connected me to Jung's knowledge of psychic life.

A distinct memory formed when I was five years old. I had traded my orange plastic grocery store watch for my friend's coloring book, something my mother did not allow in our home because she believed it destroyed initiative and creativity. When I arrived home, feeling proud of my negotiations, she took it away from me and stashed it high up in the linen closet. I stood watching her, screaming in utter outrage. I had lost both my watch and the newly acquired coloring book. It was an emotionally tantalizing, cruel, and confusing memory. We were locked in a power struggle that created a well of deep emotional waters that I drew from throughout my analysis. Within days of this event, our president, John Fitzgerald Kennedy, was assassinated, and this traumatic event in the collective ricocheted into our home. I watched as my parents wept in each other's arms. I experienced a young apprehension of empathy and recognition that the helpless hurt from loss and anger extended beyond my small world of big emotions. The complexity of these profound intersecting emotions unraveled into other painful family events that marked me, forcing me to search for ways to express the inexpressible, to take actions that affirmed my own selfhood. The intermingling effects of fate and destiny, along with the influences transmitted from ancestors and transgenerational trauma, had their import, cutting a path, reinforcing a pattern of curiosity about the shadow; the invisible, the inexpressible, and the un-worded.

I became a collector of discarded objects: pieces of wood, stones, barbed wire, and bottle caps decorated my bedrooms, creating art installations. Most of my time was spent in school music and art rooms or the dance studio. Because of my father's architectural career, we moved several times, and I learned to protect against the hurts even further, priding myself in enjoying the adventures, but lone-liness was ever present. My parents had raised two older children, and they were mostly distracted by the war in Vietnam. I turned to the wide swaths of nature near our homes and wandered in the woods, swam in nearby quarries, or in my teenage years, explored cornfields on my skis, cutting my own path in the winter moonlight. Being in nature alone was empowering. Later, as a young adult, read-ing *Memories Dreams Reflections*, Jung's weaving of dreams and image sparked a deep and warm resonance for me. My inner world, which had been trapped in the depth of winter, like the *Kore*, somehow felt redeemed and affirmed.

It was pure synchronicity that led me to Lesley College for the study of expres-sive therapies with Shaun McNiff, whose appreciation for Jung and Hillman wid-ened and deepened my psychic landscape. While the embryonic experiences with my mother inspired me to work with pregnant mothers and their young children, the unconscious pull, a thread passing through the eye of the needle, led to a Jungian analysis with an art therapist, who focused on the feminine principle and alchemical imagery. She introduced me to those obscure female voices in analyti-cal psychology that spoke deeply to me, and she encouraged me to listen to the images, respect the symbols. With her I finally began to untangle the emotional strands and knots associated with the transgenerational maternal wounding. One thread was the clinical exposure to autistic and high-risk children, as well as expo-sure to object relations, attachment, and developmental theories taught by visiting instructors from the Tavistock Clinic in London. Behind the scenes I worked with my dreams, made art, and straddled theoretical approaches. While it would have made sense to join my friend who decided to train at the Tavistock in London, my fidelity to the image and "living with the unconscious" was becoming stitched into my way of life.

While I was individuating from my parents in various ways, I had to accept that the steps I was taking towards a psychology that was not mainstream was, ironi-cally, not unlike my parents' individuation path. With conviction, I engaged with "doing the next thing that needs to be done" in my marriage to the "foreign boy," as my grandmother called my husband, while also parenting, teaching, conduct-ing perinatal art therapy research, and maintaining a clinical practice. The longing for a more rigorous theoretical immersion in analytical psychology was the path towards weaving together the many threads of my life with the commitment to live in relationship with the unconscious. While one colorful strand of early child-hood coalesced around archetypal themes such as connection/separation, sym-bolized by the chicken wishbones my mother dried for us on the windowsill, or the powerfully emotional world of pregnant woman, with the archetypal core of fusion and differentiation, I charted a circuitous path, with both uncertainty and conviction, the various unexpected challenges and opportunities that eventually gave birth to my own analytic mind.

The images of these lived experiences gathered in this volume, the imagination and synchronicities structured by time, place, and landscapes, are, as Jung says, *"meaningful and intended by fate."* The honoring of each analyst's inimitable journey, as well as their attitude towards both the unconscious and the collective, inspires respect for the wide diversity of analytic preferences. While analytical psychology emphasizes differentiation and individuation, there are shared common threads among Jungian analysts, including the appreciation for the soul, metaphor, the living symbol, fidelity towards image, with its autonomous and purposive energy, and numinous experience that connects us to the unknown and the great mystery. With the unfurling of individuation, we are reminded that our human existence, as Jungian analysts on this earth, is unquestionably insignificant, anything but glamorous, and yet also deeply influential and tremendously powerful when we are able to tend the sparks that may lead to a desperately needed shift in consciousness, one step at a time.

Nora Swan-Foster, Jungian Analyst
Boulder, Colorado
Co-editor-in-Chief – *Journal of Analytical Psychology*

Images From Early Years

Heyong Shen:

(with twin sister), two to three years old, ca. 1962

Photos from the private collections of the interviewees and used with permission

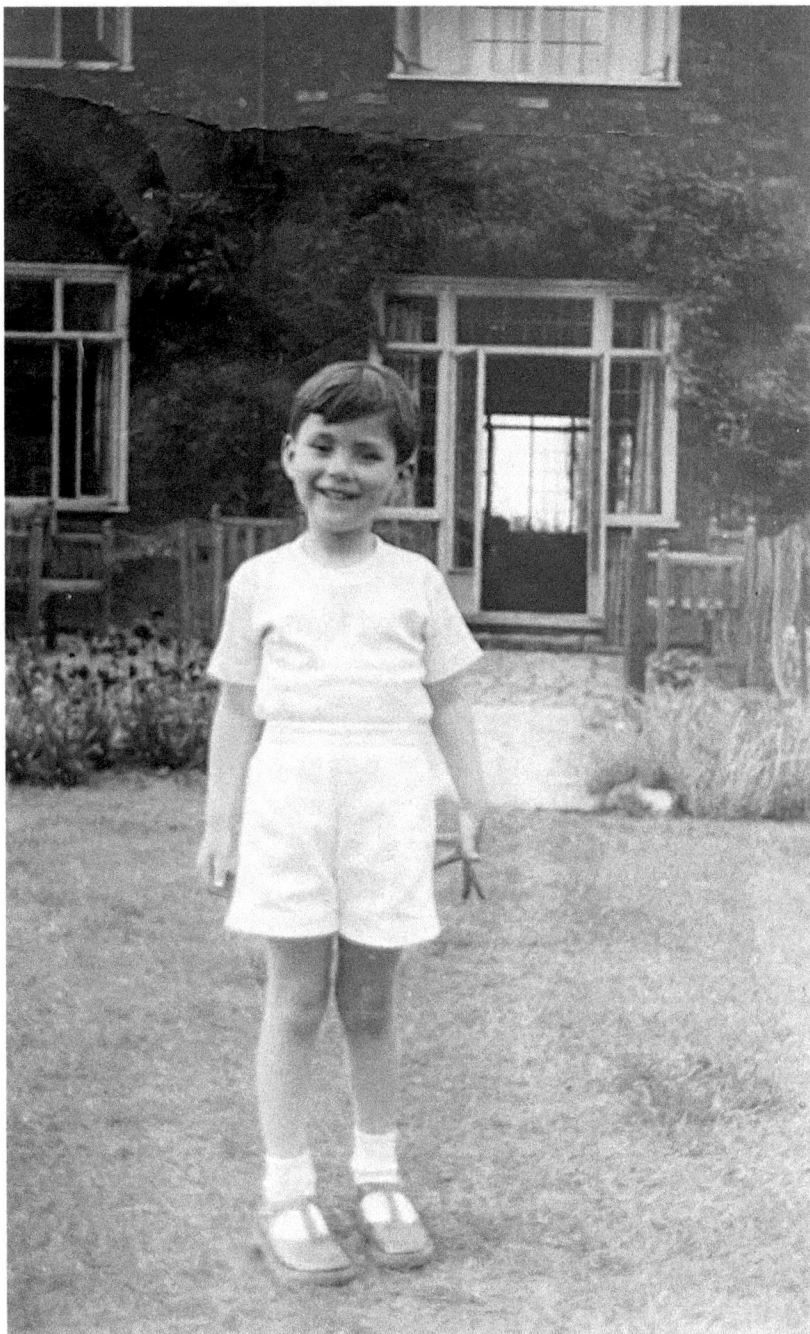

Andrew Samuels:

(in family garden in Liverpool), three to four years old, ca. 1952–1953

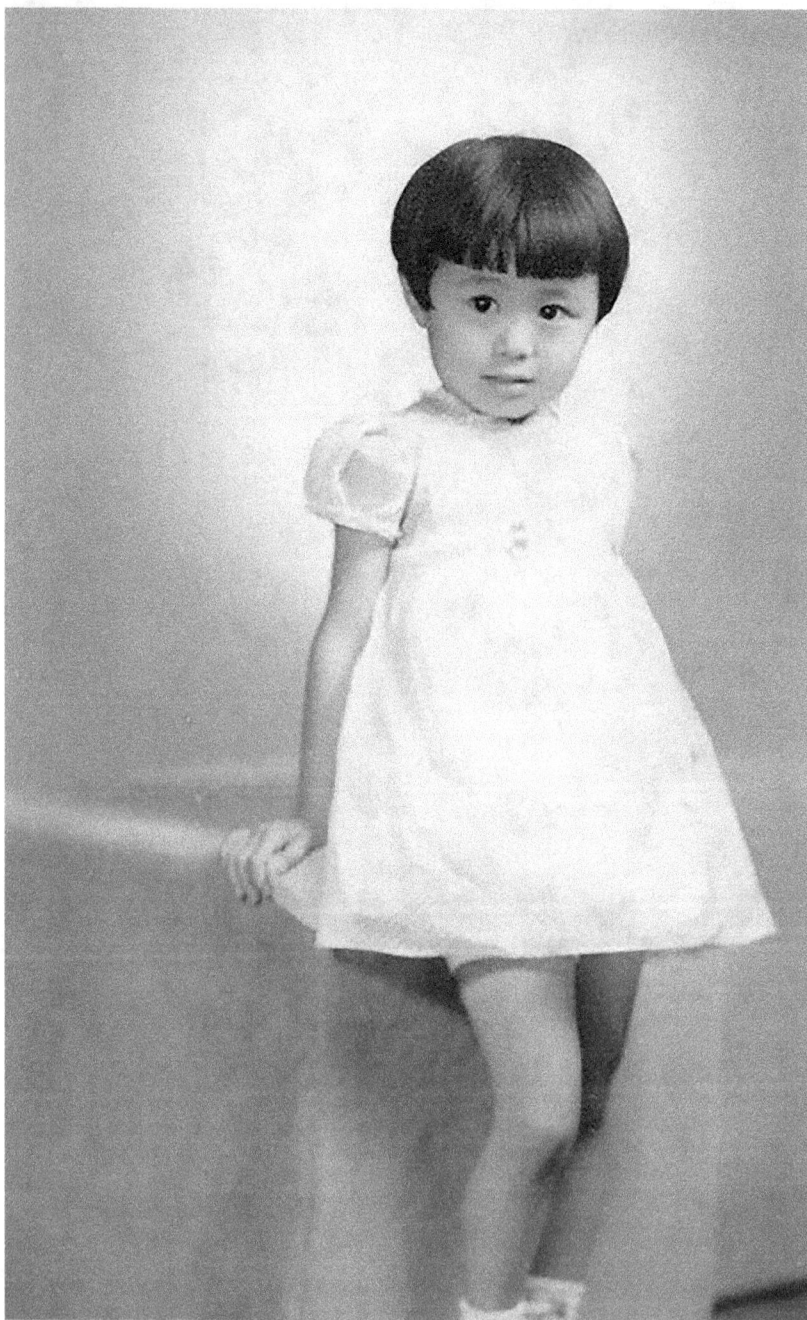

Jean Miye Shinoda Bolen:

four years old

Donald Kalsched:

ten years old

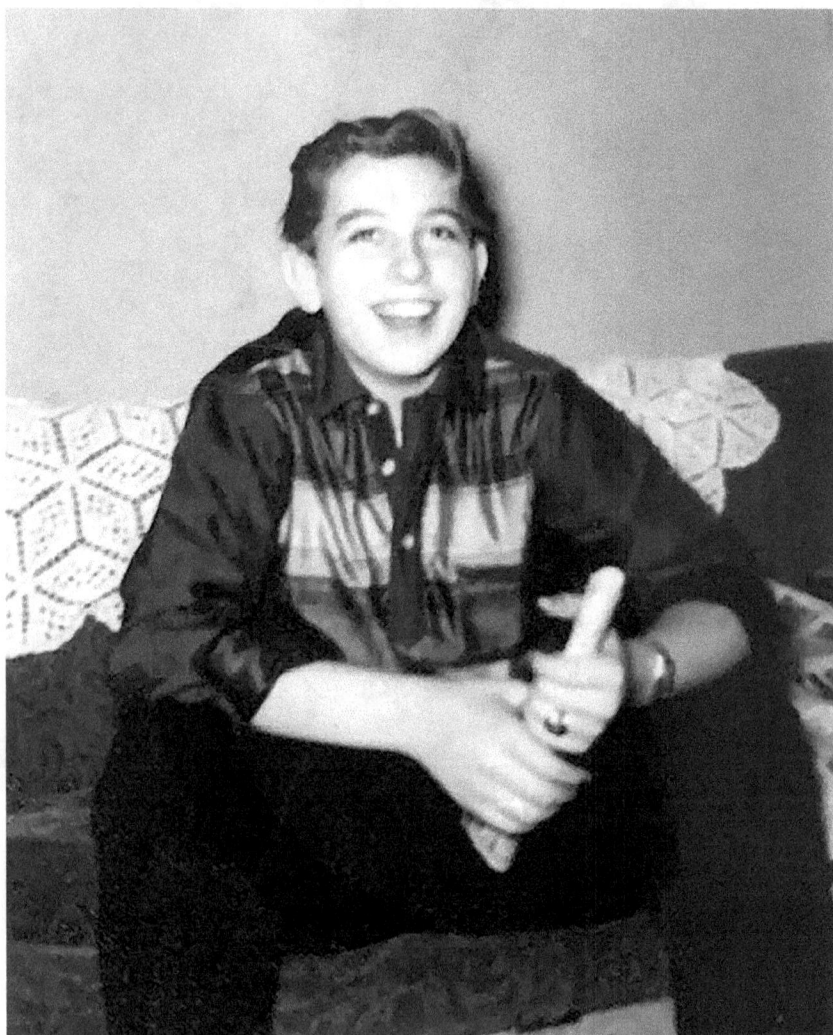

Murray Stein:

twelve to thirteen years old

John Beebe:

thirteen years old

Avi Baumann:

(with friends from the army at Kantara near the Suez Canal Egypt 1968), twenty-one to twenty-two years old

Luigi Zoja:

five years old (with his two younger brothers beside an Alfa Romeo during their first vacation at the seaside following World War II), ca. 1948

Approximately one and a half years old (winter 1944–1945 with his sled near his grandfather's villa on Lake Maggiore)

Approximately two years old (standing outside during the last weeks or days of WWII, spring 1945)

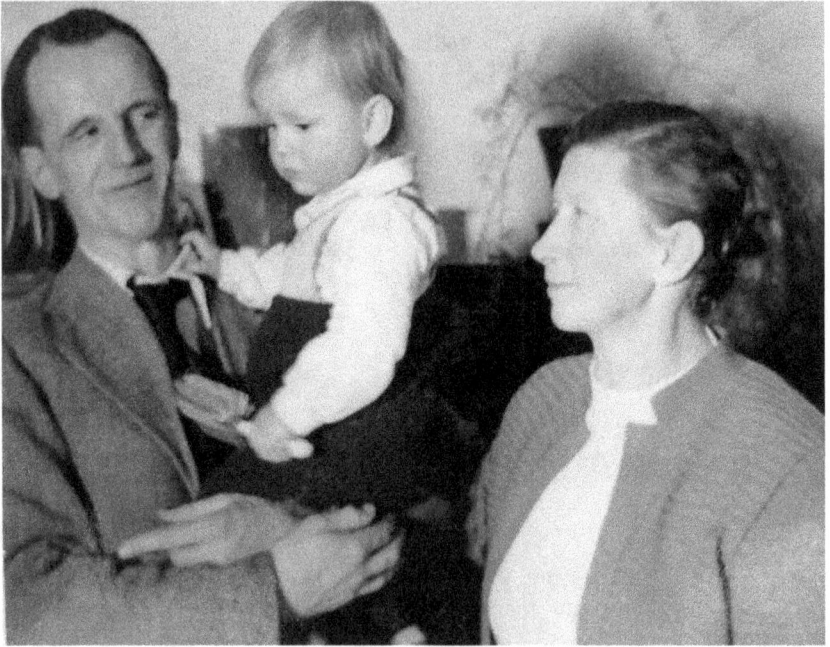

Ernst Falzeder:

two years old (with his father and mother)

Three to four years old (with his
aunt's Newfoundland dog "Assi")

Three to four years old

Introduction

This book is a celebration of humanity. It is not a mere collection of interviews with esteemed Jungian analysts and scholars of analytical psychology but a collection of gifts and a declaration of generosity on the part of each of the persons interviewed. Through these gifts an act of humanization occurs, allowing personas to fall away while revealing the human beings beneath the persona. Often it is the child in them that is uncovered.

To discuss the beginning of one's life can be insignificant to some. However, it documents the beginning of the journey towards one's unfolding Self. The beginning is often presented as a collection of experiences and qualities that have led to these individuals becoming Jungian analysts. What was it that led to this role and professional identity? What were the early elements of their lives that influenced their choosing this particular path?

It is also a coloring book, for each of the persons with whom I discussed leaves room to the reader to find himself or herself in the story and to color within its lines as they will. For this reason, it is a very personal and, at the same time, very collective book. It offers a possibility to the reader; that when he or she meets the respective person in this text, they will wish to meet the interviewee in person, to encounter them by reading their works, through engaging the people who had the privilege of working with that person or of being trained by them, or hear them deliver a lecture.

This book was born in Küsnacht, Switzerland, on the shores of Lake Zurich, in October 2010 after I visited C.G. Jung's house and garden in Kusnacht (prior to its opening as a museum) led by Mr. Andreas Jung who with a very generous, kind, and discrete manner showed me around. I was about to take the ferry to Zürich from Küsnacht. Professor Mihaela Minulescu, the professor in the group of Jungian analysts who had brought the study of Jungian psychology to Romania, had given me the telephone number of Mrs. Helene Höerni-Jung, to whom I was to deliver a book from Professor Minulescu. Although I was feeling extremely anxious, I phoned Mrs. Höerni-Jung. She answered in German but immediately switched to English. Although I had already told her that I was bringing her a book, she asked the purpose of my visit. I soon realized it might be some sort of test, but I could not convey in words all that motivated me. Apart from wishing to

DOI:10.4324/9781003148937-1

discuss her famous father, very awkwardly, I babbled a few words and managed to include the fact that I would have very much liked to talk about her mother as well. At that moment she told me that she would wait for me at 17:00 hours. I bought a bouquet of flowers and presented myself at her door three minutes before the appointed hour. She opened the door with a kind and welcoming spirit. Her home was full of warmth. She provided cookies and refreshments. I was very impressed, just as she was by my flowers. I was later to find out that this was not the practice in the local culture.

Just above the couch where I had been invited to sit there was an icon with Saint Peter and Saint Paul. A new reason for me to feel in awe. I spontaneously exclaimed: "Oh, an Orthodox icon!" Mrs. Höerni-Jung delicately explained, "My dear, there can only be Orthodox icons." When I offered her the book, she thanked me and asked me to tell her about the place where I was coming from. I told her a few things about Romania and the group of people interested in Jungian psychology. She then asked me about myself. I told her that this was my first visit to Küsnacht and that I had also visited the C.G. Jung Institute and the house where she had grown up. As our discussion moved from the collective towards the personal, I began to ask a few things about her activities and her work with icons. She told me that she saw icons just the way her father used to see archetypes, as "living gates," serving as passageways from and into the unconscious. Icons were one of the few domains that her father had failed to "tackle," which was why she had chosen to study them. She told me a few things about her work with icons, an endeavor that spanned over twenty years, working with both Orthodox and non-Orthodox in group settings. I was so touched by her emotional connection with icons and by her comment about "the balance that Orthodoxy brings in a person" and her observation, "I think that Orthodoxy is the most balanced religion of all." When I asked why, she responded, "It is because she places the feminine principle in a relation of equality with the masculine principle, which does not happen in the Protestant religion." She illustrated her answer with a personal memory from the age of seven when she used to sing in the children's church choir. On Christmas, their pastor, who also happened to be the leader of their choir, found an old song in the archives that was dedicated to the Virgin Mary. Happily, the children started singing it. Yet right after they started, a large part of the audience who had been listening to the Christmas concert stood up and left the room, including the parents of the children who sang in the choir. The children continued to sing, but the unease she felt lingered afterwards. She sadly told me that this was one of the moments from childhood that significantly impacted her; the moment when she understood that this was a manifestation of the Protestant stubbornness. It was a refusal to acknowledge the Virgin Mother, who is a symbol of the feminine principle, or offer her due place on equal standing with the Father, the masculine principle. We continued to talk for a while about her mother and her father. She appeared rather reluctant to tell me much, so I did not press her. However, she told me that she had long refused to be anything else but a tailor and a mother of three children. It was only after her father's death that she had become interested in analysis. Then she began to read her father's works and doing analysis, choosing the icon as the first avenue of accessing the unconscious.

It was so enjoyable talking with her that I really did not want the discussion to end. As if she guessed my thoughts, she asked me if I had visited the Bollingen Tower. I told her I had not, and she asked if I would like to see it. I indicated I would, but I knew that one should book a visit in advance. She said that was true, but that one of her sons was going to visit Bollingen the following Saturday, and she asked me if I would like to join him. Of course, I did, although I had no idea how to reach the place. She instantly called her son and told him that someone would like to visit the tower on Saturday.

Turning back to our conversation, at some point I asked her about her mother and how she had experienced Emma Jung as a mother. She told me that her mother had been a good parent but that the five children had a closer connection between themselves than they had with their parents. I was slightly afraid to ask how it felt to be the daughter of such a great thinker of our times, so I refrained from asking the question, yet she somehow sensed it and told me it had been difficult for them to find a domain that their father had not tackled already. But the field of icons had been one of them. I asked her if, in her opinion, her father believed in God. And she told me: "He did. In his own way, he believed."

These are the highlights of my meeting with Mrs. Helene Höerni-Jung, but I believe they provide a rich foreshadowing of what this book contains. The meeting was a wonderful moment for me; one of those "once-in-a-lifetime" moments. I began to call her annually until her passing; to hear her voice and to thank her for giving me the chance of meeting her. It was a real opportunity for me because it opened an avenue that I continued to explore with other individuals who had had chosen the path of living a Jungian life.

This meeting, which was not an interview per se, was a first taste of what was going to develop into a larger project. But had it been one of the interviews included in this book, it would surely have had, like all of the dialogues included here, a story and that would reveal to the reader who she was as a person. Each of the meetings collected here takes the reader on a journey into the soul of the person whom I have interviewed: their early joys; their favorite toy; conversations with their mother and father; descriptions of their childhood home; or the forests and valleys, lakes, streets, schools where they once walked.

This is a history book; a personal history book. It is a book that explores the early stages of each of those children who were to become role models to others later in their lives. In each dialogue one can feel the wind blowing, sense how the air smells, hear the sounds, feel the sun shining, or see the way the river flows past the boy fishing with his grandfather. One can feel the stuff their favorite toy was made of or how it felt when they touched the sticks, stones, and reeds with which they would build things with; all things that would later inspire them. One can hear the first siren's shrill sound before the bombings of World War II, as well as the touch of a mother's hand who never abandons. Presence, trust, and patience are present in these stories along with the courage to look danger in the eye.

This is a book is a ten-year-long conversation with the first generation that followed after C.G. Jung, as well as some from the second and third generations of Jungian analysts. Thus it offers an x-ray of the spirit of our times, of the various geographies, and of the ways in which Jungian analytic thinking has inspired and also been transformed. All of the interviews were personally conducted by me. In only four cases, for logistical reasons pertaining to significant geographic distance, were they conducted as a videoconference, but only after I had met the individual in person and they had already made a significant impression on me. I deliberately refrained from including many professional aspects in the dialogues. These can be found in various other collections of interviews with Jungian analysts, although, to my knowledge, at the time this project began, the last ones were published three decades ago, and only a few of them include conversations with the persons who were interviewed in this volume.

Apart from the great gift provided by the persons interviewed, this book also holds some regret that not all the persons with whom I interviewed granted me their final permission to publish their stories. Although I understand their positions, I still wished for a different outcome. I also regret that, for obvious reasons, my own analysts could not be included in this volume.

This book is about differences in the living out of individual lives and about how those differences can be integrated into our lives. It is about love and resentment toward our parents. It is also about what we have received from our mothers and our fathers, about what sticks with us from our earlier lives, about what creates trauma inside us, and the manner in which we have managed to live with that trauma. It is about conscious choices and about mercy. It is about sacrifice as well as about humiliation on the part of others; humiliation that makes us different, yet free. Ultimately, these are the stories that shaped the soul of the lives who lived the stories.

Each of these great and generous persons who I have chosen to interview has had awakened me to something unique. Each of them awoke a feeling in my heart that made me say to myself, "I would like to know how this person was when they were little and how he or she started on the path of individuation." In the following chapters, such stories unfold as the life of each individual interviewed is explored.

Chapter 1

Too Symbolic

Avi-Avshalom Baumann
INTERVIEWED BY LAVINIA ȚÂNCULESCU-POPA
(NOVEMBER 27, 2016 – BUCHAREST, ROMANIA)

Avi-Avshalom Baumann, PhD, is a senior clinical psychologist and supervising Jungian analyst. He was the president of the IIJP Israel Institute of Analytical Psychology (2012–2016), academic manager and lecturer in Bar Ilan University for the Jungian psychotherapy program, and former chief psychologist at Hadassah Medical Center in Jerusalem, Israel (1985–1991). He is the author of The Devil's Three Golden Hairs: Grimm's Fairy-Tales as a Mirror to the Dark Side of the Psyche *(2005), "Rites to create the sacred space" (a chapter in the book* The Play, from Psychoanalytic Perspective and Other Angels – *2002), "The Hidden Negatives of the Mother's Faces" (a chapter in the book:* Motherhood: Psychoanalysis and Other Disciplines – *2009), and several articles in analytical journals and papers presented in the IAAP conferences. He lectured on subjects of his interest, such as dream and dream interpretation; shadow and evil in mythology, fairytales, and politics; creativity and art therapy; philosophy and analytical psychology; the individuation process and the second half of life; two book chapters; and his blog: Avibauman.me.*

LTP: I'm interested in your story from the beginning. How did, as much as you remember, your life start?

AB: My parents were people that came from Europe. In 1939 they ran away from Europe to Israel, as young Jewish immigrants from Vienna, Austria, and Germany. They met in Israel after they were adopted by people from villages in Israel who took in these young people into their families, and they met and they went into a new settlement; a small place called Beit-Eshel in the Negev Desert. Israel was not yet a state. It was still Palestine, a British Mandatory.

LTP: That was around what year?

AB: That was around 1943. I was born in 1946. My parents already had a son, my brother David, and then I came. I was born and they named me Avshalom: which means "the father of peace." The Bedouins say, "In that place [Beit

DOI:10.4324/9781003148937-2

Eshel] a tree grows in the desert." We lived there for two years until the Independence War [the 1948 Arab-Israeli War] when Israel became a state. After the war, all the people there decided to move to the north and build a new settlement called Hyogev. In 1948, when the Independence War began, the children and women were evacuated out of the settlement. The men stayed there and fought. In 1949, after the war, they built the new place in the Jezreel Valley. That is where I grew up and where my sister was born. They came as the pioneers that worked and built the new-old land. My father, who came from Vienna directly out of high school, was very idealistic. Very quickly he had a job with the settlement. He was the Outer Secretary, someone who is called from the outside to help with building projects of new settlements in Israel, cooperative villages.

LTP: Kibbutz?

AB: It was not a Kibbutz. There were several villages that comprised a cooperative. So, he helped to build these projects. We stayed in the village, and we had what we call a *meshek* [farm], with cows, orchard groves, and hens. With my mother, I managed the farm while my father worked outside every day.

LTP: Like a small farm?

AB: Yes, like a small farm in a cooperative village, exactly. My daughter, Noa, now lives there. The place was empty for some years when my parents moved to Jerusalem, so she wanted to stay there with her own new family, not to be a farmer, but because of the beauty of the place.

All my life I knew that my parents were not supposed to be on a farm, at least my father. When one of his friends came from Vienna to visit he said amazed: "Oh, Herr Baumann is Eine Bauer? You are a farmer? How can this be?" (laugh) He was never that type.

LTP: What profession did your father have?

AB: He was in charge of building the villages and settlement planning. Later, my parents moved to Singapore for five years as a kind of diplomatic mission for international trade unions. After he retired, when he was sixty-five, they moved to Jerusalem, and he decided he would continue his education. He completed a master's degree and a doctorate then.

LTP: After age sixty-five?

AB: Yes. His subject was *The Deutsche Glaube* and the origins of a new Germanic faith – that become a form of religion for the Nazis. The Nazis had an idea to create a new religion, one not based on Christianity. The basis for the new religion came from German mythology. They wanted it to be a religion which is cleansed of the roots of Judaism and Christianity. There was one scholar, Jakob Wilhelm Hauer, a German professor of religious studies, who helped the Nazis create the new religion. My father's PhD dissertation study was on this Hauer. The Hebrew University of Jerusalem sent him to the University of Tübingen in Germany to have access to the research materials which were still stored in the home where Hauer's wife lived. It was like a healing process for my father. Hauer's wife was still alive, and she let him take all of Hauer's papers. Hauer's material was full of Germanic symbolism; the Black Sun [Gr: *Schwarze Sonne*] and all kinds of symbols which you wouldn't believe. Previously, we did not know that the Nazis had ideas about creating a new "faith" or "religion." It had to do with a new kind of anti-Semitism which is not based in Christianity. So, the Germans, after some years, took interest in the material from my father's doctoral dissertation. There is also a book about his dissertation, *Die Deutche Glaubensbewegung und ihr Grunder Jakob Wilhelm Hauer* [Diagonal Verlag, 2005]. But let's come back to me . . .

LTP: Sure, let's come back to you. During the Independence War, when you moved with your mother to the Jezreel Valley, did your father remain involved with the war?

AB: Yes, he stayed there for nine months, I didn't see him. All the men were there in a kind of siege. After the war the men joined the women and children, and they built the new place where we lived afterwards.

LTP: You were three years old. Do you still remember things from then?

AB: Yes, I have some memories from before we came into our new house in Hayogev. I remember that my maternal grandmother came after being released from Theresienstadt. She came to Israel at the beginning of the 1950s. She insisted on us speaking German with her when she arrived.

LTP: What was your maternal language?

AB: My parents spoke German, but the people that adopted them when they came to Israel had Russian origins and said, "You are not allowed to speak German." In Israel, people did not want the new immigrants to speak German. When I was a child, we only spoke Hebrew.

LTP: So, with a father coming from Austria and a mother from Germany, is there anything from your Germanic roots that you experience in yourself?

AB: After the war, everybody only wanted to be Israeli, like people from every other culture. The Israeli-ness was something that we felt we must keep. As a child, even though I studied the Bible and Jewish history in school, I did not know personally what it meant to be a Jew, because we were not religious. So, being Israeli, "*Sabra*" [one who was born in Israel] was my only identity. Only at the beginning of my second half of life did I get acquainted with what the real meaning of being a Jew, and more than this, being a German Jew. That happened at the beginning of the 1990s.

LTP: What kind of understanding did that experience translate into?

AB: It meant that I had to learn something about Judaism and about Europe, not just what we had been taught in school. I became more interested in that after I became acquainted with Jung because Jung helped me understand the cultural complexes of the new Israelis; the *Sabra* complex of my generation and the wandering Jew complex of my parents' generation. In 1981, I was a clinical psychologist in Israel. At that time, when people felt they needed a personal analysis, they went into Freudian analysis. Initially, I thought I would go into Freudian analysis and train in Freudian psychoanalysis, but I was not sure. Intuitively, something about the Freudian framework was not right for me. Too much focus on the instincts, too much oedipal stuff, and too much of seeing things from a certain point of view. It was too narrow and not enough of the symbolic, cultural, and spiritual. My main supervisor was Freudian. During that time, I thought something was not right. There were no symbols discussed. When I talked like that in my internship clinic (which was very Freudian), my internship supervisors always told me, "You're so symbolic. You are too symbolic." I did not know what to do with that. So, like a good boy, I listened, but at the last moment, I told myself I should not start. There was no Jungian approach recognized yet in Jerusalem, but I thought I should not start training at the psychoanalytic institute.

LTP: So, you were a psychologist at that time, not PhD yet?

AB: I was a clinical psychologist. In 1981 I started my PhD in psychology, and a few months later, by some synchronistic way, I started a Jungian analysis.

LTP: So, that was the moment that triggered your interest in Judaism?

AB: Not yet. Only later through individuation and the spiritual side of the Jungian approach. It was when I was beginning my PhD dissertation about lifespan development when I found out about Jung!

Going back to 1973, I had my first child at that time, after the Yom Kippur War. The Yom Kippur War was something very traumatic for me. I was an officer in the Israeli army, beginning with the 1967 war. The Yom Kippur War was in 1973, and it was a very traumatic event for me. I was obliged to go into war on Yom Kippur night because the Egyptian army was invading through the Sinai desert. At that time, I was serving in an on-call basis meaning they called you only if they needed you. I was already a married citizen and student, not a young soldier. And my wife was pregnant, we had just moved into our new house. There was no warning, it came just like that. One month later, after I left for the war and was at the front, my wife gave birth to our first baby, my daughter, and I was not there. At the beginning, it was very terrible for us. I was in the armored forces as a signal officer overseeing all the communication for the tanks. I was right in the first line with the airplanes coming. All the fighting happened there. When I first arrived there, I did not know who my commander was but there was somebody behind me. I asked myself, "Who is that man?" I had two braids [an indication of rank in the army] on my shoulder, but he had a grapevine leaf, meaning that he was higher in rank, and he was supposed to be my commander. But, at that moment, he shot himself in the leg because he did not want to be in the war; he was afraid. He shouted at me, "Avi, I was cleaning my gun and . . . suddenly . . . pfffff." After this, they kicked him out of the army. He was a professional, a signal officer as well, but because he had not experienced war, he was afraid. Anyway, I suddenly found myself in the war, against my will, thrust into the role of the main signal officer in the unit. The commander that I served under was such a harsh guy; it was not good for me. After I returned from the war I decided I really wanted to be a clinical psychologist. Something shifted in me because of this traumatic experience.

LTP: You were twenty-seven years old? Can you pick an event or an experience that was important for you related to this time?

AB: It felt like a kind of failure. Your life is in danger, you don't know what can happen, and I saw some of my soldiers becoming crazy. Soldiers that I had under me in communications and the technicians were not supposed to be there in the first line. Certainly, one was psychotic, and we had to take care of him. At that time, I was not a certified clinical psychologist, but one can see it. There was also the reality that I saw people die in the war.

LTP: So, could we say that the difficult thing was the security of the next day?

AB: Yes, definitely! I saw broken people, people reacting in a very aggressive way, and people that were imprisoned by the Egyptian army. It is like torture when you are asked to be aggressive.

LTP: At the age of twenty-seven were you prepared that you might have to go to war, by your parents or somebody else?

AB: No! Theoretically, we knew it was a possibility. In 1967, I was in the Six Days War, but that war was short: just six days. Following just behind the first line, I saw a lot of things which could affect you. I saw houses that are evacuated, refugees, houses with all kinds of things left behind when people are forced to flee, such as photo albums with pictures of the children of a family.

LTP: Very touching . . .

AB: In 1967, it was a short war. At least two of my friends were killed, but I was younger, and I did not know much about going to war. This second war was very difficult. It was impacted by the fact that I was just married and a month away from becoming a father. My first daughter was born, and I could not be there when she was born. I understand it more deeply now. It took some time until I could fly from Egypt to see my wife after the birth. I came back from Egypt after being away for five months. The war did not last five months, but we had to stay together as an army for five months. In May 1973, I was released from the army and came back home. I think my traumatic experiences during the war were very important in my decision to go deeper into the psyche.

LTP: What helped you proceed on this path?

AB: First, I decided to study psychology, in October 1970, after I finished my three years of army service. My parents thought I would study electronics.

LTP: Because you were in the communications field in the army?

AB: Because of that and because I was more realistic in my orientation to school subjects. I liked to disassemble radios and discover what was inside. A sublimation of something. (*he laughs*). I have a brother who went to the academy to become a painter. He was in heaven all the time and I was on the earth. I was born after him by one year and five months. I was the one that had my feet more on the ground, more involved with helping our mother with the farm. So, they thought I would go to Technion [Israel Institute of Technology], a university in which you study to be an engineer.

LTP: Do you think that the second child has a special trajectory, such as carrying the feeling they [need to] succeed where the first child did not succeed?

AB: Yes, I am sure. I see this in myself, and I saw this in my work. I also saw some of my parents' distress. I sensed my mother's feelings and other things that I saw beneath the surface in both of them. I see this now, but then it was unconscious. I also knew that my father went down a path which was not his real path, because of the context he was in. In his library I found a lot of Freudian books. He also grew up in Vienna not far away from Berggasse [street] where Freud lived. My first books in psychology I got from my father. He took some courses in the subject because he was interested, but he never pursued that path as a career. Underneath, I felt that neither of them was on the right path.

LTP: So, it runs in the family this appetite for psychology?

AB: I think, yes. For my father, yes, he was interested but he never really pursued it. When I decided, I had already met my wife Yael in the army and she said to me, "I remember that you told me that maybe you wanted to study psychology, but you didn't know how to tell your parents." (laughs)

LTP: To ask for their permission?

AB: Just to tell them. They would not have stopped me, but I just needed to tell them about my decision. My wife also wanted to learn psychology and in the end she did. She became a Jungian psychologist. In a way, she was part of my *anima* at that time. Back then we only spoke about psychology and literature. She told me she was considering psychology, but she also wanted to pursue theatre.

LTP: When you were younger, did you fantasize about something other than psychology?

AB: When I was younger, still in school, I was always acting on the stage, even if I wasn't thinking of becoming an actor. But when I became an adolescent, I didn't want to act anymore. I thought, "It's not for me." I was thinking, "Maybe, my parents were right, maybe I would go to Technion." But then, everything changed, and I am certain it was related to what I had seen in the war in 1967. It became clear I was not going to Technion. I went to my parents and announced that I wanted to go to the university, but to specialize in psychology. When I first began in psychology, I thought that maybe it was not the right choice, maybe I should switch to medicine, into neurology. I was interested in science, and I thought, "Maybe psychology is not enough." Also, it was a new profession.

LTP: So, how did you manage to discover Jung?

AB: After I started psychology, I thought it was okay. Then, after the first year, I had some doubts. My wife and I started to learn psychology together. I was called up for some maneuvers in the army. My wife was alone, and she thought, "I'm leaving this profession, it is only laboratory and rats," you know, experimental psychology. She did not want to pursue it any longer. Instead, she wanted to go and learn a mix of history of art and psychology.

After many doubts, she decided she would stay. I personally knew, after a short time, that I was okay with my choice.

LTP: What does it take for one to know that this is the correct choice?

AB: I would say that I was very curious as a child, watching people, wondering, "What are they doing? Why were they crying? What happened to them?" And I remember a lot of these instances, more than my brother, my sisters, more than anyone. I was very curious about people, and I wanted to understand what was happening with them. I had a need to understand things in general.

LTP: Do you think your parents cultivated any part of your curiosity or do you think it is somehow inborn?

AB: I can tell you, because of my analysis I understand all this better. It was the emotional connection with my mother and being her helper, and the intellectual connection with my father and an unconscious identification with his losses and missed opportunities.

LTP: Was your mother always a housewife?

AB: She had the farm. My father went [away a lot]. It was strange enough that during the war when we were staying in this place in Negev, she was only twenty years old, but she oversaw Morse code communication.

LTP: We say that the spark does not jump too far from the fire, or the apple doesn't fall far from the tree. (smile)

AB: Now, when I look back and I try to understand my path, I think it had to do with my parents' suffering; losing their families, fleeing, and their immigration. They were living with their trauma. Being the child who helped my mother, I understood her, and I had a father with an intellectual side but one who had a terribly traumatic past – coming to Israel, losing his family, especially his mother, and an accident he was involved with.

LTP: I believe, as you mentioned, one of the key elements in your experience with your father was the fact that your father was more focused on his traumatic past rather than on his children.

AB: That was part of the injury that we have from our father, that he was not really with us in a way. He was always, maybe unconsciously, with this (*points toward his head*). With his thoughts.

LTP: Apart from this, what was your father like?

AB: I am going to tell you something very personal and interesting. One of my first dreams in my Jungian analysis was somebody telling me that I had to bury the corpse of a deer with big horns that stayed a long time in front of my house! Then I had an interaction with my father in the dream. He told me that it all started when this person, Giveolie, died. I understood that something must be buried and finished but I did not know what happened. I did not know what the dream wanted to tell me about my father or about myself. So, I went to my father and said to him, "You know, I had this dream," and he said to me with tears in his eyes (he was about seventy at that time), "Don't tell me that nobody told you about it. I killed a man!" He assumed that I knew because we lived in a place where there were a lot of friends from Vienna, people that knew both of us well. I said, "No, I don't know what it is about, nobody told me. You tell me!" When he was around eighteen years old, they needed to protect their village from Arabs, and they posted guards every night. One evening, my father had to guard the perimeter. My father and his friend were playing with a loaded gun and there was an accident. The gun discharged and killed a man, a friend. Can you imagine? The man was injured, but he should not have died. Something was not right with the situation because no ambulance came. I don't know what happened, but something unexplained happened. My father did not tell me all the details, he only told me, "I killed a man. You must know I killed a man."

LTP: It must have been terrible for you to hear this and for him to tell this. I am sorry. In the dream did you hear the name?

AB: Someone died in the night. The name in the dream was the name of the guide for his group. It was not the name of the real person who was killed. Giveolie was the name of his guide. He was like a father figure for me. In Hebrew, Giveolie means the stalk of a flower. I went to see a friend who lived near our house, from the same group my father was in as a youth. She was a friend of my father from Vienna. She was the one who told me it was an accident and that the man should not have died.

LTP: So, your dream started when this person died.

AB: Yes. Now I know that my father's trauma was not only about what happened there but also that he had to live with this secret, and then I had to work through the trauma in my dream. Because of the context, the authorities did nothing to him as a result of the event. After some years, when we talked openly about it, he said that he experienced depression and considered suicide because it was very difficult for him. Six months later, still during the war in Europe, my father received a "healing" mission to gather a group of youth for a settlement in the desert. The group included Austrian and German youth. People from the German group thought that my mother would be a good match for my father. She was very delicate and beautiful, they met and . . . (claps his hands), from that moment they were inseparable. Three weeks later, he told her he wanted to marry her.

LTP: This is a real *conjunctio*.

AB: (he smiles) And they are still alive because they are together. They are ninety-four years old.

LTP: What do you remember from your childhood about your father?

AB: As a child, I saw a man that was highly valued from all sides. He was highly intelligent, very responsible, and took a lot of leadership in the place where we lived. He was a father that you could be proud of, but I always felt that something traumatic was haunting him. He was not a happy person.

LTP: Sadness in his eyes . . . ?

AB: Sadness . . . some sadness, yes.

LTP: What do you remember about your mother, as a child?

AB: Consciously, she was always very delicate and genuinely nice. I felt very Oedipal towards her. She was very optimistic, not like my father. She loved people and people loved her. But I always felt that there was something in what she was doing in her job, in her life, which was not right. She was supposed to do something else.

LTP: Like what?

AB: She is very intuitive, she likes people. In terms of psychology, I got all my intuition and compassion from her.

LTP: So, you both have intuition and feeling as your main functions?

AB: Yes, but because I have an intellectual father, as a child I was a bit ambivalent about intellect. But because of my father, although I was also intellectual, although I was more drawn toward the personality of my mother. My parents had a great marriage, on one hand, but I see a symbiosis, which was not always good for them and not always good for me as a child. They were so much one for another that sometimes I felt that the child for her was him and the real daughter for him was her. They were parents to one another because they each lost their own families.

LTP: Coming back to the fusion . . . the quality of the marriage . . .

AB: It is a bit like a symbiosis. It was not quite open enough, not open enough that one was independent from the other. As a child I thought they were a good couple, I saw the good side.

LTP: What is the impact this symbiosis of your parents had on your development?

AB: To feel alone. I learned to be alone. They were not intruding, but you could not come to them with terrible things; to talk about something bad that happened to you, or to talk with them about the war. Never! I had to bring the sun to them. I had a sunny disposition. I always smiled. You can still see some of that in me even today, can't you? (*laughs*)

LTP: Yes, you are very positive from my point of view. But from what you are saying, you also displayed a false face – a *persona*.

AB: Yes! In a way it was too sunny. As a child, they always called me, "the child of the sun." Do you know that expression?"

LTP: No. Does it have a name?

AB: *Yeled Shemesh*, the Sun Child.

LTP: And your brother, the painter, was he the moon child?

AB: (*laughs*) Let's say it might be. I also have a sister. She came five years after me and finally she also came into the world of therapy. Her husband is a Freudian psychologist. For sixteen years, I worked with my brother-in-law in a clinic. Not just working together, we are also the same age, in the same house, he is a Freudian, and I am a Jungian. He was from Polish origins. He came to Israel as a child and was already seven or eight years old when he arrived. He was very much into being an Israeli, he didn't want people to see that he was from Poland. He said to me once, "You can afford to be a Jungian, because you are more normal. I must be a Freudian, because I need the normality."

LTP: So, you were "The Sun Child," the one that always sacrifices himself. But what about your brother, the first one?

AB: My brother became an artist. He was an artist since he was a child. I think he was like Neptune, Neptunian in a way. He is a bit of a dreamer, like that.

LTP: Was he ever jealous of you?

AB: I think when we were children, and he was the first born, he sold me "the first born" status, like Esau and Jacob. You know the story?

LTP: Yes. How was this vivid in your life?

AB: Anytime I did better work than him and took more responsibility for my mother, he would say, "You are the first born, you are the first born." And I said, "If you don't want to be the first born, give it to me. I will be the first born." He would respond, "Take it, take it." We laughed about it as children. Sometimes we still laugh about it.

LTP: What age were you when you made this trade?

AB: I think eight or nine. He was the *puer*. Or at least that is what I feel now. He was not the happy *puer*. He is not an extrovert. He is a Pisces.

LTP: Do you think he was also impoverished by the lack of your mother's attention?

AB: Yes, he once said to me, "You were the shock of my life."

LTP: What profile suits you better: Are you "a shock" or a "sun child"?

AB: I was a sun child for sure. I identified with it as a child. Although all the problems that I had were always hidden. But there was never a problem that became too much. That is why I started analysis late in life when I was thirty-five. I am a Leo, my brother is a Pisces, and my sister is a Scorpio.

LTP: You were between two from water (astrological signs), you are a fire sign.

AB: All the family was water. My mother was Pisces, my father Cancer, her moon was in Cancer, like my father's sun, and I was the only Leo, the only fire.

LTP: How did you manage?

AB: I did not manage. As a child I thought they were so emotional, so sensitive, much more than me.

LTP: As a child, would you describe yourself as an extroverted or an introverted child?

AB: Not exactly extroverted, but not an introverted child. The role I took as a child was to be kind of a guide in the scouts. I was the leader in that group; I took all the roles as a child.

LTP: Tell us a little bit about your narcissistic wounds, as you experienced them with your father. How did your narcissistic wounds impact you becoming an analyst?

AB: First, as a child I was very optimistic all the time. Although there were problems, and I saw what happened with my parents, I never got into a depression myself. Secondly, I received a lot of attention from the people around me, not only the family. We were in a small village, and I have a smile and this ability to be loved, like what I said about my mother. I think the collective where I lived compensated for what happened in our families. It was important to me that I got attention from the neighbors, people from the village. I had a friend who was born near me, and we grew up together in the village collective, like a kibbutz, in the Negev. She said that for her the collective was terrible, but for me, no. She was shy, too introverted. She always felt that nobody loved her.

LTP: What did it take, in your case, to overcome those wounds?

AB: I think that the compensation of the collective was quite important and my ability to get what I needed, to ask for it from others. I think that my mother's love was still there, because she didn't live out of her trauma. In contrast to my father, she said, "My life began when I came to Israel." For her, it was like becoming a newborn.

LTP: And your ability to get help from the attention of others, could that ability be interpreted as being too dependent or too clingy on others?

AB: It was never like clinging. I think it is an ability to see the other. It is not only to take, but also to give, because I also have that side. I am a combination of the sun in Leo and moon in Pisces.

LTP: So, you are water on fire. A real union of the opposites! Apart from this, another unity I can see in you, I see both *senex* and *puer* in you.

AB: Yes, absolutely, because the *puer* in me was very much hidden. When I started to become interested in the *puer*, I realized it through a patient of mine. With me, I was only curious about the *puer* because I never lived out the *puer* side of me. I was always on the right track of responsibility. I married when I was twenty-three and I had a child early. If you saw my life history, you would not think I was a *puer* at all.

AB: No, but I can see the *puer* side in you by looking at how you dress. You dress quite young.

AB: People always think I am younger than I am. So, I have this *puer* side, but it was never lived out in real life.

LTP: Does it hurt to not live out life as a *puer*?

AB: No. But at that time when I discovered this quality, it hurt. At that time, I knew there were a lot of sides which I had never lived.

LTP: What do you regret?

AB: I think I married too early. All my life, I felt that I must work, I had to do things. I am seventy now and I am still working, I do not think about pension at all.

LTP: What about the *senex* part of you?

AB: The *senex* is all the responsibilities that I had, all the things that I see in life. I have an earthier side when I work with people. I am very practical. You can see it when I am doing supervision.

LTP: I would say psychology is a science for structured minds, because psychology needs thinking as well as feeling.

AB: I can tell you that my son did not want to study psychology, he wanted to be a scientist. He received a PhD in biology, but he does not want the academic role. He has the most scientific head, but of all my children, he understands psychology the most!

LTP: Are any of your children following in the footsteps of your career?

AB: Yes, one of my daughters. She is more like us, like me and my wife. She is more inclined towards psychology, and she is a therapist. The other daughter loves theatre. She is director of a theatre, but now, she has a degree in psychodrama, so she is also progressing in her therapeutic side

LTP: You have a perfect story to tell. Not to mention that, speaking about theatre, you look exactly like Peter O'Toole. The resemblance is striking!

AB: Somebody told me that. I remember it because I have this certain order in my mind – the scientist's mind.

LTP: So, this is also a quality that a psychologist, in your view, should have?

AB: Yes. I do not see practically from the side of the *puer* in the world. But in my psyche, I feel it is there. I am a *puer* from the creative side. My mind is always open. I think it is good that I have this *puer* side. It does not stop me from doing things. I cannot actualize certain aspects of the *puer*, but I can be creative, open, and accept a lot of things.

LTP: Coming near the end of the interview, I would like to discuss the blending between masculine and feminine. For me, you are like an *androgyne* because you just mentioned that you are baking cookies.

AB: Not only the cookies, I make all the sweet things in the house. But this is only a recent development.

LTP: But not just baking, you have a lot of feminine elements. I would say you are extremely masculine and feminine at the same time.

AB: You should have seen my astrology chart. My Mars and Venus are not in Leo, they are both in Libra. They are very close, and both of them are with Neptune. The water part was the moon, in the eleventh house.

LTP: And the sun is of Leo?

AB: Yes, the sun of Leo. I have many things in Leo and many things in Libra. The Libra is in house six, the house of working and health

LTP: And the aesthetic and the tendency for art from Libra?

AB: So, in Libra I have Venus, Mars, Neptune, Jupiter, twenty-two degrees, and Chiron which has to do with the wounded healer.

LTP: You are the wounded healer, but at the same time, I do not see too many wounds, you seem quite healed.

AB: I heal myself (*laughs*).

LTP: Is this a continuous work that you do, even now? What would you say is spiritual in your life?

AB: First, I am listening to a lot of music. It is the thing that I enjoy most: to be with myself and to listen to music. All kinds of music, and it depends on which day, what kind of mood I am in. I listen to all kinds of music, but especially classical music.

LTP: Can you tell us some favorites?

AB: I sang selections from Schubert and Schumann and *The Winterrreise* and *Die schöne Müllerin*. Also, from Schumann, *The Songs of the Poet*. I enjoy this music and chamber music. I very much like the music of Vivaldi, especially *Four Seasons*, and Bach.

LTP: Earlier today, you mentioned that one person normally must have two types of fathers, the biological one and the spiritual one, to fulfill the development of his psyche.

AB: Yes, but for me, since I was a child, I have had conversations with God. Since I was very young, I spoke to God.

LTP: Were you taught about God in your home?

AB: No.

LTP: You were just speaking to God, to Yahweh?

AB: Yes, that is all I knew.

LTP: Were you going to synagogue?

AB: No, but I am going to synagogue now for Yom Kippur

LTP: So, you are not a practitioner, but still it was inborn, like a natural drive?

AB: For me, it was like conversations with God before I went to sleep. I would ask him something, I said something, or I thanked him for something.

LTP: So, these are also the seeds for a future analyst, because it is important that one realizes the importance of the religious instinct for their path and individuation.

AB: Yes, I am sure. It was something that I called upon and talked with. Someone beside me, but now I know it was an inner something. Sometimes it compensates for something lacking.

LTP: For the absence of the father, because you were experiencing the absence of the father when you were three.

AB: Yes. And I experienced the absence of my father also when he was there physically, because he was very much within himself, with his job, with his thoughts, but not so much with us. I wrote a post in my blog about the unknown, about how the astronauts look outside of themselves as persons as they look out on the Earth from their spacecraft. I drew a parallel, between their experience and mine. This is the unknown of the whole world; the universe around us, which is unknown. I understand now that that part we project onto and say is God, it is more the unknown. Of course, personally, everybody has their own God, or something that is related to God. But as for humanity, for us, God is unknown.

LTP: But for the little child that is speaking to God, it is also the known person. I mean they are certain that they are talking with someone that they know. They are not talking with something that they do not know.

AB: I am saying that now I am more aware of the fact that people project something known onto something that is unknown and impersonal. Now they have become very rigid and fanatical about forcing everybody to see in the unknown only what they think is there. That is part of the problem of humanity.

LTP: Any thoughts at the close of our interview?

AB: One thing you did not touch, and I think it is very important also; the family influence, in terms of how we learn about ourselves and understand ourselves. The influence of those who are close to us, our spouse, children, and the grandchildren. I think my family is a part of me, an avenue that helped me to understand myself also.

LTP: Another thing that I would like to ask you, what is your "recipe" related to becoming an analyst? What ingredients does a person need to follow this career? What qualities would be good to have to become a good analyst?

AB: My second granddaughter, she recently had her bat mitzvah ceremony. She is very wise and wonderful. She decided that we should do something serious for her party. She decided that she and I would select twelve things that are important in life, and she would discuss them from her perspective and me from my perspective. Me at seventy years old, she at twelve. My wife asked us questions. My granddaughter spoke first and then I added to it from my perspective. One of the things that we asked: What is the most important thing in life for someone? She said so many things I agreed with. Then I added something which I, as a seventy-year-old analyst and grandfather, believe, which is the ability of a person to have his own voice, to never give up his own voice, and never to be influenced by others.

LTP: Thank you!

AB: Thank you! I was very open with you. And I want to say one more thing; for me, the idea of individuation is so important, because I come from a collective. Schools should give every student the space to be themselves.

LTP: Indeed! Avi, thank you for your openness and generosity!

Chapter 2

I Am Myself

Dieter Baumann
INTERVIEWED BY LAVINIA ȚÂNCULESCU-POPA
BETWEEN FEBRUARY 21, 2014, AND JULY 31, 2019,
IN ZÜRICH AND IN KÜSNACHT

Dieter Baumann, PhD, was born in 1927 in Schaffhausen, Switzerland, grew up in Paris until he was twelve, returned to Switzerland, and lived for a few years in the house of his grandfather, Carl Gustav Jung. He began medical studies in Zürich, continued in Geneva and Paris, and specialized in psychiatry with the son of Eugen Bleuler. After completing his analysis with the son of Franz Riklin and Marie Louise von Franz, he worked as an analyst and teacher in Zürich. Dr. Baumann was a founding member of the Swiss Society of Analytical Psychology and lecturer at the C.G. Jung Institute in Küsnacht. He was a visiting professor at the State University of New York and was the author of numerous writings. He passed away on January 30, 2020.

LTP: This is a series of interviews called *Beyond Persona*. I am interested in you as a real person. Of course, we need a persona, in the sense Jung uses it, to function in the outer world, but a lot of people build their lives only basing themselves on the persona. They don't consider who they really are, behind and beyond the persona. I'm more interested in who you are, who you could become internally, beyond persona. I'm also wondering whether people associate you with being the grandson of C.G. Jung?

DB: Yes, I understand. You see, that is very difficult in my case because, even as a boy, I liked Jung, my grandfather. I very much [liked] and admired him. My first experience that I consciously remember about him was in Schaffhausen where there was a house with a large park that belonged to my great-grandmother, the mother of my grandmother, Emma Jung.

LTP: Rauschenbach?

DB: Rauschenbach-Schenk. Her husband had died very early, in 1905, and he was blind in the last years. It was terrible. Probably he had an illness but there was a great silence about that in the family. There was a family meeting in Schaffhausen around 1932. I was about five. When you enter the garden, a

DOI:10.4324/9781003148937-3

little bit below the house, there is a fountain made of stone. There was a pipe where the water came out. It happened to be in May. And the dandelions were blossoming. You see, the one when you blow on it, the seeds fly away. They are yellow.

LTP: Yes, yes. We say *"papadii."*

DB: Yes! And if you take away the stalks, you can put one into the other.

LTP: Yes, we did the same when we were kids.

DB: Yes? We did too. And we made a long conduit into the garden and further down. My grandfather came and he remade the conduit because the old one was broken. The pipe always spat it out. That was for me an absolute miracle. I had no knowledge of capillarity. He took the end of the conduit out of the pipe and put it into the standing water. Then he placed the other end of this conduit over the brim of the basin outside. Then he bent down and sucked at it. The water came. And that was my first conscious memory.

LTP: With him? Yes, but what was your first conscious meeting with yourself?

DB: Oh, that is a very indiscreet question. (he smiles) It is difficult to say. It's very difficult to say because it happened gradually.

LTP: I read that you are part of a family with four children.

DB: That is not quite correct. I am the oldest of the five sons of my parents. The second boy was born two years after me. The third, five years after me, the fourth, ten years after me, and the fifth, seventeen years after me.

LTP: And where did you live?

DB: Until I was nearly six years old, we were living in Montmorency, to the north of Paris. And there was a street called Square Biard. There was a special entrance to that square, around which there were five houses on each side, our house was the last one to the right side. It had a small garden – for me it was big. I had some very deep experiences there. My younger brother and I had a great spirit of enterprise. In the morning, after 9 or 10 o'clock, we used to go for an expedition. We used to go out of the limits of the square and stayed on the *trottoir* (sidewalk).

LTP: We have the same word in Romanian, *"trotuar."*

DB: And our mother gave to each of us the French bread, the *"baguette."*

LTP: Yes, *"baguette,"* we have almost the same word.

DB: My mother put butter and marmalade in it and then we went there to have our picnic. I think that was my first acquaintance with the outer world. We learned to see the world because there were also very sad things there. There was already unrest in Spain at the time of Primo de Rivera. It was 1931 or 1932. That was at least four or five years before the Civil War. On the telephone pole there was a pamphlet posted about executions.

LTP: They shot people?

DB: Yes, in Spain. I saw a picture of that. That was a painful initiation. But another painful initiation, very moving, there were always horses that came along, enormous Belgian horses. Behind them were boys, poor and bare footed, who collected the excrement of the horses into the carts with their hands. They sold them to use in agriculture. Do you know something about agriculture?

LTP: Yes. You can use the excrements in the soil.

DB: So, you know that when it is cold, to make seeds grow, you put them in the manure and the fermentation keeps them warm, then you have these little seedlings which you plant. I didn't know that at the time, but it made a big impression on me. Maybe I was very extraverted at that time, but the experience of the outer world and the inner world were together. I never thought about it then, but it was definitely together.

LTP: You didn't say this in any other interview?

DB: I never told this to anyone before, except the family and in friendly environments.

LTP: I know you have a book, *Memories from Meetings with Jung*. I'm interested in what you experienced when you found out that you had a famous grandfather.

DB: That came later. That was in Paris, but during the December holidays we came to Switzerland.

LTP: But you were born in Switzerland, weren't you?

DB: Yes, but when I was six months old, I moved with my parents to Paris because my father had found work there.

LTP: What was he doing?

DB: That is a story in itself. He was in business. He was a director. His father was the owner of a firm that still exists; it is called Baumann Koelliker Gruppe, here in Zürich, where they made lamps. Now they make illumination for tunnels.

LTP: So, you had two famous grandfathers.

DB: Well, he was not so famous because, you see, he made false calculations. I don't know how to call it in English, only in German, maybe you can tell me in English. He lost his money.

LTP: He went bankrupt?

DB: Yes, bankrupt. So, my father had to support his parents when he was young. My father studied economics here, four semesters when he was twenty or so. And then came the Great Crash, and that was at the same time as the high inflation in Germany, and after the First World War. With Swiss money you could afford a lot in Germany, so with relatively little Swiss money my father went to Leipzig for five or six months. With the help of a man from Leipzig, whom he had to pay, he managed to graduate with a degree in law within five months. And then he went to Switzerland and started to work immediately. After a few years, he met my mother. He was seven years older than my mother. They married in 1926 when Jung came back from Africa. For six months they lived in Schaffhausen where my father worked. The director of the steel works in Schaffhausen was the husband of the sister of my grandmother, Emma Jung. They sent him to Paris where they had a firm called Les Raccords Suisses (that is The Swiss Fittings). You know the books with the commissaire Maigret, the detective stories by George Simenon?

LTP: Yes, I do.

DB: He lived there, Maigret. Exactly in front of my father's business house. I went there to visit and they showed me everything. When my father arrived in Paris there was a director who was very old. After one year, my father was promoted to director of The Raccords Suisses.

LTP: How long did you live in Paris?

DB: In 1933, we moved to another place, to the southwest of Paris, in the direction of Versailles. Do you know Versailles?

LTP: Yes, I do.

DB: Then, we lived in a house which was built by a Swiss architect who was our neighbor. He also had three boys and we always played together. That is where I began to go to school. Before that my parents sent me to a *kinderheim* [children's home] in the French-speaking part of Switzerland to improve my French. An uncle of mine, who came to fetch me back to Küsnacht, was completely lost because I always spoke French with him and he didn't know what to say. The brother of my mother.

LTP: Franz?

DB: Yes. I started, then at a school in Paris, the Lycée de Sèvres. That was a school for female teachers but, in primary school, boys were also admitted.

LTP: Pedagogical school!

DB: Yes, a school for future teachers. I don't know, in France it was called L'École Normale. Anyhow, I went there until the end of primary school. I learned quite easily and then, after primary school, I went to a gymnasium run by Dominican monks. So, after primary school we passed an examination and obtained the *Certificat d'Etudes*. You can go to a lot of schools with that *Certificat d'Etudes*. Somehow the school came to know that I was a grandson of C.G. Jung. So, I started to realize that my grandfather had quite a reputation. For me, I remember he was a fine grandfather. I can give you an example.

LTP: Yes, please.

DB: At home, they used to take the bones out of the sardines. We were on holiday on the coast of Normandy, not far from where the Allies landed in 1944. We started to cross the river to have a look at a new steamer, named *Normandie*. It was quite stormy when we crossed the first of the Seine to Havre. My grandfather was with me and he gave me sardines to eat. He said, "You eat the bones." He ate the sardines as well. And so, we ate them and didn't become seasick.

LTP: Oh, because of the bones?

DB: Yes, because of that. We were in contact with the water. This was very encouraging. He was an example for me. My grandfather was very courageous. A year later he was on the Blacklist by the Germans.

LTP: Yes, I heard.

DB: In 1939, we came by train to Switzerland for the last part of our holiday. When we arrived, my grandfather immediately took my brother and me to his tower in Bollingen. Despite the threatening war, he kept his courage. The Russians and the Germans made the Non-Aggression Pact. Then, on the first of September, Germany attacked Poland. Two weeks later Russia attacked Poland from the other side. It was terrible. There were a lot of Polish officers massacred. Until a few years ago the Russian leaders never admitted it.

LTP: The Russians never admitted it?

DB: (pause) In spite of all this, my grandfather initiated my brother and I to drinking. At home we were never allowed to drink wine.

LTP: How old were you?

DB: Twelve. When we had visits, we boys drank until all the glasses were empty. So, he made us drunk . . . my grandfather. He gave us wine and we were in full spirits and laughter all evening.

LTP: But he also drank?

DB: Yes, yes. But he didn't drink so much as to be drunk. But he enjoyed drinking. But you see he didn't drink when he conceived his children. He did not allow himself to damage the children. So, he made us drink. There were different other episodes. There was a boy, the son of a poor family nearby who worked as guardians of the railway (Fr. *Passage à niveau*). It was a great responsibility. Jung was like a father to him. He came with us, and we made trips and all kinds of things. That lasted about four days because then we went back to Küsnacht. We went to some neighbors in Bollingen and listened to the radio. I remember my grandfather was furious about Hitler and also very depressed by it. Then we went back to Küsnacht. After about three weeks, my parents and my grandparents agreed that we boys would stay with my mother and her parents in Küsnacht for the moment. The war went on, and I went to a school there. I knew German and also spoke Swiss German, but I had always read books in German.

LTP: But your parents spoke in Swiss German with you?

DB: Yes, at home. But at school and with the Boy Scouts [Mouvement Scout de Suisse, MSdS], I spoke French. With my brothers we spoke a mixture of Swiss German and French.

LTP: So culturally you were between Swiss German and French, between Catholics and Protestants.

DB: I went to a Catholic school. There was maybe also one occasion when I realized my identity. Dominicans were not allowed to teach in school.

LTP: Why?

DB: After the Revolution of 1789, more precisely, in the aftermath of it, the priests were not allowed to teach, except for teaching religion. But I did not have to take part in the religion classes because I was Protestant. They respected that. Also, they were always very correct and even if, by accident, I came into one of the masses, one of these Dominican fathers would intercept me and allow me to go home for one hour. The school was seven minutes from home; it was very close. I was the only Protestant and the only foreigner, the only Swiss, the only non-Catholic in my class.

LTP: How did you feel being different?

DB: I was very proud. I could do my homework during the religion hour, but I heard everything they told my Catholic classmates. But I went to the Sunday school of the Calvinist Protestants. Their temple was on the same street where we lived. So, I could always compare. I felt sorry for my classmates, I felt pity for them because of everything they had to believe in. As a Protestant, I was much freer. My parents never pushed me into religion. My father told us the story about Christ, but he did not try to influence me. Later, I went to the Protestant church, this time with the Boy Scouts who were Protestant inspired. So, I could always compare. I think it is pretty unique, that you can experience both at the same time.

LTP: Yes, it is important. I would like to come back a little bit to the moment when you got drunk with Jung for the first time. You and both your brothers were there?

DB: No, only me and the one after me.

LTP: So only two of you. But coming back to the construction with the straws, you were extremely enterprising. All of you are like this in the family?

DB: Yes, one could say so, to various degrees. Of course, when we lived with my grandparents in Küsnacht, I was privileged because I went to the gymnasium in Zürich so I could always eat lunch and dinner with the adults. Everybody was there, daily, for three years. So, Jung had an enormous influence on me. I remember him talking at the table about Paracelsus. He spoke about psychology in other ways and I felt that this was a life, you know. And, for instance, in the evening I could always eat with my grandparents, whereas my brothers had to eat before, in the office, because they needed to go to bed early, so I was really privileged.

LTP: So, you were really the only child around?

DB: Yes, I was the only one around but only regarding the evening meals. And then, you see, I made presentations for school and then I asked my grandfather, and he gave me his comments. That was very nice. When I became interested in chemistry, Jung gave me tips. At that time, he was a professor at the ETH [*Eidgenössische Technische Hochschule Zürich* – Swiss Federal Institute of Technology] and I visited him there. If it was a free afternoon, I could use his library and I made extracts with every chemical element. On one occasion, my mother said, "Well, it's amazing how the girls are more mature than the boys. Much earlier, they know about things." Then I thought, "Well how can you say such a thing, because these girls don't understand anything about chemistry?"

LTP: So, understanding chemistry was the most important thing for you?

DB: Can you imagine? I could give you another example of the fact that a man is primarily less conscious about issues regarding the relationship between a man and a woman than a woman is. The opposite is the case with the woman.

My grandfather loved another woman, Toni Wolff. Have you heard about that?

LTP: Yes, I have. I thought this was indiscreet to ask, not about your memories. (I smile)

DB: I had to turn thirty years old before I knew they had a relationship. Von Franz told me. I was blind to that.

LTP: But was Toni Wolff present or around?

DB: She would often come on Sunday afternoons at the house and would stay for the evening meal. There were also times when Toni Wolff went to Bollingen with him. On different occasions I saw her there, but it did not come to my mind that it could be an intimate relationship between them, because it did not interest me.

LTP: You were pure hearted.

DB: Thank you for the compliment, but for me, being a man, it was not important. Had I been a girl, I would have understood it clearly. But I had to turn thirty before I understood.

LTP: But your grandmother? How did she accept it?

DB: She accepted it, but it meant a lot of suffering for her. All the three of them, my grandfather, my grandmother, and Toni Wolff, they all suffered. Von Franz told me that Jung had said that if somebody dedicates himself consciously to his individuation, that means a lot of suffering. But, she also said that my grandfather had never seen a case where this would have harmed a person (for instance, his wife) or prevented her from living out her individuation consciously. It meant a lot of suffering, but it did not harm her.

LTP: Not to impede somebody else who has dedicated herself or himself to individuation.

DB: And I was so stupid as to take over the resentment my mother had about Toni Wolff.

LTP: [silence]

DB: That resentment was in my family. My uncle didn't have it because he was a man. I have begun to see that she was a lady who was very distinguished. She had hair like Nefertiti, the wife of Akhenaton. She had her hair dressed up, behind and upwards, and a cigarette holder made of silver. But then she had this little dog who was always growling under the table which gave me a certain resentment. At Bollingen I once said, "That dog always makes a nuisance of itself," and my grandfather said, "He is an animal and so he can't behave differently but you are a human being and you can do differently." That was education, that is how he educated me. I was already grown up.

LTP: That is a very fine thing.

DB: Yes.

LTP: I am very much interested in the person that you are today. I don't want to make it mathematical, but how much do you think you were influenced by the fact that you were the grandson of a famous person and how much were you influenced by the relationship with your mother, father, and brothers, apart from Jung himself? And the relationship with yourself, of course?

DB: Well, it is difficult . . .

LTP: There is a saying in Romanian, it could also be in some other cultures, that "In the shadow of a big tree, only the grass can grow." In other words, you cannot develop under the shadow of a big tree, you need to find your way out to differentiate.

DB: Yes, that is true. But, you see, I had a great resistance. I made a trip to the United States to give lectures three years after my grandfather's death. I gave lectures about things I had written about. If I had not written my material, then it could have prevented me from living my own life, as happened with different relatives. So, very early I started to write my own things. I was very much encouraged by von Franz to do that; she really encouraged me. You could say she was a genius. Also, Jung said to me once she was "a little genius," but that was an understatement which only Jung could allow himself to make.

LTP: But why, in your opinion, was this an understatement?

DB: Because she's not only a little genius. Jung could say "little" regarding von Franz, but there were people who imitated Jung, far below von Franz, and they spoke the same way about her.

LTP: Maybe, mostly because she was said to be a very direct and very rigid thinking type.

DB: Yes, very much thinking, and intuitive, but not rigid at all. She also had a very warm feeling side, but it was very hidden.

LTP: Von Franz, was she married?

DB: No. She could have married, but she felt that she had a great work to do. She also realized that if she [married and had] children, she could not do her creative work. It was a great sacrifice.

LTP: Jung had a great friendship with von Franz.

DB: Yes because she helped him very early on. You see, she was very poor because of her parents. She did work and she helped him to translate things from Greek and Latin. The *Mysterium Coniunctionis* was also von Franz's work. But there have been a lot of women jealous about that, and therefore she doesn't appear as such.

LTP: Anyone in particular that we can discuss?

DB: I must be very careful about that because they cannot defend themselves. You see, you cannot say "the tree." Jung is not a tree, but he helped a tree to grow. He always conceived it as several people doing it because he could not deal with everything. Von Franz saw that Jung did not have time to do a lot of things. Therefore, you could say, she also created one or two branches.

LTP: Yes, but is there the idea that von Franz worked on or researched Jung's ideas, the ideas that he could not spend time with, or were they her own ideas?

DB: No, no. She was original. They were her ideas. She was a creative person with her own ideas, absolutely. That is why Jung asked her to finish the book, *The*

Grail Legend, by Emma Jung. She finished it after Jung's death. She made a lot of sacrifices for Jung. When he was ill, she gave him a toad. You know, the animal?

LTP: A frog?

DB: No, it looks like a frog, but the name is [*Bufo vulgaris*]. In French it is "*crapaud*." In German "*kröte*."

LTP: I see. So, she gave him a toad.

DB: I think it was Chinese. It also had a positive meaning. It was made from metal that was quite heavy. I didn't know about it, but he told me when I visited him after, when he came back to life.

LTP: After he had a stroke?

DB: I don't know what it was. It was a heart condition and he had to exert great effort to come back to life because it was so beautiful on the other side.

LTP: A near-death experience . . . ?

DB: He described it in his biography. I visited him. I don't know how long after that. He showed me the toad and said that it helped him to find a way back into life because it helped him to touch reality. Only after her death did I come to know that von Franz had given it to him.

LTP: But was it in a symbolic way that she gave him the toad?

DB: Maybe, but she gave it to him, and it was the touch of it, having something to grasp.

LTP: Something concrete, very concrete in his hands?

DB: Yes, yes. For instance, she organized his whole library, with a catalogue for all his books. During the war, one of the most incredible things was that she worked on the interpretation of fairytales for about six or eight years. Thousands of fairytales. She worked for a woman who did all the typewriting and everything, and the woman paid her, but then the woman published it without von Franz receiving credit. The woman said thanks for von Franz's small assistance, just in a little sentence. Von Franz considered filing a lawsuit, but the woman had a man with her and they threatened Von Franz that they would slander her and reveal her relationship with Jung if she defended herself. But there was nothing . . .

LTP: Between them?

DB: Yes, there was nothing. And Jung happened to be ill at the time and so she wanted to spare him the annoyance. So she sacrificed her claim of justice for him. The book was three volumes. The first two volumes are nine hundred or so pages each. There is one volume which had only the references and an index. It is all about the interpretation of fairytales which she did before she had patients. But she could not touch that book again. So, everything she did afterwards was from scratch, using all the fairytales she had lectures on. But, of course, she had all her experiences within herself. That is how much she loved Jung and how much she sacrificed.

LTP: For him, yes.

DB: That is really so incredible.

LTP: Out of her students, who is still living? You were also her student?

DB: Yes, I did my analysis with her.

LTP: And who is still around, apart from our analysts in the institute, who did analyses with her?

DB: You see, all those people died, and . . . there are people who analyzed with her, but then could not go on because they were taken over by their own ambition. I prefer not to discuss it.

LTP: Okay. So, mainly your values emerged mainly from within you and your own experience, or were your values also derived from the experiences with Jung and others? What are the characteristics, the values, that you carry in yourself and how were they developed?

DB: It is very difficult to say. But you see, when I had my final examination at the gymnasium, I was not sure whether I was interested in psychology. So, I consulted my grandfather as to what he would recommend, and he recommended medicine to me. I'm very glad I entered medicine because it is something concrete. You see philosophy and psychology you couldn't study at that time; it was not yet a . . .

LTP: Established as a program of studies?

DB: They were not very developed, so I chose medicine. And then he told me, "You can also see if somebody has a physical disease." He told me about certain symptoms which those without medical knowledge cannot see. That is why they have psychotic patients in the psychiatric institute. So, quite gladly, I chose medicine. I started my studies in medicine in Geneva for the first year. And that included the natural sciences, physics, chemistry, botany, psychology, medical botany, and parasitology. That year, for my mind and for my intellect, was the most . . . [he pauses]

LTP: Important?

DB: The most gratifying. You see, the medical people are not really interested, very few are interested in research.

LTP: Yes.

DB: After the first exam I did anatomy and, of course, dissection every afternoon.

LTP: How old were you?

DB: I started in Geneva at almost twenty. I found that gratifying too because of the physiology, physiological chemistry, and so on. But also, with certain reservations because we had to conduct experiments with animals but I did not protest because I could have been expelled. But being conscious about it, I resent it now. After that, I went into the clinical semesters. There were four years without examinations, and we had all the examinations at the very end. Then I had to choose a specialization, and I went to Paris for half a year for internal medicine and dermatology. I also had my first experience in gynecology and midwifery. The French students looked at me and I said I would like to observe because I had no idea, I had never read anything about it. They said, "Wash your hands, there is a woman giving birth to a child." So, I washed my hands and I pulled out the child, guided by the midwife. So incredible, you know? Afterwards, when I worked in the hospitals, I learned the importance of feeling. I was really very primitive and not okay [from a feeling perspective]. So, I learned that, but the faculty never spoke about it. Some of the academics had some kind of feeling, but most of them not much.

LTP: How did you develop your feeling if there was a problem?

DB: All kinds of ways.

LTP: How did you develop this? Being in touch with the patients?

DB: With the patients of course, and then, with my family, with my wife and daughters. And with von Franz, of course, and with everybody I was in contact with. But I did not do an especially good job with it. Although I am very empathetic. Also, I am very affected by people if I don't repress it.

LTP: Do you feel pity for them?

DB: Yes, of course.

LTP: You are not the only medical doctor in Jung's grandsons.

DB: No, there are three. One is a general practitioner; one is a psychiatrist (he also worked with von Franz), and then there is also a son of the last daughter of Jung who is still alive.

LTP: Helene.

DB: Yes, she is still alive. She is one hundred years old.

LTP: Yes, I saw her.

DB: What?

LTP: I spoke with her as well.

DB: Did you?

LTP: Yes, four years ago. I also met her son who is also a doctor.

DB: The one who is a doctor?

LTP: Yes, Jost. He was extremely nice with me. I went to visit the tower in Bollingen and he received me there.

DB: I see. Yes, he was there quite a lot.

LTP: But also, your aunt, Mrs. Hoerni, wrote some things about religion, in her books on icons.

DB: Yes, that is her specialty.

LTP: She told me she worked with icons like her father worked with archetypes. Very deep work. I can see that you are the most active of all the grandsons of Jung. You are teaching and you are primarily the only one who has kept contact with the institute. Sometimes, maybe this idea that you were the grandson of Jung is abused. Because you are something in particular.

DB: Yes, and you see, when I gave my lectures in the United States, in New York, of course everybody knew I was the grandson of Jung, but I said, "You should not mention that. I don't want that to be mentioned." Of course, this was blind, but it was important . . . you see, once in Paris, somebody said to my father, "Ah, you are the son-in-law of Jung." And he said, "No, I am myself."

LTP: Yes because it is frustrating to be referred to like this.

DB: Afterwards, I had to make peace with that because this is my destiny. I was born into that situation, so I had to make the best of it. There is no sense in opposing it. But I could only do that after I had already written quite a number of things.

LTP: Thinking about you and your development since being a young boy until your current age, how important is the inner life compared with one's status in life?

DB: It's very important. I'll give you an example: I did active imagination long before I started analysis.

LTP: But was this under von Franz?

DB: A lot of it.

LTP: How did you know to do active imagination?

DB: Well, I felt a drive and I did it already on my own for a couple of years. I once had a problem. I had an examination and I wanted to read one of the three books by Lévy-Bruhl, the one in which he coined the expression *participation mystique*. I could not concentrate. I could not read a sentence. I was elsewhere and I didn't know why. Then I consulted my grandfather about it. He told me, "Look, if you can't concentrate, then something in you wants to be listened to or needs your attention." Then he spoke about his own beginning with active imagination when he was young. So that gave me encouragement and I went on. It lasted for the rest of my medical studies. It was only after I was done with my final exams and after I worked for one year in Holland that I stopped.

LTP: Your final exams in medicine?

DB: Yes. But all the time I . . . [*in silence*] . . . Once I did an active imagination that lasted two years.

LTP: Come on!

DB: Every single night I went on where I left it two days ago. Every evening.

LTP: How was it? You just stayed in your chair and . . . ?

DB: I looked inside. I looked and I tried to see and to make contact, and some things happened. It is a long story which changed me a lot.

LTP: But during this two-year period of active imagination, no one really provided support for you, no one contained you?

DB: No . . . before there were moments that I told him [Jung]. A few times I told him about what happened and later I told von Franz. But in between there were several years without anyone.

LTP: What if something of an evil nature would pop up? Or of a bad nature? What if something wrong would have happened? Were you not afraid?

DB: Oh, yes, there were moments and I had to keep my . . .

LTP: Courageousness?

DB: Yes.

LTP: Because that is a very courageous act.

DB: Well, I didn't realize then that it needed so much courage. It was so familiar in our family, and we spoke about these things a little bit too light-heartedly because there was the spiritual protection of our grandfather. There were certain things, the atmosphere, which created a certain light-heartedness about this. A little bit too much.

LTP: So, not only you were doing this? Others in the family apart from Jung were doing active imagination?

DB: I don't know, I haven't asked anybody. I know that one of my brothers created pictures, and he went to consult my grandfather to tell him about these images.

LTP: Did you do any images?

DB: Oh yes, I painted things, but also with great attention.

LTP: So, one could say that you are courageous, attentive, and industrious.

DB: Thank you very much. But I am also the opposite.

LTP: You are?

DB: I'm also lazy.

LTP: Come on . . .

DB: I have a very special side. Certain things I neglected too much. My great sin is that I never published my things, so I have about five or six books in my drawer.

LTP: What are you waiting for?

DB: The occasion. I would need a lot of time and not be disturbed. After the death of my grandfather, I left my family alone for a week or two.

LTP: What are those books about? At least the titles?

DB: About different things. Fairytale interpretations and different symbols. A lot of things; a lot of different things.

LTP: We are preparing to finish.

DB: Now it came to my mind. One thing, maybe it is pretty . . .

LTP: Important?

DB: Yes, because my grandfather never went into that, in much detail. He was so sensitive and therefore he avoided music because he was so sensitive. But I do a lot with music. Yes, I played . . .

LTP: Flute? During the life at the Fasnacht [carnival] in Basel?

DB: On the streets, with masks and costumes. I went there many years just to play in the street. I went with my granddaughter. Now I wouldn't be able to do it.

LTP: Oh, this is beautiful.

DB: And I wrote a lot. I composed a lot in three voices, but I never played it because I needed two other people to play the other voices.

LTP: But why don't you publish your things?

DB: I have some special ideas about music. For instance, do you know about the four functions?

LTP: Yes. Are you a sensory or an intuitive type?

DB: Intuitive. And so, my sensation is wild. It is crazy but it can also be very creative. And what is very interesting is that. . . . You only read about the four functions? Did you read the book by von Franz about the functions?

LTP: Yes.

DB: Okay. The same thing is in classical harmony. Do you know something about music?

LTP: Not as a musician, but yes, I do know of it.

DB: Do you play an instrument?

LTP: No, no.

DB: Do you know something about harmony?

LTP: I do.

DB: In the classical harmony you have four voices: soprano, alto, tenor, and bass. And there is one rule, between the upper three voices it will never be more distance than an octave.

LTP: Yes.

DB: But between tenor and bass it can be more.

LTP: Meaning between the third function and the inferior function.

DB: It is the same principles by which we define functions. Very interesting things. But you have to read a book by Schopenhauer. He wrote a book, *The World as Will and Representation*. He wrote it in two volumes, with the same chapters, at a distance of thirty years. The first volume he wrote in 1818, and the second in 1848. There he says that everything that exists is an objectivation of the will. He goes into all the sciences with examples; also into all the arts – painting, sculpture, architecture, and so on. Then he says all these things are objectivations of the will, except music, and music is the will itself.

LTP: The will itself?

DB: Yes, music.

LTP: Is it like intuition?

DB: Well, that would depend on the person, on their typology, and I wouldn't go so far [as to say it is always intuition]. I would just say that will is fluid. After Jung's death, a few people who had known Jung came to tell me things and to ask me things. One of them was an organist. He had consulted Jung. Jung said that in a group of people who speak together, you would want to forget about the content of their talk and only try to keep the feeling. That would be something similar to music. I thought I could create an experiment: if you could play a melody and ask the people, "What do they see when they hear the melody?" But that doesn't work because everybody has different memories. So, it is not possible. Music is a great mystery.

LTP: Indeed. You have to be born for this.

DB: Yes, but I am not very gifted. I played the piano for a little bit. I like it but I don't have a big level [of talent]. I played a piccolo flute. In Italian it is called "*ottavino*." I learned it on my own.

LTP: How did you learn it? By yourself?

DB: Yes. I was so fascinated that at the age of fifty-five or sixty, I learned it on my own.

LTP: So late?

DB: Yes, alone. Before I did not have time and it was not so important, but then it became important. I went to the streets of Basel alone or with somebody, and we just played together for a while.

LTP: Oh God, it is so amazing what you are saying.

DB: That was a great experience.

LTP: A great experience indeed.

DB: I also painted my own masks. The costumes I had made. I bought the fabric and . . .

LTP: What did your wife say about this?

DB: Well, I was already divorced.

LTP: You only had one wife?

DB: No, two wives, but I had two or three important love stories.

LTP: Right, right. But who from the family, apart from Jung himself, had much impact on you and on your development?

DB: From the family, nobody in particular, except my grandmother.

LTP: Emma?

DB: My grandmother Emma. She was very open. Of course, my parents had a great influence on me.

LTP: How was Gret, your mother?

DB: That is difficult. She was very intuitive. She was an astrologer. A very good, famous astrologer. Even to the point she was able to say to somebody, "Look, you were born a day later!" and she was right. People who came to see her also consulted my grandmother. Later, my mother tried to combine astrology with analytical work. I have always encouraged her to publish but she never published anything, except for a few things. One was about the horoscope of her father.

But I wonder why are you interested in all [this]? I think that your curiosity about these things is an aspect of your search for yourself.

LTP: Yes, I agree.

Chapter 3

Beauty Between Intuition and Intelligence

John Beebe
INTERVIEWED BY LAVINIA ȚÂNCULESCU-POPA
SEPTEMBER 2, 2016 – IAAP CONGRESS, KYOTO

John Beebe is a psychiatrist and Jungian analyst in practice in San Francisco. He was born in Washington, D.C., and received degrees from Harvard College and the University of Chicago medical school. He is a past president of the C.G. Jung Institute of San Francisco and a Distinguished Life Fellow of the American Psychiatric Association. A popular lecturer in the Jungian world, Beebe has been an invited speaker around the world and is particularly respected for his lectures on typology. He has been active in introducing training in Jungian psychology in China. Beebe is the founding editor of The San Francisco Jung Institute Library Journal, *now called* Jung Journal: Culture & Psyche. *He was also the first American co-editor of the* Journal of Analytical Psychology.*

He is the author of the books Integrity in Depth *and* Energies and Patterns in Psychological Type. *With Virginia Apperson, he is co-author of* The Presence of the Feminine in Film. *An avid student of film, Beebe frequently draws upon movies to illustrate how the various types of consciousness and unconsciousness interact to produce images of Self and shadow in the stories of our lives that Jung called individuation. Additionally, he has contributed numerous book chapters and journal articles to analytical psychology and psychoanalysis.*

LTP: Thank you for accepting to be interviewed in this project. My intention is to talk with well-accomplished professionals in our field in order to show their more human face, beyond the persona.

JB: Good. There is a persona, and a personal struggle to maintain that persona. Hopefully, it's like the bark of a tree. The tree is sturdy. It has developed bark over the years, but it also has a tender wood underneath. I like a persona to be organic; that's why I used the image of a tree. I work, like everyone else, at being clean, polished, and to become what someone else would say to me "all the things you are," but I want that all to reflect *me* too. It's not a rigid mask; for me, it's an organic thing. At the same time, the vulnerability of the

DOI:10.4324/9781003148937-4

tree and the sap underneath are interesting, and we must know more about the person to get to that.

LTP: This interview may seem a bit peculiar, because it will be like an anamnesis of the person that I am interviewing. I'd like you to tell me how your life began, as you remember it. What led you to where you are today?

JB: I was born in the United States of America, in the capital city of America, Washington D.C., in 1939. That was a very pregnant time, not just for my mother (*laughs*), but also for the world. I was born June 24, 1939. My mother had a dream close to the time of my birth. She woke from the dream alarmed and said to my father, "Where is Warsaw? Warsaw is being bombed." You could turn the name Warsaw around and say my mother "*saw war.*" The bombing of Warsaw began World War II and that was September 1, 1939. So, my mother was a very pretty woman and very intuitive. She was still twenty when I was born; a very original person and she had quite a serious social phobia. She came from a very unfortunate set of life circumstances, because when she was born, and because she was a girl, her father slapped my grandmother and abandoned the family. This was in the state of Georgia in 1918. My grandmother had no more than eighth-grade education. She had very good penmanship and a nice voice (she had worked as a telephone operator of the original American Telephone Company) but it was a real struggle. My grandmother put my mother in a series of places my mother thought of as orphanages. I guess my grandmother went to work as best she could and she eventually married again. My mother hated her stepfather. My grandmother was very strict with him, very jealous of him, because she had already been abandoned by one man. Her second husband was an honest, reliable man, and he worked as a government auditor. America, under President Roosevelt at that time, was as social democratic as it will probably ever be. Roosevelt had many projects to help people during the Depression. One of them was to bring electricity to farms. In America, even then, many farms didn't have electricity. Roosevelt had created a Rural Electrification Administration (REA) whose task it was to put electricity into country settings. My step-grandfather worked for this agency as an auditor. He carefully checked the books of the people that received federal money, which meant that he and my grandmother and my mother would travel by car from town to town.

My mother wanted nothing more than to be alone with her mother, but her mother was consumed by jealousy, keeping her new husband under surveillance lest he too would come to stray and leave her and her daughter without support. My mother's stepfather, in turn, thought my mother was entitled and lazy, and he would say horrible things to her when she went to school, like, "I hope a bus runs over you." So, my mother experienced a double abandonment from men. Nevertheless, she was a very pretty girl, attractive to her peers. At school in the 1920s other children called her "Baby Garbo." In the 1940s people compared her to Rita Hayworth, and in the 1950s, when she was still in her thirties, to Grace Kelly. She was also bright and precociously intuitive at finding interesting things to read. She would talk unceasingly about her interests at school. Once she gave a report on a new field of medical science to her classmates in a southern school, where it was valued to not to seem to know too much. She had read some reports that were starting to come out in the popular magazines of the early 1930s about allergies, and she made these the subject of a talk. As it proceeded, the teacher said, "It sounds like a witch's brew to me," and the class started laughing at her. Nobody believed that she knew what she was talking about. That was always to be my mother's story; she was always ahead of herself in the way very intuitive people often are. Her introverted intuition was accompanied by a very sensitive extraverted feeling that could be easily crushed by the depreciative evaluations of others. The result of that traumatic class was that she dropped out of school at age fifteen to go instead to the library every day and read. My mother was always an extraordinarily well-educated person. She loved to go to museums, to look at art, she loved to listen to music. She achieved for herself the education of many college graduates. But because she had little formal education, harbored tremendous fear of social criticism and a strong temper. She was not someone who could actually be taught.

I am not sure her mother and stepfather realized she had dropped out of school until long after. But her doing so made her even more vulnerable to their incessant criticism. Late in her teens she got into a terrible fight with the stepfather, and she picked up something that my grandmother had, a little ivory or plastic elephant with tusks, and stabbed my grandfather's hand with the tusks. I don't actually think he was very hurt but my mother panicked and ran away. That was in Washington D.C., and she was now nineteen, old enough to live on her own. She got a job as a clothing model in a department store and took a room in a boarding house that doubled as graduate student housing. In that same boarding house was my father who was a law student. He thought she was the prettiest girl he had ever met. My father was also very bright, but much more confident than my mother. His IQ of 165 had been published in the newspaper of Wichita, Kansas, where he grew up, and he told my mother on their first date that he was going to be the president of the United States one day. He was almost certainly an extraverted thinking type. He was very good at learning and describing what might be called received ideas, but he was not a man who could think in an original way. I rarely found his mind interesting. My mother was far more original but lacked his command of detail. They must have been infatuated, because they married a month after they met, on her twentieth birthday. They hardly knew each other, but at first their marriage was paradise for both of them, they were very much in love. Then, in the second month of the marriage, I was conceived and before my mother turned twenty-one, I was born. My father was still twenty-three, and for him, though I was a wanted child, my arrival in the midst of their still unfinished courtship turned out to be a terrible thing, because it turned my mother's attention decisively to me. When I appeared, I was the first thing she'd had that was entirely hers. She could see that I was a boy that could become a man entirely different from her father and her stepfather, if she shaped me her way. My father was lukewarm on her new project, but she absolutely fell in love with her divine child, and as soon as I could talk, my father was essentially playing second fiddle to me. He was enormously hurt and jealous, and I feared his anger throughout my early childhood. I was protected, however, by my mother. Temperamentally, I was just as intuitive as she was, but in a more extraverted way, and unlike her I was just as confident as my father. She was the first to realize my extraverted intuition. She quickly noticed that I always had a sense of what was going on in other people's minds, even from the earliest days, and she loved that side of me.

LTP: Maybe you had the benefit of both, your mother's beauty and your father's IQ.

JB: I think so. Both of them really believed in education, they were very proud of my high scholastic achievement from the very beginning. But, you see, history intervened. On December 7, 1941, when I was a little over two years old, came the Japanese bombing of Pearl Harbor which brought America into the war that had already started in Europe. Roosevelt had campaigned for a third presidential term in 1940 on a promise to keep America out of the developing European war, but his interest in supporting England as an ally was not at all disguised. Fate intervened in my family's life when the Hawaiian port of Pearl Harbor was bombed in December 1941. Roosevelt got Congress to declare war against Japan, a country aligned with the Axis powers in Europe led by Germany, which allowed America to proceed on that front as well to defend democracy. In college, my father had been in the Reserve Officers' Training Corps (ROTC), which meant that by agreeing to spend a certain amount of his college time in military training, he would, if war came and he was called for military service, be able to report as an officer. In 1942, when I was two and a half, he was suddenly a lieutenant in the Army.

Our little family's life was, from that point, shaped by his military career, which he hoped would help him realize his political ambitions. My father deeply wanted to be sent to war to get combat duty on his record, but the Army, suspicious of his eagerness, chose to have him remain in the United States, guarding against the possibility of chemical warfare and working on other forms of defense military intelligence. As a consequence, he never really got into combat and he stayed in the United States until after the war when he was assigned to the Far East to help initiate the peacetime Japanese occupation.

So, my own earliest years were spent with the world at war, and I also experienced a developing war in my home between my parents. At first, my mother had shown an interest in writing and briefly sparkled as a film reviewer for a local paper in a small Pennsylvania town. But on the first occasion that she wrote a really negative review, the local movie house wouldn't let her in the theatre again. She got so panicked at being ostracized that she became sick with pneumonia and very nearly died. I was only two. The newly developed sulfa drugs saved her life, and when she recovered my mother began to have certain ideas about how her life and mine might go; for instance, she thought we should have a house to live in, whereas my father didn't feel that we had the money for a house. They fought and they fought until she had a breakdown and became depressed enough to require psychiatric hospitalization.

That led to a separation from her of almost a year, when I was four, while she was in a military hospital on the East Coast of the United States and I was living more than one thousand miles away with my father's brother and his wife in Kansas. My aunt had suffered a miscarriage that same year so I came in as a kind of replacement baby for her and my uncle. But she was also not anywhere near over the depression of losing her own child and at that time was, in some ways, a very angry woman. There was a lot of separation from love during that period of my life. When I finally rejoined my mother and father, they had become estranged, and he was getting ready to go overseas to Japan. Suddenly, to her relief and mine, there was my mother and I, alone with each other without my father to interfere.

LTP: You were how old?

JB: About five. I turned six in June 1945, a few months before my father went over to Japan as part of the postwar occupation of the now defeated Japanese empire. This was a very complicated time in my life. Once he was gone, my mother began having one affair of the heart after another, and my father was not considered really part of any life she had chosen for herself. In November of 1946, when I was seven years old, I went with her to China. My father by then had already been in the Far East for almost a year and a half, and we were joining him in Nanking where he had been sent on a new assignment as an assistant military attaché. At this point, I was entering a country which was on the edge of a civil war. This was the last two years of Chiang Kai-shek's Nationalist regime, which the communism of Mao Tse-tung would replace on the mainland. It was also the last two years of my parents' terrible marriage. They were arguing all the time. She wanted to divorce, but he didn't want to give her the divorce. Finally, she got involved with the love of her life, a high-ranking French diplomat who was single and promised to marry her. Thinking she was looking forward to a wonderful life in France, she divorced my father. My father wrote the terms of their legal separation where she would get no money at all and I would get a very small amount for child support because she was marrying this other man. Then, after she left China with me, my father went and talked to the French diplomat and warned him about my mother having a difficult psychiatric history. The diplomat stopped writing to my mother without explanation. On her thirtieth birthday, a letter arrived from my father to her parents, telling them to tell her that her fiancé had decided not to marry her.

Without a husband to contain her, my mother had to figure out how to work to support herself, and after the brief, unsuccessful return to her mother and stepfather, who were now living in rural Georgia, which she regarded as a cultural desert, she drifted north to take a job as a secretarial assistant on the campus of Princeton University, where she hoped I would one day go to college. I quickly became her top project. Recognizing me as a gifted child (I had successfully skipped the first grade), the main thing that she put her energy into during those years was seeing that I got perfect grades at school. Eventually she started making applications to boarding schools, two of which gave me full scholarships. The second was The Lawrenceville School, [which] at that time in the mid-1950s, was the prep school for Princeton. Forty members of each senior year class could count on being accepted there, and in my first year at Lawrenceville, I was the school's top student academically.

I was my mother's great achievement. I was the one who could actually be the high achiever she might have been herself in her school years if she hadn't been so frightened, the one who carried the possibility of success for her. You can only imagine that, as I got into my teenage years, I was both: being what she wanted and also furious at her and wanting to have my own life. When I got into Harvard and chose to go there, rather than Princeton, it broke my mother's heart. But finally, my own life started to come together.

The solution to the war within myself eventually was to become a Jungian, but that choice began with the more individual solution I had found in my own identity to the problem of opposites in my parents' marriage. The opposites there were that my father was so rational, and my mother was so irrational. I think I gravitated to Jung because he was probably the only psychiatrist who was able to see that irrationality is not quite the same thing as crazy, and that is his genius. My mother, despite anxieties, depressions, and rages that were intense, was not psychotic, but she could often be shockingly irrational in the way she allowed herself to be guided by her intuition in an entirely introverted way. I often had to advise her to be more extraverted for her own good.

LTP: Were you your mother's husband?

JB: For a time, yes, but given that it was a marriage arrangement I didn't want, I was also going to divorce her. My mother and I were both intuitive and, in that sense, we were both against my rational thinking type father in that we were both irrational types functioning primarily out of intuition. But there our agreement as personalities ended because our attitude types were strongly opposed. I was an extravert, and my mother was an extreme introvert. She would have wanted us just to live at home alone, forever, and never go out or do anything. I was an extrovert and I wanted to go into the world, as I do now. So, the real battle became between her introverted intuition and my extraverted intuition. The unsuccessful pairing of my intuition with my mother's, [. . .] eventually felt like a prison to me because hers was so introverted, and mine felt like an abandonment to her, because mine was so extraverted.

Those were the dynamics that led to the divorces that overshadowed my early life, which created an early image of relationships themselves as likely to be between people who couldn't unite the opposites once they encountered them in each other.

LTP: What is your psychological type?

JB: I am an extraverted intuitive with auxiliary introverted thinking and tertiary extraverted feeling. My father, as an extraverted thinking type, had introverted feeling as his inferior function, and his happiest marriage was with his third wife, a woman from Eastern Europe who having very strong introverted feeling, [. . .] could hold her own with his *anima*, just as his extraverted thinking could handle her extraverted thinking *animus*, which gave some of her family trouble. He used to say that the secret of their very long, mostly happy marriage was that they had learned to submit to each other.

LTP: Let's come back to the inherited things from your parents, the beauty from your mother and the smartness from your father. Do you consider yourself a beautiful man?

JB: After I was eighteen, when I took my glasses off, some people whose opinion mattered to me said I was beautiful, but that was not something I thought I could sustain for very long. I had instead a long period in my youth when I didn't know how to make the most of how I could look. With my horn-rimmed glasses, chosen by my mother, most people saw me at eleven as a little professor. And I was painfully thin. But by the time I was twenty-five or twenty-six, having learned to work out and for a brief period wore contact lenses, I had perfected an all-American boy persona. I was able to maintain my weight right up into the time I was fifty-five, and I worked out enough so that I looked fit, and I can see in the pictures as late as the 1990s a persona that many would call handsome. But I think the pictures are a little better than I actually looked.

LTP: You are photogenic?

JB: I generally photograph very well. That's partly because my mother was always taking pictures of me and taught me how to pose for them, to smile down, not up, and look relaxed. But I never had the sex appeal that someone more naturally embodied has, because there was always something "less than in his body" about me. You couldn't believe I had a body, and for most people that's not very attractive.

LTP: You didn't own your body?

JB: When you are an extraverted intuitive, you sort of live in two places, your head, and the future, so people couldn't quite find me in this incarnation here and now, ready to relate to them. My body language wasn't towards them. To be sure, some people found me attractive, and I do think there was beauty to be discovered in my features, but I'm sure there was still an off-putting absence of physical presence. I worked a lot in middle life on learning to inhabit my body. It was around the time I turned forty-six that I had finally found my presence. Others were happy then with what I had allowed myself to become. My body was perfectly toned, my weight was right, and having taken up yoga I was genuinely present to others physically. A woman friend said at the time that I looked "the picture of health."

LTP: Were you thinking that you were the man to belong to one single woman? Or because of your beauty, were you thinking that you could belong to a lot of women?

JB: Neither. It was very clear to me from my earliest teen years that I had a homosexual orientation. So, to answer your question, I was looking to be in a relationship with one person, and that person would be a man. I finally achieved my goal when I was forty-seven years old, I got into a relationship with a man that I've been living with for over thirty years and with great happiness because we are a very compatible couple. Most of my adult life I have lived in a monogamous way with a homosexual orientation.

LTP: Was this clear from an early point in your life?

JB: Yes, I was already sure of that when I was eleven years old. There was never a question in my mind. The question when I was young was how do you escape from a world that is trying to cure you of your homosexuality? I had to live through the drama that had developed around this rather ordinary deviation from the statistical norm that America has since resolved by accepting marriage equality. But I haven't myself married because I've not felt I need to be married. I'm not raising children, and the relationship I am in is so natural to both of us that it legitimates itself. I should explain that both my partner and I are really committed to each other, but since both of us came from homes that had marriages that ended in divorces, neither of us wanted to take this risk of adding marriage to an already happy life. But the relationship with him has been my life's world. I suppose I seem like a pioneer or a hero to some because I was able to envision, even when young, what is now accepted as a decent outcome like this. But I hasten to add that before I got where I am, I had to go through all the stuff everyone has to go through to get to something that can work. The shifting attitudes toward same-sex partnerships remains a subject for social history because there are times in history when people have felt it's quite okay to be in such a relationship and times when the same was felt to be quite terrible.

LTP: Of course, we cannot argue with your sexual orientation, but don't you think it's a pity that you didn't transmit your genes?

JB: That was my mother's feeling. Yes, I supposed it was a loss to someone.

LTP: Your beauty and your smart genes, both of them (smiles).

JB: (smiles) Thank you for saying that. But remember the dysfunctional marriages I descended from. I felt like I wanted to break the cycle. I wanted to do something different. What I have wanted to transmit may not be a gene, but it is something generative that I've tried to transmit and pass on through my work and my teaching. I don't mean to speak against biological transmission of worthy qualities, or against marriage as a way to accomplish that, but I do feel that a lot of people marry too quickly. As a balance to that, I think a culture needs to have people who step aside and incubate values that can support a more conscious way of coming together.

But to your original question, there may be a sadness to not passing on some of my mother's beauty. My mother certainly thought it wasn't fair to her and this was not just a narcissistic remark. She was the kind of intuitive woman who knew things and she knew her beauty counted for something. I can accept that it would have been interesting to pass on her genes, and you're certainly kind to say mine might be of value, but the idea of passing my legacy through a test tube has not seemed attractive.

LTP: Not only through a test tube, but also through educating or bringing up, so to say, an improved version of yourself.

JB: You mean by fathering and raising an actual child. That would have been very nice, I grant, but you can't do everything in one lifetime. What I have been able to do, and what I wanted to do with my life, is to help as many people as possible, who are not necessarily children. I was originally drawn to working with disturbed children when I was very young, but quickly after that I became more interested in people's second birth as a person which often takes place, as you know, sometime in the teen years and from that point on. I've seen I have a gift for enabling people to be themselves and then I also try to teach theories of psychology that provide a kind of wholesome psychological atmosphere. When I speak, I probably exhale mostly carbon dioxide, but I am trying to add some carbon to the oxygen and nitrogen of collective psychology, to give it a more specific capacity to engender new life within the ocean of our collective ideas about each other. I often feel, for instance, that people have children but they don't know what they have. People go to the trouble of having children and then never inquire of themselves, "How is this child different from me?" But rather they just try to impose the same pattern on every child.

LTP: There are various theories about becoming a homosexual. Do you think anything has to do with your father's absence?

JB: Not in any direct way. The truth is I was totally unattracted to my father, rather repelled by his body. He was a little bit overweight, but he was not, by collective standards, an unattractive man. Women found him very attractive, and I think most people would say, seeing his photographs, that he was a nice-looking man. He just wasn't at all to my taste, so I'm not able to say that I was ever longing for more contact with my father. His was not a masculinity that I could use.

But I will say that I also didn't want to be stuck with my beautiful mother. Jung is very funny in his book *Aion* about the sort of mother–son marriage I didn't want. In the passage I'm thinking of, Jung is not, to any audience reading him today, even remotely politically correct. But he remains hilarious in his homophobia. He says that the homosexual son is living in a sacred archetype of Mother and Son, but when the son stays faithful only to her, and refuses to involve himself with any other woman, "This naturally causes her the deepest anxiety (when, to her greater glory, he turns out to be a homosexual, for example) and at the same time affords her an unconscious satisfaction that is positively mythological" (*Aion*, CW9ii, ¶22).

LTP: I was not exactly [referring] to longing for your father, but, in fact, I was thinking about an article by Daryl Bem that talks about homosexuality eroticizing what has been other, "What was exotic becomes erotic."

JB: That's a nice remark.

LTP: Yes, because your father and the presence of the masculine in your life and actual masculinity was missing, so to say, through your father's absence and his leaving.

JB: That was a missing masculine element that wasn't him. I had fantasies when I was a small child, it was quite erotic, that I wanted to be kidnapped by an older boy. I later learned that there was a sexual ritual in ancient Greece where there would be a young, beautiful boy, and there would be an older one who would kidnap him. That was an initiation. I definitely had that kind of fantasy when I was young and even tried to get the older brother of a girl. I knew to act it out when I was seven. This suggests a masculinity that I must have felt was missing and would not have minded being captured by briefly. But I certainly disliked my own father's efforts to make me more of a man.

And I also resented my mother's efforts to make me the man of *her* dreams. When Jung tells us that the son who stays faithful to his mother as the only woman in his life will cause her "the deepest anxiety," he adds that she still doesn't want him to go to any other woman but her.

LTP: To anybody, actually.

JB: Yes, to anybody. My mother was like a jealous Aphrodite. Whether I had a woman or a man, as a friend or as a possible love object when I was young, she was jealousy incarnate, terribly jealous and angry. Basically, what I was looking for was a quiet man who was not like my father, who was not loud, and not like my mother, who was not jealous, and so was neither an extraverted feeling type like her nor an extraverted thinking type like him. What I have now is exactly that kind of man; an introverted sensation type man who is patient, quiet, and welcoming. Who creates order that everyone likes and doesn't create drama. Doesn't make life worse, makes life better, and my friends love him, and my colleagues love him.

LTP: And, eventually, you love him.

JB: (smiles) Exactly. I sort of saw that, when I was very young, with my extraverted intuition, that that was possible, but everybody and his brother was telling me, "No, you've got to go to a psychiatrist. That is never going to happen. That is an illusion." You have no idea.

LTP: His brother?

JB: I was using American slang: "Everybody and his brother" means every collective opinion. In college very few people knew about my homosexuality, I just didn't talk about it. I wasn't terribly fond of gay culture as it was then. I was looking for a certain kind of person. By the time I got what I wanted, the world had quite changed.

LTP: Do you think that your work on integrity is somehow compensating [for] this collective idea that you shouldn't be a homosexual?

JB: I think a seed of it was there, but I was always interested in integrity. Even when I was fifteen years old, I had this idea that the three values to live by were honesty, tolerance, and compassion. I was very clear about that. These are, in many ways, integrity values. I think one piece of my interest in integrity (because I did write a book called *Integrity in Depth*) was to encourage other people to "hold on to your sense of what's right for you."

LTP: To maintain integrity vis-a-vis yourself?

JB: That's part. But the other part is to take care of the needs of the whole. I realized that I'm not doing either my parents or society a favor by letting it destroy me. The victims of society do not help society. One way to give to society is to make your life good. There was a time when I was so angry at my parents. I felt like no matter what I did, it wasn't going to work with them. When I was a little boy, my mother had me in long curls, as Victorian children were raised, so it was quite a step when my long curls were cut when I was four years old. I didn't have a boy's haircut until I was four, but that was the way so many little boys were raised. But much later, when I would come back from school, I would have to see, first my mother and then my father on the same vacation, or I felt I did. The first thing my father would say when he saw me was, "You need a new eggbeater for your hair." I didn't have a crew cut; I didn't have short hair. My father was not a very tactful man. That would be the first thing he would talk about when he saw me, so I would get a haircut. Then I would go to see my mother, and she would look at me and say, "Well, are you trying to make it grow?!," like it was grass that I had cut too much. So, my hair was too long for my father, but too short for my mother. It was maddening. I did not want to be around people who had ideas about how I should be anymore. So, some core of me came forward. But I also was so angry at them. I saw friends of mine who were very self-destructive. My generation, so many people, either committed suicide, died in wartime, died of AIDS, died in Vietnam, fell off mountains. It was terrible. My generation, the people who turned thirty in 1969, a lot of them died and very few people I know got through their lives without having been put on an antidepressant. One of the things I decided was "I am not going to be a casualty of my parents." I wanted them to feel, at the end of their lives, that maybe we weren't close, or I distanced myself from them, but I'm healthy and I survived. That would be a credit to them. That's how I can "honor thy mother and thy father," as the Bible says. I also wasn't about to let society push me into a role. A lot of gay men and a lot of men, generally, of my generation were pushed into the archetype of the eternal boy. On the model of John Kennedy.

LTP: *Puer aeternus . . .*

JB: The *puer aeternus* who then dies young. I saw that and I didn't want it to happen. In fact, that was one of my earliest conscious experiences of an archetype revealing its meaning to me, so I want to tell it in some detail.

I was about twenty-four years old. In those days in America, we often would have these world's fairs, they called them Expos. They would be rather gigantic events, and there would always be some special thing. In 1964, I was still a medical student, and I took my mother to visit the Expo that was held that year in New York. A special tent was showing Michelangelo's great *Pietà*, a sculpture from the Vatican Museum depicting the Virgin Mary and the dead Jesus in her arms. The Virgin Mary is presented in this youthful masterpiece by the great sculptor as a very young and pretty woman and holding her son in her arms. I will never forget the scene that developed in the viewing tent, which lives in my memory in present time: my mother and I walk in, and she sees it. Suddenly her eyes tear up. She is absolutely overwhelmed with the emotion of this work of art. After experiencing this in real time, I was absolutely horrified, because I thought, "That's what my fate will be. I'm supposed to die young, and she'll be the eternal beautiful young widow of the dead son." I had this enormous feeling that I was really going to have to do something for myself, that this would not become my fate. I do think many, many men of my generation were potential heroes who died young. I wasn't going to let that happen. That was when I realized the danger of an archetype. Von Franz talks in her book (*Puer Aeternus*) on the *puer aeternus* about "the terrible impersonal pattern" that can even cause a mother to prepare to enact the role of widow to the *puer*-identified son whom she correctly predicts will die young, thus remaining for eternity her boy. At that time, I hadn't read von Franz. I just saw this in my mother's face. I saw what she had in mind. Not in the conscious mind – my mother didn't want me to die – but in the archetype in which she was caught.

I did go to see the *Pietà*, at another time, in middle life, in the Vatican. Now I was a Jungian analyst, a psychiatrist, in a completely different time of my life. Seeing it by myself without my mother, I saw it completely differently. I thought this does speak to my mother and her life, but it's her problem, not mine. My mother had a very creative *animus* when she was very young, and it died young. She was one of those people who was really interesting when she was twenty-five or twenty-six, which is when I felt closest to her as a young boy. She was quite a remarkable woman. And when the French diplomat didn't marry her, after she found the courage to divorce my father, she lost her heart to live. Her *animus* died and after that she did not have the strength to go on living. She had great potential, but she never got into the world, she became a rather isolated woman as she got older. Her beauty stayed with her, but she never married again. So, another piece of my work on integrity was looking at what happened to my mother and realizing that there's more than one way to die. You don't have to die young and commit suicide, there is also psychological death. I had a strong, inner drive to stay alive psychologically and not just be a talented youth who doesn't do anything with those enormous gifts.

LTP: When did your mother die?

JB: She died in 1995, just a little before her seventy-seventh birthday.

LTP: Do you regret anything?

JB: Yes, plenty. I regret that I haven't expressed my gratitude as clearly as I should have toward people who helped me in my life. I've tried to make up for that, but I think sometimes I took the support of other people and didn't thank them enough for it. Many people have been very good to me, and I don't always tell them what that's meant to me. For instance, you are being good to me today, by giving me this interview. I have to make sure that you know that I appreciate your showing this amount of interest in me. I feel that it's important to be grateful for the people who have helped me. I haven't failed to do it completely, but there were times when I was too needy, and too narcissistic and too willing to take approval. Many people have loved me and cared for me, or I wouldn't be where I'm sitting today. I owe my life to every one of those people. They got me through. So many people saw that I had something to offer and made it easier for me to do it. I didn't fail to deliver products to them, but I didn't always show my feeling of gratitude. That's the only thing I deeply regret in my life. I didn't thank people quite enough.

LTP: Maybe for this reason only, you are not going to go to Hell, but why are you going to go to Heaven? Tell me one reason.

JB: On a few occasions, I've helped people more than anyone would be willing to help people without any obvious reward for doing so. There is plenty of reward for helping someone when everybody can see it and you know they are going to say how wonderful you are. That's not what I'm talking about. There have been times when I've gone out of my way to help people, in which no one would ever know what I did for them, even including the people I was helping, and for that I might earn a place in Heaven (laughs a lot).

LTP: Thank you very much!

JB: Thank you! You are a good interviewer. You pushed me and asked me the right questions.

LTP: Thank you!

Chapter 4

Meaningful Coincidence

Jean Shinoda Bolen
INTERVIEWED BY LAVINIA ȚÂNCULESCU-POPA
JUNE 28, 2012 – KÜSNACHT

Jean Shinoda Bolen, MD, is a psychiatrist, Jungian analyst, internationally known speaker, and the author of thirteen books in over one hundred foreign editions, including The Tao of Psychology, Goddesses in Everywoman, Gods in Everyman, Ring of Power, Crossing to Avalon, Close to the Bone, The Millionth Circle, Goddesses in Older Women, Crones Don't Whine, Urgent Message From Mother, Like a Tree, Moving Towards the Millionth Circle, *and* Artemis. *She is a Distinguished Life Fellow of the American Psychiatric Association; past clinical professor of psychiatry, University of California San Francisco; former board member of the Ms. Foundation for Women, delegate to the UN Commission on the Status of Women and Parliament of the World's Religions; and Distinguished Listee and Lifetime Achievement Award honoree for 2020 Marquis Who's Who in America.*

LTP: I was mostly fascinated with the typologies that you wrote about related to the gods and goddesses in us. Maybe you can tell us something about your beginnings, how did your life look when you were a child or a teenager, and later when you decided to become a psychiatrist?

JSB: Well, I was not even intending to be a doctor, though I have a family tradition of medicine, I have a grandfather and mother who were physicians. But I was always interested in liberal arts, in writing, speaking, and reading, and I was not very scientific. Actually, I was going to be a lawyer.

But when I was about sixteen, I had an experience at a religious summer camp that made me very much aware that I was privileged and fortunate. I was a star in high school. I was popular, a national debater, got good grades, and was a class officer. Humility replaced pride when I realized that my accomplishments were gifts: the gift of having supportive parents, the talents I was born with, and the opportunities I had been given. Up to this moment, I had thought I was deserving just because I worked hard here and there. Then I thought of my brain-damaged-at-birth, autistic-behaving, retarded brother

DOI:10.4324/9781003148937-5

Stephen who was four years younger than I. For the first time, I realized, "It could have been me – I could have been like him." In the empty chapel at night, I spent time in prayer and at some point, wondered out loud, "How can I say thank you?" It's a mystery how my profound question and the received answer came together. As a response, I promised God I would become a doctor and help people.

I came home from that summer camp and said to my parents, "I know what I'm going to do in life. They thought, "Oh my goodness, she is going to be a missionary or something," but I was just going to be a doctor, which was the family tradition anyway. Besides my mother, two of her brothers and a sister were physicians. My father was a businessman, but he always admired my mother's calling to be a doctor.

I graduated from high school and went to college and found I really had no affinity for the premedicine course requirements, math, chemistry, zoology, and physics. I loved courses like Western civilization and art history. But I had made this promise to God that I was going to be a doctor. I was taking a double major at one point, premedicine and history. When it came time to apply to medical school, I thought that if I didn't get in, "Maybe I got the wrong message. Maybe it was a mistake."

I applied to three or four medical schools and the first interviews were with my first choice. I loved being in the Bay Area and wanted to go to the University of California School of Medicine, San Francisco. When I was accepted, it was a big surprise because of how badly the interviews had gone. The first interview was with a distinguished physician, the hospital was named after his father. He seemed like my idea of a Boston Brahmin. When he looked at my academic record and saw all the liberal arts courses I had taken, he asked, "You really like this stuff?" It felt like a put-down. The second interview was worse, this time with a psychologist who wanted to know about my brother, which made me cry and left me in tears. I left that interview feeling that getting into this medical school was hopeless. I was very surprised when I got accepted!

Once in medical school I found a lot of satisfaction in working with patients as well as with courses that taught me about what a doctor should know about health and disease in human beings. The premed courses I took in college were not satisfying. Like zoology, chemistry, and advanced math. But those courses, in some retrospect, were like exercises that developed muscles; they helped develop my thinking-sensate mind.

LTP: Every course in medical school was important?

JSB: They all seemed important to being a doctor. You had to know the body, you had to know the physiology, you had to know the microbiology, and much more. Then, when I began working with patients, even though I was just a junior clinician, there seemed to be something helpful for the patients about talking with me. I felt I was in the right place.

I was not sure what specialty I would go into. I was thinking about pediatrics and internal medicine. But I also took psychiatry courses in medical school. The psychiatry department sort of turned us off as a class. The teaching did not particularly inspire us, but the clinical work, where we would see patients in the clinic and were supervised by clinical faculty who were psychiatrists in private practice, was different. Working with people, being of help as it seemed, I found fascinating. But I did not really know if I wanted to go into psychiatry, but I also thought maybe I did. And so, I took out an application for the psychiatry residency but did not finish it because I still was not sure. Eventually, I submitted the application, but I did not ask for recommendations, which were required. So, I did not think that my application was complete.

I went to a rotating internship at Los Angeles County Hospital where I started out with lots of internal medicine, because I thought I was going into that field. But I found that it was not very challenging. The patients who kept coming back to the outpatient clinic talked about their anxiety and depression and related problems. They had underlying chronic medical conditions for which we wrote prescriptions. The outpatient medical clinic was referred to by residents and interns as "The Crock Clinic."

LTP: Crock?

JSB: Crock as in broken pottery – crock pots [Ed. – an alternative term for a crackpot, a derogatory term referring to a foolish or irrational person]. About that time, unexpectedly I got a telegram saying, "We accept you into our residency, let us know by return telegram if you will accept the residency." By then I was in Los Angeles, and I really missed being in San Francisco. I loved living in the San Francisco Bay area. I accepted the residency, but was still feeling that I was not sure I wanted to be a psychiatrist, yet also feeling that a year of psychiatry would be helpful with whatever I finally decided I would do.

The psychiatric residency was in its own building on the medical campus. It was Langley Porter Neuropsychiatric Clinic, a teaching hospital at University of California Medical Center. My initial assignment was to be an inpatient doctor, responsible for five hospitalized patients on the locked ward. They were first-time psychotic patients or seriously suicidal patients. At the time, it was a teaching hospital that admitted patients who were the kind of patients that residents could learn from and who could stay until they were ready for discharge.

I found that I had a knack for it. It was the first time I really had a sense of how people suffered from psychosis. The patients who were on this locked ward did not scare me. I was interested in their plight and saw how disturbing it must be to hear accusatory voices. They were considered crazy because they were tormented by hallucinations. I found I could relate to them as people. I sympathized with their fears and learned about the situations that preceded their nervous breakdown or outbreak of their symptoms. They felt better talking with me, and as I listened to them, I not only felt for them, but my capacity for empathy grew. I could put myself in their place and see how difficult or emotionally painful life was for them. I often learned that something had pushed them over the edge, which led to a suicide attempt, or it may have been an impulse to silence their tormenting voices. This work was absorbing. I cared for my patients and knew them. I was helping them. I had found my calling! This was the first time since I had promised to be a doctor, that I felt I was in the right place. I had begun training to be a psychiatrist.

LTP: How old were you then?

JSB: This was in 1963, and I was born in 1936, so I was only twenty-seven. After I promised God I would be a doctor, I finished my senior year in high school, followed by four years of undergraduate school. I went to UCLA, Pomona College, and graduated from UC Berkeley. Then four years in medical school and one year in a rotating internship. Only when I got back to San Francisco did I find my calling to be a psychiatrist.

LTP: How did you come to being a Jungian analyst?

JSB: During three years of psychiatric residency, through some synchronicity, I was assigned several Jungian analysts as supervisors. There were very few of them on the clinical faculty. At the time, it probably was the only residency in the United States to have Jungian analysts on the clinical faculty. Additionally, there was a seminar offered once a week at lunchtime by Joseph (Jo) Wheelwright, one of the founders of the San Francisco Jungian Institute. He was a very generous, big-hearted, extroverted, story-telling Jungian who had been in analysis with C.G. Jung and after that went to medical school.

The UC Langley Porter residency was basically a psychoanalytically oriented Freudian program with Freudians on the clinical faculty who led the required seminars or did individual supervision. I had trouble accepting what I was being taught in the psychoanalytic teaching seminars, that is with the focus on the Oedipus myth. Oedipus was the main character in one myth of many, and this story was even applied to women. I had taken three years of Latin in high school and learned about the Roman gods and goddesses, who were the Greek divinities, mostly renamed. It made me wonder, "Why only this one myth – when there are so many?" Meanwhile, I was learning from my Jungian supervisors and from the noon seminars with Doctor Wheelwright. I wanted to know more of what they knew.

I had been working with dreams using the psychoanalytic approach to dreams, which was to reduce them, which usually meant reducing them into being primarily about the transference to the therapist. Here I was, a young woman resident of Asian (Japanese) ancestry, and these people are having major life problems and psychiatric symptoms. Their dreams should be interpreted to be about their relationship with me? So, I applied to the San Francisco Jungian Institute at a time when it was not popular. I didn't say I wanted to be a Jungian analyst. I said I would like to learn more about how to work with dreams and learn more about Jungian psychology. At the time I came into the Institute, I found I was in a class of one (laughs). There was a class ahead of me with about three or four people in it that I joined, and a class that came after me with three people, which I joined the following year. It would take many more years of being in Jungian analysis myself, taking advanced seminars, as well as working and writing up a long-term case with a Jungian consultant, before I met with the Joint Certifying Board (of Northern and Southern California) and was "knighted" (an expression that Wheelwright used to say when a candidate became an analyst).

LTP: So, the class consisted of only one person?

JSB: Yes, but I joined the second-year class my first year, and then joined the first-year class my second year. Encountering serendipities and synchronicities all through my life is how I became a Jungian analyst.

LTP: Do you think if something is meant to be it is going to be?

JSB: Actually, I don't think so. I do think that synchronistic events are like dreams that can inspire or warn, but it always depends upon paying attention, remembering, and learning from them. And doing something in response to the message, once you get it. I think you have to make a commitment to do what you know "from inside out." When I hear about a significant synchronicity that could affect "what's next," I think it has to do with it having a deeper call to do or becoming who you could be. I think the person who feels this then may have a choice to consider, though it may not seem like the most sensible choice to make. I think synchronicities are often related to something in us having to do with the Jungian concept of the Self, through which we may recognize something significant in our dreams or through unusual waking events (synchronicities) which happen. I should say, this has been my case.

LTP: You have been a Jungian analyst for years now. When you look back at your childhood, were you affected by events and prejudice?

JSB: While I haven't made it a point in my writings and activism, I was aware of encountering both racial and gender prejudices in my life and know that they affected me. I was in kindergarten when Japan bombed Pearl Harbor and World War II began. Everyone of Japanese ancestry, including American citizens who were living on the West Coast of the United States, lost their rights, were rounded up, and imprisoned in "relocation" camps, although we called them "concentration camps." But I missed this experience because I had an activist father (Joseph Shinoda) who prevented this from happening to us. Thank goodness! But later, when the war was over and we could return to California, it caused me to not fit in with my Japanese American peers. My father managed to get us out of California and took us to other parts of the United States such as New York, Idaho, and Colorado. The strange thing was, we were American citizens and we had the full rights of American citizenship – outside of the three western states. So, while I did not have the same experience as most Japanese Americans in California, Oregon, and the state of Washington, I was related to many relatives in the region; cousins who were my age, uncles and aunts, and grandparents (my father's extended family). My mother's family were on the East Coast of the United States. My mother (Megumi Yamaguchi Shinoda, MD) had come to Los Angeles to be an intern at Los Angeles County General Hospital, married my father, and opened a private practice for women in Japantown. Then there were covenants against nonwhites renting professional offices or purchasing houses.

LTP: As a high school student at a church summer camp, you promised God you would become a doctor and you kept that promise, then became a psychiatrist, and now you are a Jungian analyst. Have your religious beliefs changed?

JSB: Yes and no. On an intuitive feeling level, I continue to feel the presence of divinity and know that what I do with my life matters. Through synchronicity, I often also feel grace. I've been moved by the awesomeness, beauty, and splendor of Nature. I can also be moved by music, a man-made cathedral, or a cathedral of ancient trees in Muir Woods [Ed – Muir Woods National Park]. All have something to do with whatever God is, or in Jungian language, what the Self is. It is confusing when Self is often printed in lowercase in Jung's writing when Jung is translated into English. Sometimes, I direct spiritual messages to "Mother Earth/Father Sky." In my first book *The Tao of Psychology*, I wrote about the synchronicity of events that led me to becoming a Jungian. Once I learned about Jung, I was attracted to him because of his interest in creativity, spirit, dreams, and remarkable experiences.

While Jung's concept [of] Self includes experiences of whatever divinity is in human history and various religions, a shift in my concept of God came through the unexpected, and it has kept widening. Once I was asked to speak at a church that had a woman minister, she asked me to join her in prayer before we went out to face the congregation. She began her prayer with, "Dear Mother/Father God," which was totally unexpected and deeply moved me. I began using these words myself.

LTP: You are known as an activist, which is a bit unusual for a Jungian analyst. What motivated you to speak up and when did this begin?

JSB: "Silence is consent" was what made me speak up in high school before I even knew the phrase. I got in trouble for speaking up. Since then, I know the truth of the saying. I hold it in my heart and mind and make a conscious decision about what I will do about this or not. I ask myself, "Is this mine to do?"

LTP: Have you been an activist or feminist in your professional organizations?

JSB: I became energized about feminism and racial equality when I unexpectedly was appointed to the Council of National Affairs of the American Psychiatric Association [APA]. Appointments are made by the president-elect. I was contacted by John P. Spiegel, MD, in 1973, who actively sought to find a woman psychiatrist to serve on this council. Three years later, I became the chairperson of the council when the Equal Rights Amendment came up as a very big issue, and the APA was in a crisis over whether they would support it or not, after a referendum with lots of signatures was initiated asking the APA to rescind our support for this amendment.

LTP: What did you do?

JSB: Several women, Alexandra Symonds and Jean Baker Miller, and I who were active at the national level started the organization called the PFERA

(Psychiatrists for the Equal Rights Amendment). The next national annual meeting was months away and would be held in San Francisco. This council had many committees and task forces including the Committee on Black Psychiatrists and the Committee on Women Psychiatrists. There was a task force on Asian-American Psychiatrists that I helped become a permanent committee in the APA as the Committee of Asian-American Psychiatrists. I was a "two-fer," that is, one person who could represent two minorities.

LTP: What did you do next?

JSB: I was the only one of us who lived and worked in the Bay Area, though others would be coming out for it. I thought of Gloria Steinem. I hadn't met her before but knew what she stood for and that she did help women, and I admired her. So, I called, told her what was happening, and asked for her help. She came through for us! Gloria came out to San Francisco and held a press conference, drawing attention to our issue. She got media attention for us about the effort to suppress women's equality within the APA. She put me in touch with local feminist leaders, such as Del Martin and Phyllis Lyons, who taught us women psychiatrists how to demonstrate outside the entry area to the annual meeting where most psychiatrists would be coming and going. We made signs, used a megaphone, and picketed. We drew the attention of the psychiatrists attending the convention who were mostly male, but also received publicity and local media attention.

LTP: What effect did this publicity seem to have?

JSB: When the APA board of trustees met at the end of the annual meeting, they listened to what we PFERA women had to say and then met in their executive session. We waited outside while they discussed it. They not only voted continued support for the ERA but even donated money to the effort to get ratification from the few remaining states. While we were waiting, a personally significant event happened, I got a message that my book proposal for *Goddesses in Everywoman* had been accepted by Harper San Francisco.

LTP: What happened next?

JSB: The effort to pass the ERA failed when it did not pass three-fourths of the state legislatures by the 1979 deadline for ratification. Shortly after this, Gloria Steinem nominated me to be a board member of the Ms. Foundation for Women. The Ms. board members included the original founders Patricia Carbine, Letty Cottin Pogrebin, Gloria Steinem, and Marlo Thomas. My first meeting was a residential retreat in which new members and founders met, talked, and bonded.

LTP: What about your activism at the United Nations?

JSB: The next time I became involved in activism was at the United Nations. I was in the delegation that advocated for a Fifth World Conference on Women (5WCW), a movement that for me had its beginning in 2000.

LTP: How did you get involved in this?

JSB: A rather circular story. I had written a just-published book, *The Millionth Circle*. Peggy Sebera, who went to the Parliament of the World Religions in Cape Town, South Africa, in 2000, had taken it with her and shared it there. The workshop had been organized by a circle of women in California which included Ronita Johnson, a black woman and member of the circle. And who showed up but Elinore Detiger who had several years previously invited me to come to the Netherlands to meet the Dalai Lama in 1986. Elly Pradervand, the founder of the Women's World Summit Foundation in Geneva, Switzerland (a UN nongovernmental organization [NGO]), was there with Elinore and invited Peggy to visit. After she returned to California, Peggy called to invite me to a meeting that several women who headed UN NGO organizations would be attending. They wanted to use the name *The Millionth Circle* and wanted my permission to use it. My intuition said, "Yes!"

LTP: How did you manage to be in a man's world but still retain the beauty, elegance, and femininity that I can see glowing from you? Because there are women that are invested with management positions or something similar and they often seem to lose connection with this glow.

JSB: I kept learning, feeling, doing, making choices, and appreciating beauty in nature. I feel a sense of deep gratitude for the life I have, so much of it is a gift. While at the same time, my commitment to taking on "an assignment" persists and making a difference that matters to me continues to give me a sense of purpose. Work done out of love that is meaningful could be the source of the glow!

LTP: Could you talk a bit more about what you mean "to take up or take on an assignment"?

JSB: This is something that comes along that calls you, seems meant for you. Whatever it is, you have a choice to take it on or not. It may seem to be a small step. Or could even feel like a huge decision. This can happen over and over depending on how much freedom and health you experience, how your heart and mind [are] functioning. When an "assignment" comes along, you can take it or not. But if you do, it becomes part of your personal myth, part of your individuation, and it may not be easy.

LTP: Could you define "assignment" for me.

JSB: There are three questions that only you, each individual, can answer to define "an assignment." One: Is it meaningful – to you? Something that matters to your heart and soul? Two: Are you with good people? Do you trust each other? Do you share laughter, outrage, joy, fun, and sorrow? Three: Is it motivated by love? Love sustains and energizes what you are doing when it becomes a commitment.

When you take on "an assignment" and it is with others who share your values, you grow together. You get stretched, learn, accomplish what you probably would not have been able to do alone. And there is the sharing of fun together, as well as sorrow. When love motivates you to do heart-committed work or love is the reason to help a person or a cause, more love grows in you, and you have more to give. Love is unlike anything else. Love is the only energy that the more you give away, the more you have and the more there is.

LTP: Do you have children?

JSB: I have two. I had two. My son Andy died when he was twenty-eight.

LTP: I am sorry to hear that.

JSB: Andy (Andre Bolen) was born with a "bump" on his forehead near his hairline. We had it removed when he was five. It looked sort of like a wart and turned out to be a neurofibroma. This didn't affect him until his growth spurt in adolescence. His diagnosis was neurofibromatosis type 2, in which non-malignant fibromas grow mainly on the cranial nerves, eventually causing him to lose his hearing. Andy loved music. He was a musician who began with perfect pitch and played the guitar. As the fibroma on one of his auditory nerves grew, it shut down his hearing and had to be taken out surgically. Usually, the auditory nerve and the fibroma are surgically removed through the ear canal without involving the brain. There was another option, which might restore his hearing but required a much more complicated surgery and potential complications. I could find out what was possible, but it was up to Andy to decide. He chose to have implants in the midbrain that brought back his hearing. Less than a decade later, he tripped and fell, damaging the spinal cord in his neck because the bony protective cover had been removed during the surgery. It happened at the entryway to our house. He was taken by ambulance to the hospital where he was examined. When nothing could be done, he was sent home paralyzed and only able to communicate in a whisper. He had a daytime male nurse who could lift him. He seemed at peace. When I asked him how he spent his time, he said he was reviewing his life. I slept on the sofa in the room we called the library where he had his hospital bed. I would wake up to go to his bedside when he needed something and called "Mom" in a whisper. The night he died, I heard him call "Mom" in his old voice. It startled me. My first reaction was "How could he do this?" I went to his bedside, turned up the light, expecting to see him looking at me, but his eyes were closed. I heard him take a few breaths, and then he stopped breathing. He woke me up so I wouldn't find his lifeless body in the morning.

LTP: You mentioned your son. What of your daughter?

JSB: Melody was born first. The two were only eighteen months apart. My first pregnancy, labor, and delivery were an initiation in which I was awake throughout, but probably in an altered state and very tired. It was a normal vaginal delivery and while I was being tended to, my newborn daughter was cleaned, wrapped, and placed in my arms. Whatever the labor pains were, I immediately forgot them. What a miracle it is to give birth to a new life, to have a baby! She was taken to the newborn nursery, where most other babies were larger and asleep. When I first saw her through the window, Melody was alert and seemed to be looking around to see where she was. She was a beautiful baby. Nursing her in the night sitting in a rocking chair in our apartment in Sausalito, looking out over the bay was a sacred experience. Even though I had delivered about a hundred babies as a medical student and as an intern, to be the birth mother through which new life comes was very different! Melody grew up, became a psychologist, worked in a nonprofit clinic in Santa Fe, New Mexico, and married. When New Mexico decided to turn its health and mental health services over to Optum, a national health insurance company, Melody applied for a position and was put in charge of mental health services for the entire state.

LTP: A question about transgenerational transmission of symbols from your ancestors: In your dreams, do you have symbols that belong to Japanese culture?

JSB: Not particularly. But I am quite aware that though I am third-generation Japanese in the United States, and I don't speak the language, there is an aesthetic sensitivity that is quite Japanese. There is also something in the way I was raised which I passed on to my kids. But I don't recall seeing any Japanese symbols in my dreams.

LTP: But how are you as a person seen as Japanese, not just appearance but style perhaps?

JSB: Yes, I think perhaps honor and decorum; Japanese behave well. The expectation was that I would behave well and my expectation of my two children was that they would behave well also. We all pretty much did. But maybe there is also something that emerges from their combined genetic makeup, both of my children are half-Croatian and half-Japanese.

LTP: Oh, your former husband is Croatian?

JSB: His grandparents came from Croatia, as mine did from Japan. The Euro-Asian combination resulted in beautiful kids.

LTP: What do you see going on in the world that you see as significant and yet may be going unnoticed?

JSB: Power over others, which is a patriarchal principle, is losing ground. Democracy and the inclusion of both women and men in governments, universities, the arts, and in the armed forces are increasing. Now there are internet visual meetings that cross time zones and continents, as well as virtual personal conversations – all of which, as technology advances, get taken for granted. Just as there were consciousness-raising groups, just women talking, that resulted in the women's movement five decades ago, now there are in-person women's circles, internet women's circles, and women's international meetings that are going unnoticed that help women to grow into who they truly can be!

LTP: How might I be in a circle?

JSB: It is now easier to form a circle or join one if you want to be in one. The pandemic and sheltering-in-place coincided with being able to form virtual circles, which are proliferating. "Circle" rather than "group" is now in common usage. Some circles begin like a reunion and check in with friends who were in college, various trainings, or summer retreats together. So, maybe with others who were with you in Küsnacht? *The Millionth Circle* describes a model built around a sacred center with silence for meditation, prayer, or receptivity. This slender book was like a seed packet and led to *www.*

millionthcircle.org, which brought me to the United Nations. Many of the virtual online courses have break-out rooms after lectures, where smaller groups of people are brought together randomly for a circle discussion among them about what they had taken in from the talk. It has led to many virtual circles, some of them international. Many people have regularly met in circles for years, maybe for the rest of their lives.

Like any new kind of a relationship, you have to learn by trying. Just as consciousness-raising groups led to the Decade of Women in the 1970s, women's circles are proliferating now. They support the women in them to speak about their feelings and share what they may aspire to do, want to do, or could do. I also have become aware of a growing number and influence of men's circles and mixed circles. I talk about the invisible power of circles – like the formation of geese in flight when leadership is shared. When the lead goose tires, it rotates off and another goose takes the lead position. When geese fly together, they fly seventy-one percent further than if they fly alone. It's a metaphor for what we humans in circles can also do with our activism.

LTP: Thank you very much for your time and sharing!

JSB: Thank you!

[Ed – What follows is a brief update between Lavinia and Jean in February 2022, prior to the publication of the original interview from 2012.]

LTP: A lot has happened with you since I interviewed you a decade ago.

JSB: I think that this was when you were in Küsnacht as part of your Jungian training program. It may have been the time I was there and was unexpectedly surprised to find myself at Bollingen with one of Jung's grandsons and Robert Hinshaw, an old friend, Jungian analyst, and founder of Daimon Verlag publishing house. I remember that I had entered the grounds and was in the courtyard before it sunk in where I was! This is Jung's Bollingen! Jung's retreat.

LTP: How is it that you are able to add to the interview while keeping the format?

JSB: When I learned that the title of this anthology was *Beyond Persona*, I met virtually with you and Mark Winborn, the co-editor and another Jungian analyst. When you requested photographs of me as a child and maybe as an adolescent, I got it that we analyst-subjects were being encouraged to share information about our childhood and the journey that led us to who we became. I read our transcribed interview and knew very well that I had left out personal and difficult details of what my early life was like and how I came to be me. The longer responses to this question-and-answer format are the additions. I went into details, most of which I had not shared before. I shared more about what was in my mind and heart in the midst of historical events and racial prejudice. Thanks to video technology, all this is possible, with you in Bucharest, Romania, and Mark in Memphis, Tennessee, we three can meet together.

LTP: Thank you very much for your time and sharing! Any last words?

JSB: Yes! I'm not done yet! Thank you very much!

Chapter 5

The Princess of Color

Penny de Haas Curnow
INTERVIEWED BY LAVINIA ȚÂNCULESCU-POPA
(MARCH 17, 2017 – LONDON)

Penny De Haas Curnow is a Jungian analyst practicing in the United Kingdom. She originally trained as an artist at Camberwell College of Art. Penny de Haas Curnow is a training analyst of the SAP. She has presented workshops and papers internationally and in the UK for many years. She developed a program titled Activating the Artist in the Analyst which includes the study psychically and visually of transformative processes. Her particular interest is in an aesthetic representational imperative, trauma, and the unrepressed unconscious. In 2019, she presented a paper titled "Imagination, Aesthetic Processes: A Guide to Otherness within the Self, and Culturally, A Preventative and Curative Crisis Intervention" at the IAAP Congress in Vienna.

LTP: Having attended years of open lectures at the Jungian Institute in Zurich, I had an idea to collect interviews from the people in analytical psychology, discussing the beginning of their lives, their paths that led them to become Jungian analysts. Especially since analytical psychology is quite new in Romania. The first six of us, Jungian analysts, were just admitted during the IAAP Congress in Kyoto.

PDHC: People in Romania or in the UK?

LTP: Not necessarily just from the UK. People who were giving lectures at the Jungian Institute, for instance, or whom I met at conferences, or I had read their work. My method of selection was not random. It is related to how I connect with these people. For instance, I felt an instant connection with you, having heard that you are not only an analyst but also an artist yourself and blend these two fields together; that is analysis and art, and the manifestations of art. But the intention of this interview is to discuss anything that led up to your becoming an analyst.

PDHC: Up to?

LTP: Yes, what influenced you to make the choice to become an analyst, maybe in your teens or in your childhood? Anything you would like to share.

DOI:10.4324/9781003148937-6

PDHC: So your method of selection is not something you can really define; rather it is an instant knowledge that you connected, right?

LTP: Right.

PDHC: Okay. From what you're saying, the discussion would point to what led people to become the persons that they are?

LTP: Yes.

PDHC: I just want to ask you, are there other analysts, Freudian analysts, in Romania? You said there were six of you . . . ?

LTP: Yes, Adlerian also. Freudians are more developed in Romania than Jungians are, in terms of international membership. They are also larger in number, whereas there are one hundred of us in our Jungian society. We only started to connect with the IAAP and enroll in this path for certification as Jungian analysts ten years ago. In terms of interest, I graduated from college in 1998, but in 1996, twenty years ago that is, I attended an optional course in Jungian psychology, right after the revolution in Romania.

PDHC: Okay. That is interesting. I would quite like to know about that. I believe that it is what we do together that matters. I mean, I don't want to just talk about what led me to be an analyst, because I have been an analyst, I have been in this profession actively since a very early age, since I was twenty-two. That was a long time ago, so in a way it is like the first twenty-two years went just like that. . . . I started really young. I was the youngest person in my training, twenty-five, so I have done a lot. I first trained as a psychotherapist and then later started doing what I do. Let me go back to how I started. How exposed do you want me to be?

LTP: Very much so if you want.

PDHC: Okay. My father was a bit of a mystery, a bit of an enigma. He had an extremely difficult time in the war and was apparently tortured. He was quite decorated. He was an extremely difficult man, and he did not want a child. He was very angry and had violent outbursts. It was quite difficult. My mother was a sweet person, but underneath her sweetness there was a terrible sadness. So, I was an only child, which was difficult, and my way of managing that was to disappear into storytelling and to tell wonderful stories and draw the stories I told. So, by eighteen months old, I was drawing on walls and tables and so on. I was getting bits of paper and I loved telling these stories and drawing them because of the feeling that gave me.

Some people say it is escapism, but in my understanding, it was a sort of aesthetic experience even then. The pleasure of seeing a leaf sitting in the shadow of a tree in autumn and the feeling it could evoke and telling the feeling it would evoke, enjoying that feeling, the magic, the shivers down the spine, it was right . . .

I had a lot of friends, and I was sort of the leader of the gang, so that kind of compensated for the loneliness . . .

My mother's family was warm and lovely and full of song and music and laughter. They were just a plain, middle-class family, whereas my father's was more aristocratic. His history goes back to a home in South Africa, but he really could not tell us about it, so there were things I did not know. I did not know about the war stuff until later, but the atmosphere was in the house. As a child I used to have this picture in my mind, of hundreds of airplanes flying. In those days some of the airplanes had two wings, and I didn't realize until later that he had crashed; he had flown people over to France. He was in the intelligence branch and had information to provide. They made intelligence drops; it was very dangerous. He had a terrible crash and was imprisoned. So, all that was terribly present in the house. I was a naughty girl. I went to different schools. I went to drama school and then I went to a school for young ladies, which was lovely. Then I went to a big posh school which I didn't mind.

I remember at the school for young ladies, it was charming really, I was sitting in a classroom and the teacher was saying, "Today we're going to do a special kind of drawing. The drawing we're going to do is how to make something look good. If you do a shape like that (a triangle) and you put three chairs like that and you get a cocktail glass, you've got something trendy because that's very 1950s." I was so angry at the idea of anything contrived or stylized. What I felt was the need for integrity. We are artists, we should do something original. I remember doing paintings about a television series about a pit in outer space, a science fiction thing. I thought it was awful because I was doing a thing (not going through my head), but the teacher said it was wonderful and I could not believe my ears. I was sort of picked out as being really good at art at that school, but I did not love that piece. I was taken away from that school because I was considered too bright for it. I was sad to leave it, I loved the art.

Another thing that was relevant was that my best friend was Jewish. In those days, there was a lot of nastiness around Jewish people. She was sort of attacked. I remember standing by a table (I was six at the time) and saying, "The next person that speaks to her like that has got me to contend with." So, you know, that kind of protection wall was relevant to what came later. I found myself very interested in the war and I read. I knew every battleship, every airplane, and all about submarines.

LTP: Was your father dead by then?

PDHC: No, he was alive, but he didn't tell me any of this. I studied it by myself. Also, my father had Freud in his bookcase, so I looked at that.

LTP: He did?

PDHC: Yes. My father went to Oxford and studied philology, then psychology, and eventually he changed to economics. He became very well-regarded in this country. Then he died. My mother died when I was eighteen, it was a catastrophe. . . . But, as I was saying, I was studying the war. I was sitting in the library one day and I started to read a book on Auschwitz. I was fourteen at the time, and it was a shock. It really got to me, and I started to make a painting about it. I've still got the painting. I could show you . . . I might. . . . Anyway, the teacher very nicely put it in a prominent place so it got a prize. I was really amazed that it did. Kids do this, so I was not so different from other kids, but when I look at the picture, I can see those things about the war that had infiltrated from my father. It was all there. Then there was also another little life . . . it might not be interesting for this interview . . .

LTP: But it is.

PDHC: I was made for horses. We moved near the country, and I made friends with someone who became my best friend. She had a horse, and I bought a horse too, out of my pocket money, despite what my parents said. I rode, got quite good at it, competed, went hunting, all that. It was wonderful, because I loved it, I still do. But it was also because my father was so possessive about my mother, he would never let her support me or come to anything. So, I went with other people's families. I was part of them, they welcomed me. I loved them and they loved me, so I survived. Also with my mother's family, those who were in London, they were joyful, funny, humorous, normal people. My mother worked at the school, and she died when I was just eighteen. It was awful because it was very sudden.

LTP: I am sorry to hear that. Why did she die?

PDHC: She had cancer, which got everywhere in her body. She swelled up and I looked at her swollen, bloated legs and I guessed something was not right. She was taken to the hospital. And then, the next day, I got a phone call and my father told me, "You should come, but you don't need to hurry," so I knew. She was in the loo [bathroom] and had an aneurysm and dropped to the floor. Her last words were "Doctor, I . . ." and that was it. It was very, very sad. My dad took it very hard. He was in a terrible state. We went to Paris, it was awful. We didn't speak to each other, it was awful. But by that time, I had been accepted at a prestigious modern art school. Just before she died, my mother had told me, "I wish you wouldn't go to that awful art school, I wish I could see you happily married instead," so that was . . .

LTP: It was like a testament . . .

PDHC: Sort of. . . . We had a couple of lovely days just before she died, we went out and . . . (long pause). So, I went to art school for the first two weeks while she was still alive, and I was just like any other student. At the end of the first week, we had a critique and my painting received first prize. It was a painting of a woman saving a drowning man at the bottom of the sea, and the teacher said, "This is different from any of these other paintings." The other paintings were all so lovely. I came home and, by the end of the weekend, my mom was dead. I went back to the school afterwards, but it felt different. I sold my lovely horse. It was sad and I became immersed in poetry and philosophy and Sartre . . .

LTP: Who were you saving with your drawings?

PDHC: Who was I saving? When I was drawing as a kid?

LTP: Yes.

PDHC: I didn't know that I was saving anybody but what I thought I was doing then . . . I am not going to analyze it now, but some of my drawings were of a very happy family, which mine wasn't, so I was creating a happy family to be part of. I was creating what I didn't have . . . I still get enormous joy out of keeping my eyes open and telling what I see, only now my stories are my patients' stories and stories about myself. . . . So, I guess, what you mean by your question is that by telling those stories I was being a mother to myself. It was self-care, not an omnipotent kind of self-care, not the "I know best" kind.

In teaching analysts to be artists – a big jump of thirty years now – one of the things I am aware of and speak much about is that sometimes, when you make a mark, say you look at a table and get the character of it, you become it. You get into it, and you become it. So, when you are making that mark, you are repairing it through the making of the mark. The mark is the incarnation of that re-creation and so the mark will have a resonance. So, when you say that marks will get you, which they often do, it is because of that. If I show you drawings about my family, you will see that the drawings show things about me, a very penetrative me. But anyway, to go back . . .

LTP: In the picture of the drowning man, who were you saving?

PDHC: The way I felt at the time, in my young girl mode, was that I had this incredible feeling of compassion for men's suffering. I used to feel it. I first listened to it through a tenor singing and I could hear it in the voice. I got it from *The Magic Flute* and it made me crack up. And I had all these images juxtaposed in my mind, all kinds of images like Mary, Christ, and Mary Magdalene, and all that. It is hard to think about it, but whenever I thought about men's suffering, I had this overwhelming feeling of rescuing the drowned. I guess it was the drowned male, but, of course, not knowing consciously then. . . . There was obviously this notion that I was being Mary . . . and there was Christ on the bottom and my father was Christ and . . . I don't want to be reductive about it, but the truth is after that I had the feeling I wanted to go to prisons, to talk to men that were on death row. I guess you could say there could have been something of the hysterical young woman. This notion of the compassionate heart and all that, it is spiraled through everything. At the art school there were all these expressionist paintings, all the artists I loved back then. Now, they are back in fashion. I remember, for instance, a huge painting by André Breton, and the first line was, "in depth of the sunshade I see the marvelous prostitutes," but he saw something else in these prostitutes and he was painting that. . . . After that I went to University of Bristol to study other things. Then I went to study psychotherapy and became a psychotherapist. I suddenly thought of something else. . . . Shall I go somewhere else? How long have I got?

LTP: Seven more minutes.

PDHC: Okay.

LTP: I see a lot of religious symbols around; what kind of importance does religion have for you?

PDHC: I was very influenced in my late twenties by a very powerful man. It was a disastrous relationship; it was particularly terrible for him. Of course, I can't name any names, but at that stage it was the love of my life. He also was my mentor, he saw what I could become and recognized my ability. It was such a love. . . . Love has always been hugely important, and I am not just talking about partners . . . but it is massive. I feel I have the capacity to love big. I had cancer myself when I was much, much younger, thirty years ago. I lost two babies as well. I think out of that, but particularly with cancer and surviving it, I survived through painting. I really knew the meaning of compassion. As it was, I like John P. Dourley very much. The process in which I work is very different from Dourley, but the core of the matter is that the process of transformations and stretches, as Dourley calls it, is ultimately a consequence of your own wound, a consequence of the shifts inside yourself, and it is very important. I don't know if this fits into your interview.

LTP: It surely does. Please continue.

PDHC: I walked away from my mother's church because I loathed the fakeness of it. I walked out of the confirmation process. It was terrible there. I converted to Catholicism because I liked that and because it was a true mystical spiritual process. I think I am in love with the Jesus story. It is totally compatible with me. If I take Mass, which I don't often do, there is a transformation process, just as there is with my patients. I spoke earlier about Mary Magdalene and of the Hail Mary prayer, which is a mantra. The point about it is that it describes a capacity to love with the hugest heart possible, however much shit you have done. It is not that it wipes it out and it is super-soppy [self-indulgent or lacking strength], which I think is a misconception. It is not at all soppy, but it is if we cannot take in that capacity to love, then we cannot change anything. What we are talking about is that we must undergo some significant changes. That might answer the bit you were asking me.

LTP: All those elements, how deep did they blend together in you being a psychotherapist and a psychoanalyst? Into being a guide for others?

PDHC: I don't think of myself as a guide; I think of myself more as a co-traveler. I suppose it is a starting point for me. It is not the answer that you are looking for. As Caravaggio said, I learned that the artist in me will, instead of falling apart when something is terrible, I can stay with it. I endure it. You journey inside yourself, and it transforms through and in you, and then it rematerializes. The most toxic things re-materialize in the most informative and the most beautiful forms. It is not deliberate, but I am applying that in my work so that I do not shirk from things, however ghastly, and I always ask myself, "what is the consequence for staying?" If the consequence is truth and what we want, then it is alright.

My great passion is allowing things – as in the title of my paper, "the good of things as they are." To allow for things as they are, not to impose upon them, but to let the object serenade us in all its innocence and originality and be allowed to be what it is. Of course, we kill it all the time, because we are too frightened of that presence because it is too painful. After art school, I kind of had a breakdown. I got to a point where I was so tense, and I took about five pharmaceutical prescriptions. It led me into the hospital, and I had these incredible, lovely two weeks where I had sanctuary. I had peace, I had space, just to know me, and I started breathing again. I started a degree for myself; it took me about two years. When I was recovering, I asked myself, "What is most important in life?" People and creativity. Put them together and what you have is an analyst. That is how I started the journey.

LTP: One more question. Since you were saying you took care of a colleague in your teens, is there a connection between counseling yourself and other people and sacrifice and grief? In other words, do you think it is necessary for a person to sacrifice and grieve in order to transform the inner pain into joy or into something bigger?

PDHC: Put it like this, although it is making it rather cartoonish and popular, remember the story of Abraham and Isaac? God instructs Abraham, "Kill your son." Abraham wanted to obey and the angel appeared and so on. . . . The point being, when I taught analysts how to be artists they said, "But I can't do it. Oh, it's too painful. Oh, it's too difficult." They did not want to do it. I said, "Look at that body there. What is that person going through? Can you see the pain in that body?" "Oh, yes," they would reply. I would say, "Can you recognize that part in yourself?" Again, they replied, "Oh, yes." I would ask, "Can you make a mark?" but they would say again, "No, it's too difficult." They did not want to do it. This is true, and they were analysts.

So, you see, what they had to learn was "If you want truth, there is a price." You have to let go. Bion calls this negative capability. We can call it what we like, but it is a big thing. A huge, complicated thing. That is to surrender, that is to sacrifice. And so, it is the sacrifice of knowing, of being right, of relinquishing the feeling, "That's not fair, I'm going to call it off!" It is the sacrifice of all of that. It is the sacrifice of what you see, and it is the entrance into darkness, and then the vision. So yes, I think it is necessary.

LTP: Thank you very much. A moving interview, indeed.

Chapter 6

20,000 Books – Or More

Ernst Falzeder
INTERVIEWED BY LAVINIA ȚÂNCULESCU-POPA
(MARCH 11, 2018 – LONDON)

Ernst Falzeder, PhD, is a former teacher at the universities of Salzburg and Innsbruck (Austria), as well as a senior research fellow at University College London and editor and translator for the Philemon Foundation, whose aim is to publish the complete works and texts by C.G. Jung. He is also a former research fellow at the University of Geneva (Switzerland), Cornell University Medical School (NYC), and Harvard University (Cambridge, MA). He has written more than two hundred publications, including as chief editor of the Freud/Ferenczi correspondence (three volumes, Harvard University Press); editor of the complete Freud/ Abraham letters (Karnac); translator of Jung's seminars on Children's Dreams *and* Dream Interpretation Ancient & Modern; *co-editor, with John Beebe, and translator of the correspondence between Jung and Hans Schmid-Guisan; editor and translator of Volumes 1 and 2 of Jung's lectures at ETH Zurich,* History of Modern Psychology *and* Consciousness and the Unconscious *(all Princeton University Press); and of* Psychoanalytic Filiations – Mapping the Psychoanalytic Movement *(Karnac).*

LTP: These interviews are focused on a hypothetical exercise: about what is present when you are able to perceive your persona and if you somehow managed to remove that mask.

EF: Yes, but you know, the persona is very important too.

LTP: It is indeed!

EF: You couldn't survive without it.

LTP: I understand; that is why there are people who censor their material a lot.

EF: I mean, we are talking abstractly, but surely there are things which are not for public consumption, you know what I mean? I wouldn't like to strip before the public eye, so to speak.

LTP: Yes, it is an exercise of striptease, but it's an intellectual sort of a personal striptease that goes just so far, not entirely. So, you may keep your pants on.

DOI:10.4324/9781003148937-7

EF: I will try, yes.

LTP: I heard the speech you gave in the Library of Congress.[1]

EF: Yes, what has been called the "*condom talk*."

LTP: To be honest with you, I did not really understand it fully in terms of English; obviously I am not a native English speaker. At one point, everyone in the room laughed, it seemed like a very good joke. Can you tell it again?

EF: I tried to show that Freud and Jung are still well-known figures. To give an example, I quoted a piece from *The New York Times* which had appeared just a few days before. It mentions an exhibit in the Museum of Sex in New York City which was about the history of the condom. The author of the piece, Edward Rothstein, wrote, "The condom is a declaration of sacrifice in the midst of indulgence. It is evidence of civilization and its discontents."

LTP: Yes, it was discontents I did not understand.

EF: The point is that this is a reference to a famous work by Freud, *Das Unbehagen in der Kultur*, which appeared in English under the title, *Civilization and Its Discontents*.

LTP: I see. I translated part of Renos Papadopoulos's *Handbook of Analytical Psychology* into Romanian. Having worked on translation, I'm glad that you were the translator of Jung's seminar on *Children's Dreams*. That is a unique piece. I guess Jung was not that much interested in children, was he?

EF: He was not interested in the sense that Winnicott or Melanie Klein were. He didn't work with children, so you're right, but that doesn't mean he didn't think about them: their education, their problems, their growing up. He often stressed a key fact, that children fulfil the unconscious demands put to them by their parents. So, a child's neurosis can be seen as a symptom of the parents' neuroses, a view that is mainstream today, but was quite innovative at the time.

LTP: To come back to you, after this introduction, I know that you are a historian of Jung's activities, but not just that. As we speak, you are also the co-editor of the correspondence between Jung and Hans Schmid-Guisan. I know that you also were involved in the preparation of other correspondences. How did you get interested in this subject, all in all?

EF: Well, I started as a Freud scholar. I don't know if you've read my interview with Brett Kahr. There, I talk about my past, what interested me.

LTP: But in short, you graduated from two fields of study: history and psychology?

EF: No, I studied just psychology in Salzburg, Austria. But my teachers were always very interested in history, so it was kind of "part and parcel" of my training. It all started when I became fascinated by Freud at the age of sixteen, and by the time I was eighteen, I had read everything by Freud. So, when I started studying at the university, I had already read Freud's collected works and many other psychoanalytic books. And then I became a Freud scholar, but, of course, only *peu à peu* [trans. gradually]. It's a long journey from being an eighteen-year-old freshman to becoming an expert and teacher yourself, a long way indeed, which would not have been possible without help and mentors.

LTP: Yes, sure.

EF: And I also had personal psychoanalysis.

LTP: With a Freudian?

EF: With an eclectic Freudian, you know, a modern kind of . . .

LTP: A Neo-Freudian, so to say?

EF: Well, one could say that, although the term is usually used to describe the work of authors such as Harry Stack Sullivan, Erich Fromm, Karen Horney, Clara Thompson, or Frieda Fromm-Reichmann. But on the other hand, there are practically no Freudians who are one hundred percent Freudian nowadays, with the exception of a few dinosaurs.

LTP: Yes.

EF: It's much more about object relations today, you know, the interpersonal approach, relational psychoanalysis, about the "here and now" in psychotherapy, countertransference, and all that. But yes, Freudian. But I also had an analysis with, let's say, a part-Jungian.

LTP: Who, if I may ask?

EF: Rudolf Bock, in Salzburg. His wife was a prominent Austrian Jungian herself.

LTP: In Salzburg. Both analyses were in Salzburg?

EF: Yes. All in all, I had four analyses.

LTP: Four, both women and men?

EF: Yes.

LTP: Very good. Myself, three analyses.

EF: In English?

LT: Two in English and one process in Romanian.

EF: It must be difficult.

LTP: It was, indeed.

EF: When I really want to talk about very intimate things, I use my own regional dialect. I never lost that. You know, I spent years in America, and I was fluent in English, much more than I am now. I read in English, wrote in English, gave talks in English, dreamed in English; everything in English. When I came back, I had trouble finding words in what is called High German, or standard German; I would stammer, but my dialect was always there, I never lost it.

LTP: It's your mother tongue.

EF: Yes.

LTP: Coming back to you, tell me about your childhood and how old are you?

EF: I'm sixty-three.

LTP: Sixty-three, so you were born in 1955. In a family of how many kids?

EF: Two older sisters.

LTP: How many years after your sisters were you born?

EF: One is eight years older and the other fourteen years older.

LTP: And what were your parents' professions?

EF: My mother was a housewife. But she was very intelligent, she had also studied at university. She had completed gymnasium, as we call it, and she began her university studies, but didn't finish. Then, after her marriage and with children, she became a housewife. My father was a bookbinder.

LTP: A bookbinder?

EF: Yes, it's a handicraft, although the situation has changed of course. My father was born in 1909 and, at the time, bourgeois people often didn't buy bound books. They bought the uncut printed sheets, without a cover, because they had personalized libraries. So, they took the sheets to the bookbinder.

LTP: And had it personalized?

EF: And said, "I want this leatherbound, or in linen," or "I want gilt edging, or this or that."

LTP: I didn't know this.

EF: Then go to the Freud Museum, it's a five-minute walk, and look at the books he had. They are all bound by a bookbinder. Look at Freud's books, you couldn't buy them like that in the shops.

LTP: So, was your father's job something that influenced you as well, in reading?

EF: I was always a ferocious reader. Greedy, never satisfied – I read, read, read. Reading was my world. It still is. I estimate that since the age of four I have read an average of between two [and] three hundred pages per day.

LTP: Oh, my God!

EF: So, reading is very important to me.

LTP: Who taught you?

EF: Myself.

LTP: You taught yourself to read?! That means you also had a context in which your parents read as well, or you had books in your house.

EF: We had books, although not very many, perhaps one hundred or so. But it was not an intellectual household. My parents did read, but, you know, like things you buy at the kiosk, pulp fiction, dime novels, Westerns, love stories between a doctor and a nurse, or the knight in shining armor. All the clichés. They were actually members in a book club, so every month they would get a book, but those books just sat there.

LTP: So, you got your Viennese style from your mother.

EF: My mother was born in Olmütz, today Olomouc in the Czech Republic, in 1912, because my grandfather got a position there as a teacher for some time, but grew up in Vienna, and then after her marriage moved to Upper Austria. My parents witnessed both World Wars and were poor and hungry for long periods of time, until things got better in the late 1960s and 1970s. I think these experiences were extremely formative for them.

LTP: They were Austrians, but did they also have a Jewish background?

EF: Austrians, yes, but not Jewish, as far as I know.

LTP: Did your father fight during the war?

EF: Yes, I think so, but only at the end. His job in a printing plant was considered important for the war by the Nazis; they needed people to print and to bind propaganda material.

LTP: So, they needed him.

EF: Yes, but towards the end of the World War, they needed every male person to fight.

LTP: When you are saying that something from your mother's Viennese style stayed with you, what are you referring to?

EF: Well, the dialect, and the humor. You know, what the Viennese call *Schmäh*. This is the Viennese version of satirical, sometimes even cynical humor, but also laughing about oneself. It's quite influenced by Jewish culture. Jewish jokes are always about themselves, making fun of themselves.

LTP: So, this came from your mother, she was quite open. When you exert humor, you are not only very intelligent, but you are also . . .

EF: Yes, it's a double-edged sword because it can also wound the other person.

LTP: Was she ever bullying towards you in this way?

EF: This is getting very personal. I think it was just like in any other family. I am a parent myself; I have two kids and I make mistakes. Every parent makes mistakes, so I have nothing negative to say about my parents. It's just how it was. I mean, they had a very hard life.

LTP: Yes, it's not negative, it's a construction. It's something that contributed to who you became. Sometimes, we can perceive some things as negatives, but in time they may prove to be constructive to the personality, not a negative.

EF: Yes, my mother was handicapped. It was painful for her to walk, she had to walk with crutches, and she was often in the hospital or receiving treatments. My father couldn't look after me because he had to work long hours, so then I was sent to relatives. So, from an early age onwards, I spent a lot of time with other people. Also, directly after birth, I was separated because my mother nearly died when I was born. She had to stay in the hospital for a long time and I was taken to a crèche [day nursery]. It was the 1950s, they changed your nappies [diapers] and gave you a bottle and nothing else. No love. Then, as I told you, when I went to elementary school, I spent months here, months there, you know, with an aunt or with an uncle. Then, at the age of ten, I went away to boarding school.

LTP: How did it work?

EF: All year long except for the holidays, nine months per year. The entire school year.

LTP: How was this experience for you?

EF: Negative. It was all male, you know. Only boys and only male teachers who also lived at the school. Later, we also had a few female teachers and a handful of female students, but only as so-called "day students," who went home after classes. It was like a prison, we were not allowed to leave the premises; that was not nice. But it was an elite school, with a different curriculum than the other schools, and I learned a lot. We had exchange programs with schools in England and France, had English conversation lessons with a native speaker, and also six years of Latin. I still can read Latin fairly well. But it was also strong in the sciences, physics, chemistry, and mathematics. Just to give you a little history of this boarding school, it started out during the monarchy as an elite boarding school for training officers, military officers, and then it was transformed by the Nazis into the NAPOLA – another elite school – *Nationalpolitische Erziehungsanstalten*. This became an infamous institution because it was a school for training Nazi officers and ideologues. Then, after 1945, the new Austrian state transformed it into *Federal Erziehungsanstalten*, but we still had a number of Nazi teachers; it wasn't a clear break. The headmaster was a Nazi.

LTP: Why did your parents choose that school?

EF: For two reasons – we had no money and I was obviously bright. They couldn't afford the fees for a regular gymnasium [college preparatory]. They couldn't afford it because at that time you had to pay tuition. You also had to pay for your schoolbooks. You had to pay for everything, like excursions, or any extracurricular activities like skiing, and they simply couldn't afford it. So, I would have had to go to the regular local state school. Because it was a very good school, and I was bright, for my parents it was a win-win situation. They didn't have to pay tuition, and I could receive a good education and take the entrance exam for the university. The Austrian state paid for my education and upbringing.

LTP: So you received a scholarship . . . normally the other students paid or . . . ?

EF: At the boarding school? It depended on the income of the parents; the more money the parents had, the more they paid. At the beginning, my parents paid nothing at all, and then, when things got a bit better, only a nominal fee.

LTP: What year did you begin attending boarding school?

EF: At the age of ten.

LTP: At the age of ten. So that was fifth grade?

EF: Yes, after four years of elementary school.

LTP: Could you say you had a unique treatment compared to your sisters? Did your sisters follow the same path or not?

EF: I am actually very sorry for my sisters, because my sisters are at least as bright as I am, but they were girls.

LTP: And . . . ?

EF: My parents apparently didn't think it necessary for them to have a very good education because they would marry anyway.

LTP: Ah, okay.

EF: My parents were old-fashioned in that respect. It would be easy to criticize them, but as I told you, my mother was handicapped so my sisters had to look after me.

LTP: Ah, so, they were parental children, so to say.

EF: Yes, especially the older one. She was fourteen when I was born. I mean, there were times when she had to stay home from school, when she couldn't go to school because she had to look after me, which she didn't like very much (he laughs). Imagine a sixteen-year-old girl who must look after a two-year-old all day long. It was not funny for her.

LTP: But who do you think cared for you the most?

EF: At the risk of oversimplifying, books.

LTP: You see, that's a surrogate mother.

EF: A surrogate world. I mean, a whole world opened for me once I could read. I could just say . . .

LTP: Goodbye real world, I am going to my world?

EF: Yes, correct.

LTP: How large, if I may ask . . . how large is your library?

EF: It used to be about 10,000 books. But I already gave away about 5,000.

LTP: Are you mad?! (we laugh)

EF: I didn't have the space. I've also made arrangements for my specialized books to go to the Viennese Psychoanalytic Society when I die.

LTP: To donate them?

EF: Yes.

LTP: What did your books teach you?

EF: Language, grammar, orthography [spelling], syntax, style, composition. . . . But not by studying these things; it was a kind of osmosis. When you read a lot, automatically you know where to put the commas or how to write a word.

LTP: Did it somehow craft your personality as well?

EF: I couldn't tell you . . . I have nothing to compare it to. I just know how it was for me.

LTP: I know, but, for instance, did books help you to form your reflective function or your patience, or your steadiness, or . . . ?

EF: I think it changed over time. I think in the beginning it was just escapism. It was to escape reality, to just go into a fantasy world and live there. I am sure it was neurotic. But later, books also served as a bridge to reality or as an explanation of reality. So, I was really dumbstruck when I first read Freud. I thought, "Here is a guy who knows what it's all about. The first adult who understands me: It's all about sex." I was sixteen.

LTP: Ha ha. (I laugh)

EF: (He laughs) Yes, that was my feeling. Until then, the priests, the teachers, the parents . . . I mean, sex, you didn't talk about sex, and when you did, it was something bad. You know, masturbation made you blind or whatever. . . . But Freud said it outright; this is what it is about. It was a revelation; it was a bridge back to reality. It was also rebellious. Freud was still anathema in mainstream society, and so this was also a good way to show my adolescent rebellion.

LTP: So somehow, Freud, through his works, gave you revenge . . .

EF: Well, that's too strong. Not revenge. *J'était soulagé* . . . I was relieved.

LTP: Relieved. So, your books were your fantasy world. What about toys?

EF: Very few. This is not like today, when children have their own room, and they have so many toys, they don't even know all their toys. We made most of our toys ourselves. We went into the woods, or to a little brook [stream] and built dams, and with a pocketknife made ships. There were animals.

LTP: But did you have something like a transitional object?

EF: I remember a small wooden car. That was my treasure. I got it as a present and for me it was a very big present, like "this is yours." I mean, most of the other toys were handed down from my sisters, they were inherited, but this was just for me!

LTP: You said that children nowadays have their own rooms and toys. What was your space, your private place, before you went to boarding school?

EF: Inside my head. . . . There wasn't a private space, neither at home, where I slept in the bedroom of my parents, nor later at the boarding school. Nothing.

LTP: You slept in the same room?

EF: Yeah, we were five people in a small apartment, so there was no privacy. There was always somebody there. So, I read. And I can still do it like that . . . I just concentrate automatically. I can sit anywhere and read. It can be very loud, but if I have a good book, I forget all about what is going on around me. I'm just in the book. I made my own bookish fantasy world.

LTP: How did you pick your books?

EF: Mostly libraries, public libraries or the library of our church. Well, first my parents' books, obviously, but they had very few that were literature for kids and adolescents. I mean you can't read Goethe at the age of five or eight. So, I went to the local branch of the public library and within a short time I had read all the books they had for boys. Then I thought, "What shall I do?!" So, next I read all the books for girls, because I wanted to read. I remember my parents were troubled; they felt there was something wrong with me because I was reading girls' books.

LTP: Oh, my God! (I smile) How can a person, a child, only four years old, eagerly want to start reading? If the environment had been different, maybe you would have acted differently than you did. You might have played more, or you might [have hung] out more with other kids, and so on. But you chose reading . . .

EF: You know, it was one way. It was not the only way. Music was another; when I started to play the piano. After a time, I also became very physical. For instance, I had an uncle, my mother's brother, who had money. He was a lawyer and he was my godfather. So, he was, so to speak, responsible for buying me the more substantial presents, because my parents could not afford much. When I was ten years old, he gave me a bicycle, and this was another new world to me. At the age of ten, shortly after I got the bicycle, I went alone from Linz to Spital am Pyhrn, where we spent our holidays with my aunt and grandmother. I traveled one hundred-thirty kilometers on my bicycle.

LTP: Wow, ten years old!

EF: Yes, ten years old, alone. I remember my mother gave me a five-shilling coin, maybe the equivalent of 10 € today. It was just to use if I got lost or too tired to go on biking, then I could buy a train ticket. But I didn't need to do that. I arrived and she said, "Oh, yes, finally you are here, give me the five shillings."

LTP: Give me back my money! (I laugh)

EF: Give me back my money, funny, yes. But this was also very important for me, you know, physical endurance, exercise, being in the mountains.

LTP: Aha. Do you ski?

EF: Yes, I even became a skiing instructor.

LTP: Yes, now I remember that Joe Cambray presented you at the Library of Congress as a skiing instructor.

EF: And music also, I am a reasonably good amateur pianist.

LTP: What are you not?

EF: Everything else. I am not a psychoanalyst, for instance.

LTP: Even if you said that you are a Freud scholar. What do you mean by Freud scholar, scholar means an academic?

EF: Yes, I am not a practitioner of psychoanalysis.

LTP: Why didn't you become one?

EF: I started to train, but I didn't complete my training, partly because there were conflicts with the local group. They wanted me to undergo the complete training, including the basic theoretical courses. I said, "No, I won't do that because I know more than my teachers." Some of those teachers had actually been my students at the university, so I didn't want to pay my former students to teach me what I had taught them. Or like, reading Freud as a course. I mean, this was ridiculous.

LTP: Reading Freud for the third time . . .

EF: More like the tenth or twelfth time. So, I quit.

LTP: Were you an outsider throughout your life because of your different way of being?

EF: I don't know. The word outsider is perhaps too strong. A loner perhaps. But a loner is also . . . somebody going his own way . . .

LTP: On the hero's journey?

EF: Hero . . . oh no. . . . The German word is *Einzelgänger*. . . . In English, "lone wolf" or "loner." I was never much for groups, that feeling of "togetherness," of having a group identity, of "belonging." I would say, "I don't know you, why are we talking about 'we' and 'us'?"

LTP: Yes, this attitude towards life has its benefits, but it also has its shortcomings . . .

EF: On the other hand, I think I have been a fairly good teacher. So, this was a way of coming back into group life, with my students. It is also a kind of group feeling.

LTP: And later, did you also choose a loner as a wife?

EF: (he smiles thoughtfully) I was married once. She's not a loner.

EF: Are you divorced?

EF: Yes. We were together for sixteen years, so, a substantial period of time. I have had five significant ex-relationships in my life. I'm still on excellent terms with all five women. As a matter of fact, next week, I will meet with three of them.

LTP: Together?

EF: Together, four of us. We have a regular round of card playing. Three of my ex-women are members of the group, so we meet regularly.

LTP: What do you play, poker?

EF: No, Tarock, like Sigmund Freud. (he laughs)

LTP: Ah, okay.

EF: It's a Viennese game, very Viennese. My parents played it quite a lot, and I had to step in when the adults were one player short.

LTP: Ah, you were the dead hand . . . "come here" . . .

EF: Come here . . . at the age of five or six I was a stand-in.

LTP: So, my question was, how did you pick your partners?

EF: They were very different women.

LTP: Did you select them, or did they pick you?

EF: Who knows?

LTP: Did you ask for the marriage, or did she propose?

EF: No, with my wife, one and only wife, I proposed. But it was after we had talked about it for years. I mean, it was not out of the blue. It was just until one of us said, "Okay, let's risk it."

LTP: Risk it?

EF: I don't remember the exact words. In any case, it was not the most romantic of moments, you know, with going on my knees before her, or with an engagement ring.

LTP: But all the women were different?

EF: Yes, very different. You know, small, very tall, very thin, substantial. . . . All very different.

LTP: What about their personalities? Did anyone resemble you?

EF: The one thing they had in common is that they were, still are in fact, all very strong women. I couldn't stand a woman who always said, "Yes, yes." (he imitates a moody attitude)

LTP: Coming back to you now. When you were sixteen, how did you discover Freud among all those books?

EF: Yes, that's actually a nice story. Basically, I developed a crush on my psychology teacher.

LTP: Ah, that's a good start.

EF: Yes. I think she also liked me very much. So, she gave me a present, a book by Freud. It was *Das Unbehagen in der Kultur*, the book we mentioned at the beginning of our talk. At the age of sixteen. I didn't read it at first. I read other things. Why should I read Freud, just because a teacher gave me a book? But she kept asking me, "Have you read it? Have you read it?" And I said to myself, "Actually, I should read it, to get this over with." That's how I got started. It's a nice story.

LTP: But symbolically, were you fond of Freud because of this incipient love? She gave you this book because she liked Freud as well? Or because you were convinced that Freud was great?

EF: There's a nice book by an Austrian emigre who then went to California, Rudi Ekstein. It is called *From Learning for Love to Love of Learning* and I think that's what happened with me. First, I read Freud to please her, and then

I read more and more by him because it interested me, and I wanted to learn more.

LTP: So, by the age of eighteen you had finished what Freud had written. What about Jung? How did you come across him?

EF: Well, when you read Freud . . .

LTP: You read Jung . . .

EF: Not necessarily, but you realize that Jung is obviously important, and so is Alfred Adler. So I tried to read the most important works by those so-called dissidents and other analysts. I read Adler, I read Jung, I read Rank, Abraham, Ferenczi, all those guys. I knew what Jung was about. I read *Memories, Dreams, Reflections* (MDR), and maybe three books, apart from MDR. But just as a sideline. My work on Jung really started because of Sonu [Shamdasani]. I think that was in 2001–2002 when I was jobless. He said, "Ernst, would you like to work for us, for the Philemon Foundation?" I asked him, "What do you have in mind?" Sonu said, "*Translation from German into English.*" I replied, "Are you crazy? I mean, I am not an English native speaker." Well, I had done some translation work before, but never into English. Sonu said, "Oh, you can do that," and I asked, "Are you sure?" He said, "Yes." So, I did it. That was Jung's *Children's Dreams* seminar.

LTP: How did you meet Sonu?

EF: It was at a party at his place. I had a friend at the time, Peter Swales. I don't know if you know the name, a very important Freud scholar, and he knew Sonu very well. So, I met with Peter in London. I think I gave a talk there or something and he said, "Hey, there's a party in the evening at the home of a friend of mine, would you like to come?" That's when Sonu and I met for the first time. We looked at each other, we went for a short walk and talked a bit. Since then we've been friends.

LTP: Very nice. To come back a bit, do you maintain the same distance from Freud as you are of Jung? Do you feel neutral or are you more biased towards Freud?

EF: I consider myself an intellectual historian. I am not an "-ian." I am not Jung*ian* or Freud*ian*, or whatever. But Freud simply writes better. His German is better. His style is better. He is the better writer. This is important for me. I think Jung is very important, obviously. I mean, I've done the editorial or translation work for several of Jung's books, not all of them yet published. So, of course, I think Jung is important, but if you ask about my sympathy, Freud is probably closer to my way of thinking and writing. Also, culturally I'm probably closer to the Austro-Hungarian background, rather than to the Swiss German one. Despite the similarities, it's a different culture. I feel closer to Freud's way of writing and thinking. But, of course, in my scientific work, I try to be as unbiased as possible.

LTP: So, you are an "-ian," you are a history-ian.

EF: Yes, you are right. If I have to be an "-ian," it is a history-ian. (he laughs)

LTP: Do you think that becoming a historian has anything to do with your life history?

EF: Yes, I'm sure. But that's like a pleonasm, it's true for everybody. I mean, everything I do has also to do with my life history.

LTP: Not for Sonu. Sonu answered "no" to this question.

EF: Well, I answer "yes!" (he laughs)

LTP: It's a good mixture, so to say, because you are quite different, even if you are friends.

EF: Yes, that's perhaps one secret of friendship. If Sonu were exactly like myself, I wouldn't need him as a friend. You know, *vive la différence*!

LTP: (laughing) I really like the mixture, not only of the culture but also of languages related to you.

EF: Yes, French also used to be important. You know I worked in Geneva for ten years, which is French speaking.

LTP: Yes, I read your vita. You worked for a lot of prestigious universities, including Harvard. Did this have any impact on you? Are you arrogant?

EF: Oh, that's for you to decide.

LTP: I believe you are not, but what do you think?

EF: Sometimes I am, especially with people who are both ignorant and arrogant. That combination can be . . .

LTP: Deadly?

EF: Deadly. But I don't have anything against stupidity. I worked with mentally challenged people, Down's syndrome, hydrocephalus, epilepsy, brain damage. I loved those guys. I also worked as a psychotherapist, with very simple people, if you want, stupid people, but I loved them, and they loved me. But what I really don't like is the combination "I am brilliant and I'm right," when in reality the person is in fact stupid and wrong.

LTP: Yes, but he may be also narcissistic.

EF: Yes, but that goes hand in hand, you know? Seldom right, but never unsure.

LTP: Approximately, how many books have you read?

EF: Pfaaa . . . !

LTP: Give me a figure, please!

EF: Yeah, when I say on average between two and three hundred pages per day, that's the equivalent of a book. So, you can do the math.

LTP: Let's say sixty years. Let's say fifty-five.

EF: Yes, let's say fifty-five years times three hundred and sixty-five days, and you have the approximate number of books I have read.

LTP: Do you consider yourself a savant?

EF: Well, I am intelligent, but I am not a savant, or a genius, or whatever. Let me tell you. My first university was the University of Salzburg. I moved to Salzburg at the age of eighteen and I was soon a kind of a star pupil, you know? I was really naïve. I told myself, "I am becoming a university student! Wow! I have to be well-prepared. The others will be so much better!" So, I felt I had to read. I really read a great deal and I just let it show. Then I started publishing articles and I thought, "Oh, I'm good!" Then I came to the University of Geneva and was impressed, "Wow, I still have so much to learn." It was a better university, in a different league. Then, in Geneva, I also became kind of a small star. And then I went to Harvard. There I realized, "There are so many other people who are better."

LTP: Who is your milestone, your comparison pillar?

EF: Sonu, for instance.

LTP: Oh, come on, you are two brilliant individuals that can compare one with the other.

EF: Sure, but the comparison tells me that Sonu is definitely better than I am. There is no question; he is the alpha dog intellectually, and I am the beta. Some of my teachers and mentors, like Igor Caruso, André Haynal, Axel Hoffer, Pat Mahony, John Kafka, Peter Heller; those were my role models. Daniel Stern, he was a professor in Geneva. I worked with him. Have you read his works?

LTP: Yes, his writings in children development.

EF: He's good, isn't he?

LTP: Very good!

EF: I mean, I am not as good as those people.

LTP: What do you lack?

EF: Originality.

LTP: You are not original?

EF: I am to some extent, but not as much as those people. I mean, Daniel Stern really brought about a turn in developmental psychology. He was an innovator.

LTP: Yes, but I am also talking about being human and still modest. I mean, having read 20,000 books and still be so modest, even when you are being interviewed by a no-name, like you are now, with me. Because for me, a person that is very high up and does not want to have a discussion with a regular person is not . . .

EF: My motto has always been, "Just ask them." The worst thing that can happen is that they say, "No." So, what do you have to lose? If they don't answer, it is also an answer. And the second thing is, in my experience, most of the really exceptional people are modest.

LTP: I have the same opinion.

EF: They know how much they don't know. The more you know, the more you know what you don't know. I mean there are arrogant assholes who are good, but not exceptional. Like climbers, who still have to use their elbows, "No, I have to get to the top." But if you talk to Noble Prize winners, like Eric Kandel, for instance, or other really exceptional guys, they are so modest. Most of the best are modest.

LTP: Apart from your upbringing, that you brought to yourself, did anything else matter, like religion, for instance, spirituality of any kind?

EF: Yes, I was brought up as a Catholic and I was a brave little soldier for the church. I was an altar boy.

LTP: Ah, you were? In the church?

EF: Yes, yes. I still play the organ at Mass from time to time.

LTP: When did you start learning to play the organ?

EF: At ten or eleven.

LTP: This is when you went to boarding school?

EF: Yes.

LTP: So, you learned it in music class?

EF: No, I started to learn the piano at the age of six or seven. Then I went to boarding school and continued my piano lessons, and I was obviously gifted, so my teacher suggested that he give me organ lessons free of charge. I thought it was because he liked me, but then I realized it was because he wanted me to play the organ on Sundays, so that he could sleep in. (he laughs)

LTP: So, you are again the replacement dead-hand child, moving from the card games to the organ.

EF: Yes, now in a Catholic framework. I was also a member of a choir.

LTP: Yes, I was about to ask . . .

EF: I was a bass, but after some time the choirmaster said, "Hey, Falzeder, you play the organ, or the cembalo, or the piano," because then he didn't need to do it himself while conducting at the same time. We also performed in churches and sang at Mass, so this too was in a very Catholic environment. But then, of course, everything changed when I began to read Freud.

LTP: Did he become like your religion?

EF: No, not religion, more like an antidote. At the same time as I became interested in Freud, I also had a very religious phase and initially I sought to combine those two fields.

LTP: Was it possible?

EF: No.

LTP: I am trying to do the same with Jung and Orthodoxy [Eastern Orthodox Church].

EF: With Jung it should be easier. For me, it was not possible, at least not with that kind of religion, which was very evangelical, very strict, hierarchical, and very much about guilt. So, I read Freud's *Future of an Illusion* again, and I thought, "Ah, yeah, that's it!" So, I came to see religion, or at least organized religion in a hierarchical church, as *kindisch* or at least *kindlich* – as a childish or infantile thing, like Freud described it. I am not talking about deep spirituality. I'm talking about religion as I experienced it in school and in the countryside, among the ordinary people, the old women with their rosaries. This was an infantile way of thinking, in my mind. I still think, "If there is a God, why should He care about me, of all persons?"

LTP: There is a saying: "God only knows how to count up to one. So, for Him, every one of us is important." It is not that God is interested in you only, he is interested in you also.

EF: I am no longer religious. I like how Freud dealt with it. A stubborn atheist.

LTP: Are you an atheist now?

EF: Yes, I guess I am.

LTP: You don't seem to be. You seem to be very kind, and kindness comes from God.

EF: I think kindness is something you have to learn. I don't know if you have read Schopenhauer.

LTP: Yes, of course.

EF: I mean, he's the ultimate misogynist and pessimist. Nevertheless, I like Schopenhauer very much. Surprisingly he makes a strong *plaidoyer* for being polite and friendly. Whether it comes from God or not, the important thing is be kind!

LTP: To live it.

EF: Yes, live it. I don't need a God to be nice. That's what I think; you may think otherwise.

LTP: Well, we are free in thinking. I respect you; I accept your position. In Romania, we recently had an earthquake. Quite a serious one, 5.3, maybe 6 [on the Richter scale]. That was quite shaky. On Facebook a phrase circulated, "At 6 on the Richter scale the atheism is disappearing."

EF: (he laughs)

LTP: Yes. What do you do on Sunday mornings, apart from interviews?

EF: Usually, you mean? The mountains. Hiking, skiing, mountain biking, cycling. . . . That's what I like to do. But sometimes I sleep in.

LTP: Currently, are you living with someone?

EF: No.

LTP: You came back to become a loner. But you are living with your books.

EF: And my piano.

LTP: What's your favorite composer?

EF: Bach and Mozart. This is true genius.

LTP: Maybe you can give us an example of your playing in Vienna next year because the next International Congress of Analytical Psychology will be there [2019].

EF: We will see. I'm not a member of the IAAP. I'm not an analyst.

LTP: Oh, I understand. Are you performing anywhere?

EF: Yes, every now and then. Not at the moment, but let's put it differently. I like to make music with other people, because doing it alone is boring. At the moment, I have no one to play with. But I know somebody will come. For instance, a year ago, with one of my former relationships, we performed for an evening. She's a very good singer, a mezzo-soprano. She has a very beautiful voice, very musical. I accompanied her and we had a mixed program from pre-Baroque to Bach, up to Duke Ellington.

LTP: Duke Ellington?

EF: Yes, like mainstream jazz and blues. Some time before that, with a male singer, a tenor, we performed Schubert, *Die schöne Müllerin*, the song cycle. So, on an irregular basis I perform.

LTP: The last questions – in your opinion what was the life lesson that you remember from your father?

EF: The life lesson is humanity and inner kindness.

LTP: And from your mother?

EF: Let me tell you an anecdote about my father. My mother was a very difficult woman, but I think I understand that now, from her point of view, being handicapped and all. She came from a bourgeois Viennese family and married a poor worker. So, there were problems from her family, like "Why did you choose that man?" Also, she was always in pain. She had terrible migraines, she could hardly walk, and would become narcissistic and hysterical. There was one situation when she went into hysterics, and I was confused, maybe even a bit terrified, as a child. I looked at my father, and he said to me something like, "Boy, this will pass. She will stop, and after all I love her!" That is the life lesson he gave me.

LTP: Very touching. Very nice. Your father taught you that the most important thing is to love. If there is love, there is everything . . .

EF: And patience, as if he were saying, "Right now, it's a difficult situation." He didn't literally say that, but that is how I feel it in my memory, like, *"She's in a difficult situation now, and try to understand her! This will pass. She will again be a very nice woman. After all, I really love her."*

LTP: What life lesson did you teach your kids?

EF: Ha! I will ask them.

LTP: What do you think?

EF: I don't know, I will have to ask them.

LTP: Yes, I understand. Please do. Is it a boy or a girl or two boys?

EF: Boy and girl. Man and woman now. My son is thirty-three and my daughter twenty-eight.

LTP: Okay.

EF: Be decent! Don't be evil! Learning is important. Languages are very important. Both my children speak several living languages, apart from German. There are also two mottos which I like and which I borrowed from Ernest Jones, of all people. One is, "Do not complain, go on working!" The second is, "There is always a place on the top!"

LTP: Is there?

EF: Yeah. My son switched from studying theoretical physics to history and philosophy, and some were concerned that he wouldn't find a decent job afterwards, but I supported it. There is always a place on the top if you are really good. You will get recognition; it doesn't matter what you do if you are exceptionally good at it. So, maybe these are the messages I conveyed. Also, physicality and love of nature. One of my former relationships, the singer, is also a skiing instructor. She comes from St. Anton am Arlberg, a world-famous ski resort. She also has a son who is as old as my daughter. So, when Caroline and I and our three children, when we went skiing, we were a sight, you know? People would turn their heads and watch us.

LTP: At the end of our interview, I have a few questions about your publishing activity. Have you ever been rejected by a publisher?

EF: Yes, a few times. Everybody gets rejected now and then. But then I tried another journal, and they took it.

LTP: On the same manuscript?

EF: Yes. Or I translated it, for instance, into French, and then it was accepted by a French journal. So, I just keep on trying. Everything I wanted to get published did get published, one way or another.

LTP: That's a good thing because that's a good impulse for all the young people that want to publish.

EF: Yes, I mean just look at the numbers, about how many manuscripts are submitted – books and articles. I'm also a reviewer for publishers, like university presses in America, and also for journals.

LTP: Which ones?

EF: Like *Psyche* in Germany, the *International Journal of Psychoanalysis*, or the *International Forum of Psychoanalysis*, those kinds of journals. I'm also on the editorial board of *Luzifer-Amor*. Just a week ago, I rejected a paper. But the good thing about peer reviews is that, as a reviewer, you must give reasons why you rejected something. So, as an author, you can learn much from a rejection. Because those peers can help you by asking, "Why did you do it that way? It would be much better if you would have done it another way."

LTP: So, they are not just saying, "This is not good." They are saying, "This is not good because . . ."

EF: Yes, "because." If it's a good journal.

LTP: This list of good journals, ones with an impact factor, they are very difficult to get published in, especially [in] our world.

EF: Yes, I know. For instance, it took me a long time to get published in *The International Journal of Psychoanalysis*.

LTP: Which is really the highest.

EF: Yes, the Holy Grail, or at least it used to be.

LTP: You were published there yourself, or as a co-author?

EF: Both.

LTP: Both. And who did you co-author with?

EF: With John Burnham. And a short piece with Judith Dupont.

LTP: Were you invited to co-author, or did you initiate it?

EF: John said, "Ernst, let's do a piece together," and we did it. Then he said, "You have to be the first author," because alphabetically Burnham should have come first, but he insisted.

LTP: That you had to be the first author?

EF: Yes. We submitted it to the journal, and they said, "No, it's too long." So, we shortened it, and it was accepted.

LTP: The paper was on?

EF: It was entitled, "A Perfectly Staged 'Concerted Action' Against Psychoanalysis: The 1913 Congress of German Psychiatrists" [2007]. A historical piece. The title is actually a quote from that congress by one of the leading German psychiatrists at the time who said, "Psychoanalysis is a perfectly staged concerted action," which was indeed against psychoanalysis.

LTP: Thank you for those two meanings. And thank you very much for the interview!

EF: Thank you!

[Editor's Note] Prior to the publication of the interview, we received the following update from Dr. Falzeder about how his children saw him, as a father and the lessons they learned from him. Here is what Eva Erhart and Florian Falzeder wrote about their father:

> The most obvious and (deceptively) superficial answer would be three folk wisdoms on how to deal with difficulties in life our dad once or twice (or rather more often) liked to recite to us. Handed down to us in Upper Austrian dialect, they could be roughly translated as follows: (1) "Life is hard." (2) "Really, are you sure?" (3) "Who knows what it's been good for?" The latter is a bit like the English phrase, "This too will pass" or "Always look on the bright side of life."
>
> There's much to read into those: a humorous way of coping with life, a smile about the many things you don't get, perhaps even a Socratic philosophy. You don't need fancy words or awfully long sentences to wax philosophical.
>
> On another existential level, money. The bohemian lifestyle of the freelance researcher has taught us that, indeed, life can be hard. But almost always you can cope. We both have a rather basic need for some financial security in life, however, so this life lesson may have backfired a bit . . .
>
> In any case, we have always admired our father's generosity to help others in need, when you have the means to – and you almost always have.

Note

1 Published under the title, "Freud and Jung, Freudians and Jungians," Jung Journal – Culture & Psyche, Summer 2012, Vol. 6(3): 24–43.

Chapter 7

Mysterious Combinations

Miriam Gomes de Freitas
INTERVIEWED BY LAVINIA ȚÂNCULESCU-POPA
(MARCH 4, 2015 – KÜSNACHT)

Miriam Gomes de Freitas, PhD, finished medical school in Brazil in 1973. In 1974 she went to Paris for a period at the Salpetrière on neuropsychology. She attended courses at the Jung Institute in Paris and afterwards went to the Jung Institute in Zürich. Her training analysts were Prof. C.A. Meier and Mrs. Pope. She went back to Brazil in 1981, after giving lectures on her dissertation subject of "Electra and the Father Complex" at the C.G. Jung Institute in Zürich. She has also lectured at the C.G. Jung Institute of Chicago and at St. George Psychiatric clinic in Berkeley. Dr. Gomes de Freitas lectured on analytical psychology for decades in Porto Alegre. She taught at the Psychiatry Department in the medical school for a year, in Porto Alegre, conducted study groups for years, and gave many lectures at universities of psychology and medicine in Brazil. Her interests are wide, from Greek mythology, Hebrew tradition, sociology, and philosophy.

LTP: In this series of interviews my interest is finding out how Jungian analysts became the people that they are today. But first, how did you get to study Jung?

MGF: It was 1974. I entered medical school because I wanted to be a psychiatrist. I have read many things by Freud before, but at that moment there was nothing of Jung in Brazil. We had almost no translations of Jung, very few things. The university and all the academies were entirely dominated by Freud. There were many things that I did not understand or did not quite agree with in Freudian theory, but I have always thought, "Well, maybe it is because I have no practice and when I start practicing it will all make sense." So, I was very eager to become a psychiatrist and a psychoanalyst. At this point, the two were not so separated as now. I wanted to resolve the doubts that I had with my readings. I started to ask the teachers and instructors. They had no answers though, and not only did they have no answers, but worse, they made me feel that it was just "resistance" asking those theoretical questions over and over again. Seeing that there was no space for questioning anything,

DOI:10.4324/9781003148937-8

that it was a sort of dogma, apparently too high to be grasped by an inexperienced student, I started the practical work. Things simply did not fit, and the theory did not help my understanding of the patients. I was asking myself: "What am I going to do now? I came to medicine to be a psychiatrist and now I find it scary. . . . " The closest thing I could do was to go into neurology, because in Brazil at that time, there was nothing outside.

LTP: Outside of . . . ?

MGF: Outside a psychiatric training with a Freudian or Kleinian perspective. The Freudian approach to psychodynamics or medical psychiatry was dominant and exclusive. But I wanted a psychological approach, not only the medical approach; I wanted both. I did not think that we should exclude one or the other. For me, the medical approach together with the Freudian psychoanalytical approach was not workable. So I decided on neurology and went to Paris to study neurology. I went to the Salpêtrière [Pitié-Salpêtrière Hospital]. That is where Freud started, as well as Pierre Janet and Jean-Martin Charcot. Every Wednesday we had a meeting of the neurology corpus, where the instructors and professors of all the specialties of neurology would offer their contribution to the case. There were also psychiatrists working there too. There were representatives from neuropsychology, neuroimaging, the neurological clinic, and neurophysiology. I realized that there were other approaches to psychiatry, that other physicians were having similar doubts, and that they were discussing these doubts. That was also Lacan's time; the 1970s. This rekindled my interest in psychoanalysis. I started to look for books and read. I read a bit of Lacan and then I read a book by Jung. I was fascinated.

LTP: What book was that?

MGF: It was the book that he wrote with Karl Kerenyi, about the maiden, the young maiden and the child, the original child.

LTP: The divine child. The mythology book?

MGF: Yes. I liked it very much. . . . One of the things I liked very much before going into psychiatry was Greek mythology and theater. I had thought about going into theater to become a director, not as an actress. I was fascinated by Greek tragedy and Greek mythology. This book somehow gave me a psychological insight into the Greek world that I could not get through the Freudian approach. Then I started to study Jung, and I began to go to the Jung Institute in Paris. I went to Eranos that year.

LTP: Excellent! What year was that?

MGF: It was 1974.

LTP: Who presented then?

MGF: It was James Hillman, David Miller, Antoine Faivre, Gilbert . . .

LTP: . . . Durand?

MGF: Yes, I believe Gilbert Durand. He talked about mythology. James Hillman was there and also Shmuel Sambursky with his paper on I-Ching.

LTP: In 1974, who were you invited by? Because I know that in Eranos, everything was by invitation only.

MGF: I was invited by a professor of the Sorbonne, Antoine Faivre.

LTP: So you were one of the students?

MGF: I was one of the students.

LTP: You really made an impression on him . . .

MGF: You can say that . . . and I was going to the Jungian Institute in Paris. That is where I met Antoine Faivre, who wrote a book on esotericism. He is a specialist in 19th-century esotericism and teaching at the Paris Institute. Gilbert Durand was also teaching there. So, it was their invitation.

LTP: By that time you had already started in analysis?

MGF: No, I was not in analysis. I was just fascinated by the Jungian ideas. I went to Eranos and I realized that I wanted to go to Zurich, because Zurich was where things started. At this moment, the situation in Paris was not very well organized in terms of training. Zurich was the source.

LTP: Yes.

MGF: Zurich had a much more organized training. I knew that James Hillman was teaching there. I talked to Hillman in Eranos and I asked, "I would like to go to Zurich. How can I do it?" He said, "Well, you have to wait to enroll." Because this time there were many students coming and I had to wait. But I wrote to Guggenbühl-Craig, who was the president of the Zurich institute at that time, to see if there was anything I could do. I needed some letters of introduction, maybe two or three.

LTP: Referrals?

MGF: Referrals, yes. Antoine Faivre gave me one, and James Hillman gave me another. I was to start my analysis in Zurich. I wrote to Guggenbühl-Craig again and, since I was a medical doctor, I was wondering if I could work in Zurich. I did not know anything about the working situation in Zurich.

LTP: You already finished medical school by then?

MGF: Medicine, yes. I had already finished. Also another year of neurology, a training that I did not finish.

LTP: Okay, so you are already a physician in psychiatry. And after this, you began a specialization in neurology that you didn't finish?

MGF: Correct. So, I wrote to Guggenbühl-Craig and I asked if I could work in the clinic with him. He answered: "Yes, I believe we can work together. I think we can work analytical well together." But I did not understand that he was referring to being in analysis with him . . . I did not understand English very well and I did not understand the jargon "to work with someone." I didn't know it meant to be in analysis with someone.

LTP: You thought "work" meant to work as in having a job, not analysis.

MGF: Exactly. I answered Giggenbühl's letter saying, "When I come to Zurich I will look for you." I was thinking about a workplace. So, I came to the institute that was still in the old institute location on Gemeindestrasse.

LTP: Where the Psychology Club is now.

MGF: Yes. Frau Baumann, who was the secretary back then, was a nice dragon. Everybody was afraid of her because she put enormous bureaucratic tasks on us, so we would have to fulfill this and that. A lot of things. She asked me, "Who is your analyst?" I said, "I don't know yet. I just arrived here. I'm not in the training program yet. I'm just applying." She said that I needed to have an analyst and she gave me a list of them to select from. She convinced me I was too slow in getting things done. I didn't know how to move about in the city, how to go to Küsnacht, or to Erlenbach, or anything. Everything sounded very complex to me. German names sounded rough to my ears.

LTP: Mystery?

MGF: A mystery to move around and a misery as well. I saw in the list a man called Meier. A very simple name.

LTP: C.A. Meier?

MGF: Yes, C.A. Meier. He spoke French and Italian and lived on a street that I had already seen, very close to the institute. So that is what I wanted; I went to see Meier to start my analysis with this person who had a name I could easily pronounce and lived in a street close to where I was staying. I did not know who he was. For me, he was the easiest person to find and he had the quality of knowing Latin languages, which set him sort of close to my background. I didn't know anything about the Jungian world. I wanted to wait to call Guggenbühl-Craig until I had done everything to show how efficient I was; I was proud to do everything by myself and wanted to tell him, "I have met an analyst, I'm fully registered in the training program, ready for work." After solving these urgent tasks, I called Guggenbühl for an appointment. The appointment was sort of odd because, supposedly it was an analytical hour, whereas I thought he was going to give me a job. (She laughs)

LTP: So, initially it was a job interview . . . (I laugh)

MGF: (She laughs) He didn't know it was a job interview, and I didn't understand what was happening. At some point in our conversation, I told him that Professor Meier was my analyst. Once he understood that I had already started my analysis with Professor Meier, it was "Goodbye!" I still didn't understand anything, only that there was no job waiting for me. Many months later, I was introduced to the jargon. People would ask, "With whom do you work?"

LTP: Meaning "Who is your analyst?"

MGF: Yes, that was the meaning. First I used to answer, "I don't work here, I am studying!" Then, I started to understand what had happened. But, it was already done. I was working with Meier and only later on did I come back to see Guggenbühl-Craig.

LTP: You only worked with Meier as your analyst? Or did you have a second analyst?

MGF: After a certain period of time, I started to work with Mrs. Pope [Ed.- full name of analyst not known].

LTP: I see. Coming back to your family, were you a unique child in your family?

MGF: For a long time, I was an only child. I was nine years old when my brother was born.

LTP: And your parents supported your passion for Jungian analysis?

MGF: Yes.

LTP: What were the professions of your parents?

MGF: My father was an engineer and my mother was a psychologist.

LTP: Oh, what kind of psychologist was she?

MGF: She never really worked. She finished her studies and worked just for a while with psychology in the schools, child psychology. She was more education focused and had a pedagogic approach. She never worked clinically with psychology.

LTP: What first attracted you to psychiatry?

MGF: I had to understand, I wanted to understand . . .

LTP: The madness?

MGF: Yes and why we become what we are. It is really a search for understanding.

LTP: Yes, it is important to have doubts, to have questions. . . . What I liked about your story is that you did not quit the fight because you believed that there were still questions to be answered. I found the same attitude when I heard you talking about Job from the Bible and his courage to state, "No, I didn't do anything bad." This steadiness and consistency in your work, I now discover in your life also. What age were you when you knew that you were going to study psychiatry?

MGF: Well, I had to decide what to do when I was about eighteen years old. I considered different options: architecture and construction, theater, and medicine. In medicine, I liked psychiatry because of its human aspect, I always was more attracted to this. Although, even in analytical psychology we discuss inner structures, so there is a technical part. I like both; to mix the technical, scientific side of medicine with the matters of the soul. Architecture is a result of a sort of combination between art, mathematics, and physics. I like that. So my choices were between architecture, medicine, and theatre. The university entrance exams for medicine and architecture were more or less at the same time. So, I had to choose between one or another. The exams for theater were at a different time. So my choices reduced to medicine and theater. I didn't know if I was going to get into the medical school because in Brazil it is very difficult to enter the university.

LTP: High competition, I assume.

MGF: Very high competition. After you are inside you can continue, but before entering it is difficult. I signed up to take the exams for medicine and theater. I decided to give up the theatre examination when I learned I was admitted into medical school.

LTP: But you still have a loving side for theatre?

MGF: Yes. I wrote two plays and directed them. One play was called, *The Dreams of Reason*.

LTP: Wow! So, you wrote and directed this play? Where was it performed?

MGF: In Brazil. At the Goethe Institute. The other was about one of Kafka's plays, I don't know if you want to hear this.

LTP: Of course I want to hear this. Which of Kafka's plays?

MGF: Do you know Kafka's writings?

LTP: Yes. Some of them.

MGF: It was over *Josephine the Singer, or the Mouse Folk*. It is about a singer who is a mouse. And the whole thing is that they have forgotten the tradition of singing. They didn't know how to sing anymore. The tradition was lost. So Josephine is the singer and they gather around her. She emits some sounds and they try to remember what singing is (or was) through her. In my play, after his death, Kafka goes to Jerusalem and visits Gershon Scholem's room. There, the dead Kafka discovers Scholem's correspondence with Walter Benjamin about his work through the sound made by the mouse. So the whole thing is about lost traditions and our efforts to obtain even the slightest idea of what it might have been before.

LTP: I noticed in your lecture your interest in traditions and lost traditions. Do you think something in your life was lost and that you have looked for it?

MGF: I am thinking in terms of our collective world. Of course, we have lost traditions in terms of humankind. We don't know, but something is lost. Some connection with a deeper reality is lost, both on a personal and on a collective level. Otherwise, the world would not be in the trouble that we are [in] now.

LTP: I agree with you!

MGF: You see it? Of course it is through the individual that we are arriving at this understanding because there are no institutions to promote this recovery. Or, if there are, they are not fully effective if the individual does not change, because it starts with the individual even if the problem is collective. But I don't know if only individual solutions will be enough.

LTP: But at least on a smaller scale, if every one of us would make a small change in this life, a small effort to recover something for his or her own life, things could be changed.

MGF: Yes, I think so. I think this is what we can do.

LTP: You cannot fight with the system, at least not the entire system in a country. You cannot fight something that is much greater than you. What we can do is claim space, time, and peace. We can create little changes and those changes can lead to changes on a larger scale.

MGF: I think that is the way!

LTP: I can see in your talk and in your attitude, something about you that is quite different from some teachers, which may also be cultural. You are somewhat of an outlier. You are not very common.

MGF: (she laughs) I know.

LTP: It is not a bad strangeness or oddness, but you are kind of a strange presence, which is truly great. Exactly as you said about Job, it takes courage to stand up for what you are, to be what you are, and to assert what you want. Did this also lead to loneliness?

MGF: No, I think this is individuation. This is the aspiration to be unique, to be what you are. This is the process. If others don't do it, what can I do? (she laughs) I'll do it myself. But I will always keep some space for the others.

LTP: Indeed, but this has also shortcomings doesn't it? Not only benefits . . .

MGF: Of course. You cannot have everything. But the satisfaction of being what you want. . . . There is nothing that compares with that. I gave up the academic world very soon. I dedicated myself almost entirely to clinical practice and study groups.

LTP: You are right. At least to discover who you are.

MGF: Or to discover what we are not.

LTP: That's true. But of course, in the course of our life, we develop continuously. Can one say that we have a core that is stable and a lot of other developments within ourselves that change? Talking about the God image in us, can we say that we transform part of what we are, or does it remain stable from the moment we are born until the moment we die?

MGF: Let me see. . . . In terms of the human soul, which is the human personality, each one of us is a particular idea of God, okay?

LTP: Okay . . ..

MGF: A unique idea of God and that is what we are at the bottom. Hebrew tradition says that this soul, the Yechida, which means our own uniqueness, is what we are in God. It remains in God and never incarnates. What we have is a virtual image of it. So all our efforts would be to realize, to make this to become real through our lives. Of course, we have many choices: we can betray this, we can develop one side, or we can develop here and there but leave lots of holes. Everything is possible because we are free people. We have the freedom to be what we want. Of course, there are certain circumstances and determinations limiting our possibilities. I was born in Brazil at a particular time. . . . So you have certain unescapable conditions, but in the context of these conditions, we are free to choose and try to become what we are, by activating our Yechida historically, through our deeds and choices. It is a choice to achieve, to reach the fullness of our Yechida, which is the best idea of God in each one of us.

LTP: Like the initial idea of God; a God that is within you. Like you said, God puts in you a unique image; a new, unique expression.

MGF: He [God] doesn't put into me. . . . When my soul is conceived in heaven, it is conceived according to one unique idea of God, which is the Yechida. The rest is my job.

LTP: This one unique idea stays or has many manifestations, which are our life developments. Or is this something that we could call our destiny, our path, our life script?

MGF: You could call it that, but I'm not so deterministic because, to a certain extent, I can follow, betray, or even reconfigure that path.

LTP: But sooner or later, one could take another path on the street but the GPS [global positioning system – as a metaphor for the Self] takes you back on the right track.

MGF: Not necessarily. I have a GPS but I do not necessarily listen to my GPS. Or I listen, but I don't understand it – maybe it is talking in another language. We no longer have the prophets to say where to go or to translate the GPS instructions.

LTP: Isn't the prophet inside of us, isn't it part of our voice of consciousness?

MGF: I don't think this voice is so transparent. If it were transparent, it would be so easy to be on the right track. I think we make so many unnecessary mistakes in life.

LTP: Are you still making mistakes?

MGF: Oh, of course. And I'll make more, I've done a lot and I will make more, for sure.

LTP: But what do you consider your greatest success?

MGF: I think my greatest success was to be faithful to my own life, even when I was wrong.

LTP: Even when you were wrong and you had to admit that you were wrong?

MGF: I have, yes, of course. Otherwise, there is no point. But the point is, sometimes you can only admit the mistake afterwards, not before. Most of the time, you only see your mistakes when you look back.

LTP: But to admit the mistake previously, or even after, is a virtue. Even after the mistake, to admit it is a virtue. You could continue rationalizing it until the end.

MGF: No, no, no. Mistakes are something that I have to admit. This is my law, my ethics.

LTP: Towards yourself?

MGF: Yes, and towards everyone as well.

LTP: What is the important thing that you would say to a young analyst from your own experience?

MGF: It is a daily process.

LTP: Do you have a method for that process?

MGF: Well, you look to your dreams. This is one of the methods. Using reflection, you think about what you did and what it caused in your environment, towards other people.

LTP: So, you have to be curious and be reflective . . .

MGF: And you have to try to be objective about things. Many things, you may not understand at first and then you understand them, maybe years later.

LTP: So you also have to be patient, because one day understanding may come. Were you a curious child or you became curious?

MGF: I always was.

LTP: How did your parents get along with this?

MGF: I had great opportunities because one of my mother's sisters had a farm, and I would have lots of time and space there to explore. There was a whole world of nature to explore, completely free. This was very important for me. And I continue to cultivate it to this today.

LTP: Do you have a special place you go in nature now?

MGF: Well . . . no. I like to discover new places. Brazil is a terrible country in terms of the social and political aspects, but in terms of nature it is great. So, I travel a lot in Brazil, but not to the tourist places there.

LTP: The Amazon jungle?

MGF: No, I don't like the tropical areas.

LTP: Where do you like to go?

MGF: I like the southern lands of Brazil; the mountains, the lakes, the rivers, the southern forests. Sometimes I go with someone, sometimes by myself. I've never visited the tropical forests, there are too many snakes and mosquitoes.

LTP: Do you tolerate loneliness well?

MGF: I like to be by myself. I don't call it loneliness, I call it independence.

LTP: Yes. So you make a distinction between being alone and being lonely.

MGF: Yes, it is a very big distinction. You can be lonely with someone by your side. I think independence is the word.

LTP: I perceive you as a very calm person. Is this something that you worked on or have you always been like that?

MGF: I have always been like that.

LTP: Were you an independent child?

MGF: Yes, very much.

LTP: You had your own room and your own toys or . . . ?

MGF: Yes.

LTP: Who did homework with you?

MGF: No one. I did my homework. Actually, I started school in the second grade because the material of the first grade I had already learned by myself.

LTP: So you were very conscientious as well.

MGF: Yes, I would say so. I always enjoyed studying.

LTP: Would you also say "wise"?

MGF: I would say that I had a very happy childhood, no doubt. My childhood was very happy. I was very free, especially at the farm with my aunt. She was my godmother too. She was much older than my mother because they were from a family of eight children and she was the oldest. My mother was the youngest, so there was a big difference in their ages. My aunt had three boys who were about fifteen years older than me and she had always wanted a girl. So I held this space in her heart and I would stay with her at least four months of the year on the farm. It was really a paradise. I had three months in the summer and one month in the winter and a few other weekends and holidays.

LTP: Every holiday you went there?

MGF: All the time.

LTP: She was your godmother, but was she like a mother to you?

MGF: Yes, she was a very active woman. From morning until night she worked. It was a big farm, and there was a beautiful orchard with fruit trees. It was marvelous just to go into this orchard with all the scents. The fruits today don't smell anymore. Those fruits had a marvelous smell. Everything, all the food, came from the earth. They had animals and they planted everything. There were about eight women and thirteen men working for her to manage the farm, the horses, and other things. It was a world in itself. I would wake up in the morning to gather my egg from the chickens, drink the milk from the cow, eat the bread that they just made in the oven, and then a piece of fruit. It was all there! Even the flowers from the garden.

LTP: So you were actually in heaven!

MGF: I was in heaven and I really thought that it was paradise. I remember when I was about six or seven years old, I would ask her, "Are you sure that paradise is not here?" And because it was a closed universe, I had tasks. Brazil is a country that had slavery until 1888. So, many of the employees of the farm were descendants from old slaves and still lived on the land of the owners. There were some old people that lived there. My aunt would make bread, biscuits, cheese, and other things. When I was eight or nine years old I would take my horse to deliver these things to various people. I felt like an adult delivering these things; crossing rivers and going through the woods, and sometimes I would eat at their table before coming home.

LTP: So you were actually in charge of the deliveries?

MGF: Yes, I was. That was magnificent because my aunt gave responsibility to a child. I had to be responsible in order to carry the food to different homes.

LTP: Would you advise parents to give children similar responsibilities?

MGF: I would. But it has to be in a safe place. Today, places are no longer safe. There are certain things that you have to do to protect the children. I had the opportunity because children didn't need so much protection then, the place was very safe. I was free to do all my exploring. Sometimes there were other cousins that would come and we would go in groups, but I was my aunt's favorite. So I was the chosen one and that was a good thing.

LTP: Is she still alive?

MGF: No, she died. But I think these experiences gave me a sense of confidence about walking by myself in the world. Brazil is a dangerous country. Sometimes I hear, "How do you dare to travel by yourself?"

LTP: But later in your life, did you marry or have children?

MGF: No, I didn't marry. I never married.

LTP: And no kids?

MGF: No.

LTP: I thought you seemed lonely . . .

MGF: Really?

LTP: Yes, I feel you are. In your look one could say that you are an adult, but in spirit you are definitely a teenager.

MGF: Really? It's funny that you say this.

LTP: I feel it this way, even the way you dress, like a teenager . . .

MGF: Come on! (she laughs)

LTP: But I say it in a good sense. Your clothes are extremely colorful and free. I believe there are important things in what you say, but not only in the content, in the spirit of how you say it. I saw in your lectures, even if it was difficult to digest, that your experience was lived.

MGF: That is true.

LTP: Your words did not sound like they were taken from a book, like, "Here is a copy . . . now let's discuss it." That would be very dry. But no, it is lived. So talking about how you went to work on land and connecting that with Adam's punishment felt alive. Speaking of work, how many books did you publish?

MGF: Two books. Both in Portuguese, but I still have a lot of material to publish.

LTP: Yes. You should. Personally, I look forward to reading your work. Do you have any hobbies?

MGF: Well, music. I love to listen to music and I love movies. I like art and for a while I painted a lot of paintings. But it has been a long time since I've painted anything.

LTP: Why?

MGF: Because I moved to a place where I don't have an atelier. And I don't like to do small paintings.

LTP: Do you have large paintings?

MGF: Yes, meters and meters. I couldn't build an atelier. I could not paint inside my home.

LTP: Did you ever have an exhibition?

MGF: I had a few exhibitions, yes.

LTP: Any portfolio somewhere?

MGF: No. I am not a person of portfolios.

[Editor's Note] Prior to the publication of the interview, we received the following update from Dr. Freitas: "So much happened after the interview. I'm now working [on] a historical trilogy. It's about a civil war that took place in the 19th century in Brazil. I was moved by a dream I had more than forty years ago, even before the beginnings of the 'Jungian adventure.' In the dream I come into an old farm, in a rural landscape. I enter the room and see a man, dressed in 19th-century [costume], working at his desk, with lots of books around. When he sees me, he stands up from his chair and hands me a telegram, with some solemnity. I ask him, 'What is it?' He answers, 'It is a telegram from the past.' In the telegram it is written, 'Do not allow infamy to be the currency among you.' I didn't understand anything about the dream. A few years later I went to a town in the innerlands, the place where my paternal family came from. I went to the museum, and the first picture I saw was of the old man in my dream. I then discovered that this man was my great-great grandfather, who lived from 1811 to 1888. Back home I interrogated my father about his family. He never talked about it; we had no pictures at home. I barely knew the name of my grandparents. It took me some time to get the facts, forcing him to tell something and then filling out the information with one of his sisters. I discovered that my father was born in Uruguay, not in Brazil, something I had ignored. I discovered that he was born there because the family was exiled after his grandfather was assassinated, together with some other people in the family. It took me years to discover the whole thing, finding facts, digging through documents, old newspapers, and unpublished manuscripts in libraries until I understood what the 'infamy' was about. It took me a whole life to get to this 'lost tradition.' The official history books don't tell it. You see how this 'wanting to understand who we are' and 'lost traditions' were the most crucial themes of my individuation, both on the personal and the collective level. I recently published a book on Walter Benjamin, focusing on his theory of history and applying it to a Brazilian case. I see a most fruitful association between psychoanalysis, on a personal level, and Benjamin's work on a collective level."

Chapter 8

A Tuesday Night Course for Twenty Years!

John Ryan Haule
INTERVIEWED BY LAVINIA ȚÂNCULESCU-POPA
JULY 5, 2012 – C.G. JUNG INSTITUTE, KÜSNACHT

John Ryan Haule, PhD, is a Jungian analyst in private practice in Boston and a training analyst at the C.G Jung Institute, Boston, as well as teaching periodically at the C.G. Jung Institute in Küsnacht. He is the author of six books: Divine Madness, The Love Cure, Perils of the Soul, The Ecstasies of St. Francis, Tantra and Erotic Trance *(two volumes), and* Jung in the 21st Century *(two volumes). He may be best known for his courses on* The Collected Works *of C.G. Jung. He had been teaching* The Collected Works *at the C.G. Jung Institute, Boston almost every semester since the early 1980s. In addition, he also writes and lectures on a variety of topics related to the psychology of C.G. Jung.*

LTP: How have you come to teach Jung's *Collected Works* repeatedly over the last twenty-five years?

JH: Well, it's hard to know where to begin to answer a question like that.

LTP: Shall we start with childhood?

JH: Let's start a little later than childhood. I had a close friend when I was about twenty-three, and he talked about Jung all the time. Everything that came up was an inspiration for him to have something to say about what Jung would say about it, and I thought that the things that he said were really very interesting. So eventually I started reading Jung a little bit here and there. Around that same time I fell profoundly in love with a young lady about my age. We immediately found we had a telepathic understanding between us, the things that go on in love relationships, which previously I never believed in. Meanwhile I was reading Jung's idea of the *anima* and *animus*, where these sorts of things are described, so then I really [began] studying Jung in earnest. I thought, well, if Jung knows something about this, how many more things can he teach me?

So, that was really the beginning and I was very much interested in matters of religion. I had had what I considered to be a religious experience that completely changed my perspective on life about five years before that. The only

DOI:10.4324/9781003148937-9

way I could understand that religious experience was on the basis of Christian theology. Having been raised Christian, this was the only means I had to try to understand it. Jung gave me the idea that what had happened to me was not necessarily a Christian experience at all; it did not belong to any denomination. It was just a deeply human experience. So, by this time I was interested enough in Jungian psychology to want to study at the Jung Institute in Zurich. I did not know how many other institutes there were, but this seemed to be the place where Jung had been and I had to prepare for it. I thought I really ought to have a doctorate to do that, and religion seemed to be the field for me, not psychology, because the psychology that was taught in American universities back in the late 60s, early 70s, was more experimental psychology and behaviorism. It was dominated by the idea that you don't look at the mind at all, you look at stimuli and what the responses to those stimuli were. The mind was a black box that we don't even try to understand because it's so difficult.

So, I wanted to study religion because it seemed to me that the most important parts of Jung were closely connected with religion, and I wanted to know whether what Jung said about religion was true. So I got into a program studying religion from various points of view. I studied world religions and philosophy of religion and tried to find courses that were oriented towards psychology in religion. Once I had the degree, I thought I needed more experience and I managed to get a university position teaching philosophy and religion for three years. Then I felt I was ready to apply to the Jung Institute here in Zurich. When I finished that program, I went back to Boston to practice.

On your question, though, of why I began teaching Jung's *Collected Works*, I just thought it was what I needed to do for my own grounding. I had written my doctoral dissertation on Jung and had read *The Collected Works* some ten years earlier. I thought I needed to read them again, now that I'd had all this experience of training and also had been practicing as an analyst. I knew Jung's writings would hold new meaning for me.

I thought the way to study *The Collected Works* deeply was to try and teach them. So, that's what got me started and by this time there was a small training program in Boston. Because most of the analysts wanted to be able to teach the trainees, I had only limited opportunity to do so. So I began offering a course in the evening that was open to the general public and any trainees who wanted to join it. So for fifteen or twenty years I had a Tuesday night course.

They were devoted to Jung, and I had to spend more time studying Jung so that I could present the material in those classes. I did find that my understanding of *The Collected Works* was growing and deepening during that time. As a result, I also began to read all the material I could find on Jung's life and the early works, I mean the origins he came from, which Jung called the "French School." Part of that research was in my diploma thesis in Zurich. In order to force myself to master what Jung's main French influence, Pierre Janet, had written, I offered a course in Zurich in the year following my graduation. Because it takes a long time to develop a practice, I had a whole year when I had very few patients. During that year I devoted most of my attention to reading Janet so that I [could] provide a clear picture of what his perspective was and how it influenced Jung.

LTP: I see you are a researcher, you are very curious, and you go deep. Were you that curious in your childhood?

JH: I never thought to ask myself that question. This is probably an oblique way of answering your question, but what I noticed, though, I've seen that trait in my son, who was born in Zurich during my training. Whenever he got interested in something, he had to know everything there was about it. If that's a trait he saw in me, maybe I had it too as a child. But it isn't a trait I knew I had.

I don't know what I discovered when I was a child. I was a dreamer as a child. It seemed to me I did not want to be tied down to anything, but I had a secondary school experience that changed me. I went to a Jesuit school in Detroit, and they challenged me and gave me really interesting material. I became very interested in a lot of the subjects that I studied, so I began taking them on with great interest, learning as much as I could about those things. Fortunately, I got responses from my teachers that suggested I was on the right track. I remember that I was a bit of an inspiration to my brother, who was about four years younger than me. He started writing by the time I was at university. He was starting to write papers in secondary school, and he would show his papers to me and I would critique them, showing him how he could make them better. He and I both earned PhDs. He is an English professor.

LTP: And your PhD is in religion?

JH: Yes, mine is in religion.

LTP: After you studied religion, you became a priest?

JH: No, I did not become a priest. A piece I left out of that earlier story was, at the time that I fell in love and discovered Jung, I was a member of the Jesuit Order. I was living like a monk in an attempt to follow that religious experience I had. I felt I had to do something serious because I felt I had learned there is something about religion that could not be avoided, that was of primary importance. I didn't know what to do other than enter the church in some way and try to put myself forward as a person who would lead other people in the direction that I felt that I was going.

But as I said, Jung converted me from belonging to a single religion. So, when I went to graduate school, I became very much interested in Islam, Hinduism, and Buddhism. All those things enriched my understanding of the experience I had. So, when I discovered Jung, there was no longer any desire to be a priest. It seemed to me the monastic life was much too limited. In fact, I spent my last year in the Jesuit Order teaching chemistry and geometry in a secondary school in Cleveland, Ohio. As I looked at the priests in their forties and fifties that were working at that school, they all seemed to me to be less than fully rounded. There was something about their personality I called "flat-sided," and I thought, "If I stay here I'll be flat-sided too."

LTP: So currently, are you a practitioner of any kind of religion?

JH: No, no. I don't go to church and I don't practice any religion.

LTP: Do you miss anything?

JH: No, I don't miss anything. I learned how to meditate in a certain way during that time, I can still do that, but I don't practice meditation on a regular basis. It has changed me to have meditated for thirteen years, and so I can use that practice from time to time as I need to. But I find that living my life on a deep level is itself a sort of religious or spiritual undertaking.

LTP: So, you may say you have a relationship to God, but not through a certain religion?

JH: That's right, yes. My idea of God does not much resemble Christianity's image of God. I don't see God as a very large and powerful person who lives outside the universe and somehow pulls the strings that makes things happen. God, in my view, is really the *anima mundi*, the world-soul. We live in what seems to be an eternal universe that is always growing. Just as you might think of an amoeba as having purpose, always to make its life better in the next moment than it is in the present moment, by getting to a better location where the environment is more comfortable, finding more food, escaping from enemies, all that sort of thing. That would be intentionality in an amoeba. That's the same as having a soul at a very low level. I think if you go down even beyond life, the *anima mundi*, the soul of the world, is still operating. I think that is God. God is in everything. It is a sort of pantheism. God is in everything, making everything work. For Jung, the most important thing was individuation, and individuation is the tension between the ego's project and our wholeness, because the ego can get out of harmony with our wholeness. We human beings are the beings in the universe who get most out of line with *anima mundi*.

LTP: Let's hope we're not upsetting her or him or it very much.

JH: Well, you see, I don't think *he*, *she*, or *it* is upset. This is simply what is happening. Take global warming, for example. If we follow the desires of our egos and end up destroying this planet as a habitable environment for us humans, the planet will survive, the universe will survive. Very likely many new species will appear to take our place. Global warming may turn out to have caused another colossal die-off of a huge portion of the species now living on Earth. There have already been four or five major die-offs in the history of the planet. Each is followed by a huge explosion of new species evolving to fill all the ecological niches left empty. That's all part of the process of the *anima mundi*, which, as I see it, is the source of evolution as well as synchronicity.

LTP: Returning to this life, apart from your professional life, is there another life? What do you do in your life outside of your professional life? Do you have any passions, hobbies, things that you are focused on, or is it just your work?

JH: Well, I think my work is in the Jungian line. I would say that if you take on Jung seriously, it is a way of life. So a lot of the things I do are in line with that. But I make room in my life for other things, I mean, I swim every day.

I prefer to swim in a pool so that I can count my laps and keep myself in good shape. I also follow some sports teams.

LTP: Which ones?

JH: Well, the Boston Red Sox baseball team, for example.

LTP: I can see that you are competitive somehow. Do you get along with humbleness as well? Do you have moments of humbleness, and if yes, in what?

JH: Well, I like to think that my ambitions are unusual ambitions. For example, I don't wish to have an administrative position at the Jung Institute in Boston, or in Zurich, or in the IAAP because I want to devote my time to study, because the studying that I do is also studying me. There is something reflective about it. So, I do have ambitions to improve the Jungian world. It's the reason I do these courses and spend the time that I do and the reason that I pass on the PowerPoint slides to the students, because I want Jung to be understood. I'm not trying to make a name for myself. My goal is making students enthusiastic about Jung and about how serious Jung was about what he was doing. I think Jung was motivated by a deep spirituality. You can't go very far in reading Jung without encountering religion. He often says that if we still had religion that worked for us, we wouldn't need psychology. In other words, psychology is an attempt to get us in harmony with ourselves, which is what religion is always trying to do. Getting in harmony with ourselves on a deep level and on a high level.

LTP: So the spiritual part of Jung is not limited to the one volume called *Psychology and Religion*. You're saying that everything he wrote is somehow connecting all the little details with something else, something greater.

JH: Yes, I think you'll see that in all of his late works. He wasn't as explicit about that in many of his earlier works, but after he had that near-death experience in his sixties, he became determined to speak more openly about what he really thought. So, for example, we have the article *Synchronicity*. In the first chapter he describes synchronicity, in the second he describes his own failed experiment in synchronicity, and then in the last chapter he knows that people need some rationale for how these things could be possible. Basically what he says is that our Western metaphysics, our unconscious assumptions about how the world is constituted, is uniquely limited. If you look around the world you see in the Far East the idea of Dao, the wholeness, and how the wholeness is constantly changing. If you go back to "our closest cultural relatives," as Jung calls them, the people of the European Middle Ages, what you find there is the idea of the *anima mundi*, the world-soul, which is very similar to the idea of the Dao. So, he's saying we need a metaphysics that takes that sort of thing into consideration.

Right now, we have people willing to speculate on the basis of how our understanding of physics has changed. One of them trained here in Zurich and graduated just as I was beginning, Jeffrey Satinover, who has later in life become a physicist. He is working on this issue, and I noticed a book of his for sale in the library downstairs, *The Quantum Brain*. I'm going to read his book next because I think he is working in this realm too, a realm in which we see there is a unity in the universe. The universe is an organism of a certain kind, and our brains are not simply the biochemical machinery that we've thought them to be, they are operating at another level. When we start looking at Higgs bosons and fermions, for example, we are getting to a realm of how matter comes into being, how choices are made at this pre-life level.

LTP: So, can we ourselves explain everything?

JH: Surely not. But I think what will come out of such speculation will be new developments. What will come out will be a view much closer to the Dao or the *anima mundi* than we've been able to consider for the last five hundred years. Jung wasn't exposed to such ideas because he was born in 1875 and died in 1961, but I'm sure this is the direction he was going.

LTP: Thank you very much!

Chapter 9

A Deepening Conversation

James Hollis
INTERVIEWED BY LAVINIA ȚÂNCULESCU-POPA
DECEMBER 21, 2016 – VIA SKYPE

James Hollis, PhD, is a Zurich-trained Jungian analyst in Washington, D.C. In the professional Jungian world he is a co-founder of the Philadelphia Jung Institute, a co-founder of the Saybrook University program in Jungian studies, and past executive director of the Houston and Washington Jung societies. He is also vice president emeritus of the Philemon Foundation. He is married to Jill Hollis, a retired therapist and artist, and together they have three living children and eight grandchildren. He is the author of seventeen books and two audiobooks on analytical psychology.

LTP: I would like to thank you for agreeing to this interview, which is an act of openness, of generously sharing from your experience of life with people interested in Jung and its psychology. I would like to start from the beginning. How was your childhood as you remember it?

JH: I would say that there were two major forces at work in my psychological formation. One was that I was born at the beginning of World War II, and even though I was perfectly safe 1,000 miles from the ocean, I was very aware that the world was not safe. I was aware that the big people around me were anxious and there were people being killed, and a great deal suffering was going in other parts of the world. So, that had a big influence upon me.

I realized also that some of those people were not coming home because I saw the results firsthand. That gave me a strong sense of human suffering on one hand and also underscored the fact that my rather protected existence was perhaps an exception in the world.

The second thing was, in our family of origin, although I didn't know it then, my mother had been a very abused and troubled person in her formative years. She suffered considerable mood swings, anxiety states, depressions, and, of course, we tend to consider whatever we are dealing with as normal, and we make adjustments. So, I learned two things: one was, perhaps, to stifle my own voice and my own needs at one level and secondly, to do what I could to try

DOI:10.4324/9781003148937-10

to improve her mood or speak to the issues that [seemed] to be distressing her. So, as I know now that was significant conditioning toward what we call "co-dependence" today. It meant that I was constantly trying to be mindful of her emotional state and to try to adjust.

Also, my parents had been born into poverty, and my father worked all his life in a factory, and later, I worked in the same factory building tractors. My mother had a high school education and she worked as a secretary all her life. But the core message to me from them was, "The world is big and we are not, it [the world] is powerful and we are not, so, stay home, stay out of harm's way, and we will just try to take care of each other." It is an understandable ethic of survival and adaptation, and it took a long time before I began to question that.

I also know that as a child I learned something different, something better, and it was a delight, and therefore I started reading very hungrily, just as a child might hunger for some kind of food and not know what she or he is hungry for. I think I read biographies because I was unconsciously looking for some alternatives in this world and some sort of bridge to move out into the world.

So, today I can see that probably the first half of my life, certainly the first twenty years or so, were defined by extreme introversion and avoidance and, of course, that is not very helpful in the outer world. Slowly, I learned to make the necessary adaptations and step into the world, but I didn't realize fully the weight of that early conditioning until, at midlife, in my thirties, I hit a significant depression. I was, at the time, a university professor in the humanities. I enjoyed teaching very much and yet the depression pulled me down and away from my work and sent me to my first year of Jungian analysis, back in the early 70s. At that time, I had no intention of changing my career: I had no intention of entering that world at all. But increasingly, I became fascinated with the presence of dreams, with the dialogue that occurred there that seemed to me to be more real than what went on in academic classrooms, as much as I valued that.

So, when I went to Zurich, I believe it was simply the next extension of my desire for self-examination and personal development. At that point, I still had no thought of transitioning from my teaching profession. But each year I went strengthened that possibility further, and I found myself valuing the dialogue that occurs in the conversation with the unconscious. I came to value that more and more and slowly evolved in a recognition of a need to leave academia. So, I left a full-time tenured position at the university that was very hard to attain. A lot of my friends thought I lost my mind and perhaps I did, but I haven't looked back.

LTP: What age were you?

JH: I was thirty-five when I went to Zurich and forty-one when I left academia.

LTP: So, you came back from Zurich as a Jungian analyst, having already decided to quit, or did you make up your mind after a few years of practice?

JH: It took a while. First, economically, I needed to earn a living, so I kept my teaching job for a couple of years. But as I slowly built a practice, I found myself valuing the conversation with adults, with real-life issues, as being more intriguing and more interesting than talking to eighteen-year-old students. There is nothing wrong with teaching young students, but you have a different kind of conversation with them. So, I could stay involved very organically and naturally both in teaching and in a deepening conversation around the meaning of this brief journey we call our lives!

LTP: Right! But if we can come back a little bit to your childhood, to your first years of your deep introversion and to the depression that hit you later at around thirty. Would you say that you didn't enjoy your childhood?

JH: I think we can say that, yes! I think that it was defined by a constant attentiveness to the environment, namely to the world and to the household, and it was filled with a great deal of anxiety. My only escapes from that, during that time, were reading and athletics. I spent a lot of time playing sports.

LTP: Were you the only child?

BH: No, I have a brother who is five years younger. That is a big difference biologically and socially, so my brother and I were never very particularly close, because I was always significantly ahead of him in terms of age. So, when I left high school, he would just be entering, when I left college, he was just entering and that sort of thing.

LTP: Tell me about the toys from your childhood!

JH: I think, initially, my toys were nature. I spent a lot of time outside, and I loved to climb trees and would imagine myself as the master of a ship when I was on the top of the trees where I could see forever. I also was fascinated with airplanes. I always wanted to have an opportunity, someday, to fly on an airplane. I certainly have plenty of experience doing that now.

LTP: Flying an airplane or flying with an airplane?

JH: Flying with, not as a pilot. I think sports was my primary toy. Initially, I know that I used my mother's clothespins as toy soldiers, when I was very young because again, we were a very poor family, so we didn't have a lot of toys, so I think I gave free rein to imagination.

LTP: Right! That was really my next question because these days, the children have tons of toys and sometimes they cannot discriminate between what they like or not. How important was it for your imagination not to have as many resources available?

JH: I think that my imagination had been stimulated by my reading and by seeing adventure movies, so life was never uninteresting when I was on my own. I had some friends in the neighborhood and we would get together and play what we used to call "Cowboys and Indians," those kinds of childhood games. As we got older we got involved in baseball and football.

I think it was an active childhood; I wasn't passive. In that neighborhood, we all created our own recreation. I remember none of us had enough money to buy a new baseball, so we would make one out of cloth and stuffing. So, this says something about the neighborhood that I grew up in.

LTP: Right! With regard to basic things like food and clothing, were you used to, perhaps not hunger, but experiencing frustration of your needs and still being tolerant of the situation?

JH: Yes, absolutely! First, I want to say we never lacked for food; for one thing, my father always had at least two jobs. So, in addition to working for the factory, on the weekends he would shovel coal into people's houses. Most people, at that time, still used coal. So, I should say that three things I most learned in childhood were: work, war, and worry. I saw my father working all the time, and I have never not had two or three jobs myself. I still do it at this age in my eighties. I have literally three different jobs, so work is always a part of my daily life. But my father developed epilepsy in my teen years. He could not drive for a while. My mother learned to drive a car and went back to work, so that was another profound influence there. When I look back on it, work, war, and worry were the three main messages.

LTP: Coming back to your development, in terms of ways of dealing with frustrations around the lack of resources, how do you recall it?

JH: I think when I experienced significant frustrations, I went off on my own and talked – so to speak – to the sky or to the trees, because I knew enough not to disturb the family atmosphere anymore. So, I [learned] to suppress a lot of emotions which partly, I think, contributed to a midlife depression. Psyche revolted.

LTP: You said your mother was one of your key areas of focus, trying to deal with her mood swings and with her condition. Now, would you see it as something that impaired your development or emotional understanding about who you really were or who you should have been?

JH: Yes, definitely! First of all, as I said, I learned to suppress my emotional expressions, because they would further destabilize the environment of the home. Looking back on her life, I have an enormous compassion for her. She was not bipolar, but she cycled between anxiety and depression. At times, she would go away, in the house, and would not speak at all for three days and everybody would try to figure it out "What did I do wrong? What do I need to do now?" It was essentially orienting one's life around a mental illness.

My father was a good man but also his understanding was the same, "Be supportive of the system, don't do anything to disturb it!" There was no model there for any kind of permission to have one's own life. When I look back upon it today, it is with sadness that my mother suffered so much and my father never lived his own life. I think, as I became more aware of the influence of that upon me, it strengthened my resolve in the second half of life to risk more and to step into life more. I find with a lot of clients, no matter how successful they might be in the external world, many still lack an elemental permission to be who they are and to pursue what their soul wants them to pursue. I certainly experienced that myself. I think going to Zurich in my thirties was a significant break from that psychology of suppression and adaptation, because there was nothing in my life then that supported it other than an urgency of psychological pressure from within.

LTP: Would you call yourself an "adapted difficult child" or a "well-behaved child but not necessarily adapted"? Were you naturally kind and at peace, or did you become this way?

JH: I think my nature was to be introverted. It still is, even if I live an extroverted professional life. I have always felt that kindness was the best way to be in this world, whether we receive it from others or not. I think that was always part of my nature, and it was part of my brother's nature too. Interestingly, my brother also went into a mental health field, which I think is not an accident. He was a social worker. He died of Parkinson's disease a few years ago.

LTP: I am sorry to hear about your loss.

JH: I think it is no accident that both of us undertook, in our later life, the study of psychology to understand where we come from.

LTP: How can a person experiencing a deep depression in their thirties recover without being stigmatized or without feeling that they are inadequate?

JH: Well, I certainly felt stigmatized at that time. I was one of those who felt that one needed to do everything on one's own and to do it through heroic effort. Yet my depression kept defending against that. So, I entered my first analysis, not as the beginning of the second half of life, but as a confession that I was not able to solve everything by myself. I think part of why Jungian psychology became so important for me is I began to realize that there was meaning in that depression. As Jung said, "There's always a bottom to the well," and once we get to the bottom, there is always a task there. Your life is asking you to address something, to respond to some challenge, and to stimulate growth or development. So, I came to realize over time that depression was meaningful and that it transforms everything.

The way I put it to people today, when talking about depression, we must ask, "Why has this come, and what changes in your life are being asked of you?" rather than asking, "How quickly can we get rid of this depression?" To ask, "Why is your own psyche withdrawing approval and support from you? Where are you, or your complexes, or the pressures of your life asking you to invest your energy? What corrections or changes in life are necessary here?" This moves one from the sense of being a victim to an active participation in the construction of one's own life.

LTP: Yes, indeed! Coming back to your thirties, were you already married then?

JH: Yes!

LTP: How important was your wife's acknowledgement that you were experiencing a difficult time?

JH: It certainly placed enormous stress on the marriage. Ultimately that, and my analysis, led to the end of that relationship, to ending that marriage. So, I was unmarried for most of the time I was in Zurich.

LTP: Oh, you divorced!

JH: That's correct! I think the factors that led to my initial choice of partner were part of the reasons for the depression. We make choices when we are young, not knowing the nature of the unconscious influences at work in those choices. I have great respect and affection for that person and yet, we had both outgrown the reasons that brought us together in the first place. That was very difficult and certainly that, combined with the depression, was the most difficult phase of my life. Yet, out of that, came a new sense of possibility and choices.

LTP: Let's return to your childhood. You said that by nature you and your brother were kind. Did you receive any support from your parents related to a spiritual life? In your opinion, were you "trained" to be kind, or do you think that you were born just being kind?

JH: I think we were essentially born to be that. My father was very kind, very thoughtful. In later years, he lived in a retirement community and was very helpful with people there. He outlived my mother. At his funeral, person after person came up and talked about the kindness that he had given to them. In terms of our spiritual life in childhood, my parents went to a neighborhood church, and I went there too. It happened to be one of the historic peace churches and certainly the ethic of a human sympathy, sacrifice, and commitment to others was profoundly reinforced there. But I think it did have a reinforcing effect upon what I've thought was my natural being anyhow.

LTP: How important was the experience of being in church and the presence of God in the early years for you in moving through life?

JH: At one level it was supportive, and on the other level was an impediment. I remember from childhood on, I had serious questions and doubts about what I was hearing in terms of theology. I also appreciated the values of the people around me and the support that community offered. So, I had two different experiences. One of substantial doubt, that I kept to myself. On the other hand, a lot of feeling of community and support. I left that religious community when I went to college and never returned to it, but I have enormous respect for the people who had been part of it.

LTP: What denomination was it?

JH: It was a small group called The Church of the Brethren which is very similar to the Quakers [the Society of Friends] in terms of their theology. The importance of inner light and of social service [was] central to them.

LTP: Can you describe the young James?

JH: Well, it's hard to see myself from outside. I think, genuinely speaking, I was friendly, quiet, and in my own way tried to show up either in sports or school. Never in a way that was proud or boastful. I always found that to be very embarrassing.

LTP: To be proud and boastful?

JH: Yes! One of the things I had [learned] from my parents was basically, "Don't show up!" Because if you are out there, you are at risk. The whole family was very subdued. As a matter of fact, in the last conversation I had with my mother, when she was literally on her deathbed, I mentioned to her that I had a book out, which had been published in Swedish. Her ancestors were Swedish, and I thought that would be pleasing to her. But she was very anxious for me because she was afraid people would not like the book and then they would not like me. It shows how sensitive my family of origin was. Here she is dying, and yet her bigger worry was what other people would think of her son. That happened in 1992 and she was in her eighties. It took me back in my childhood, and I realized that was the way she had been all the time.

LTP: How did your shyness and introversion influence your relationships with the girls in your adolescence?

JH: I dated very little, as you can imagine. I was very shy in approaching girls and that continued into college. I got married at the end of college. I don't think my future wife was my first date, but maybe in the early group of dates. As I look back on that, especially given today's values, I realize how unfortunate that was. It affected me also in other ways. I did not have good grades through high school and early college. I think the depression was showing up then; it's just that I didn't recognize it. I read a lot, but I did not put effort into my classes. There was even a question about whether I could go to college, but I did very well in the exams, which showed that I had potential. In fact, I had the highest verbal score of the entering college freshmen class, which did not match my transcript of grades. I was completely committed to sports in college. I was on the football team, but I developed a bone disease in my legs and arms which I still have. At the end of my second year, I underwent significant surgery. I was lying in bed wondering, "What I am going to do now, because I can't play sports anymore?" I thought, "Well, I guess I have to be a student." So, overnight my grades moved from average and below average, to the straight A's [highest marks] and that is what allowed me to go to graduate school.

LTP: But internally, did you have a sense that you were intelligent, even if the outside evidence did not demonstrate it?

JH: I don't think so! On the contrary, I think that I did not value my capacity and academic abilities because [they were] related to a negative self-image that our whole family carried. Again, that contributed to the depression that was probably there in childhood, but passed unnoticed by the others.

LTP: Were there any supportive adults or the supportive elements that helped you? How did you manage to grow up so well?

JH: It is hard to know. I certainly had childhood friends as playmates. My best friend, who lived across the street from me, happens to live in Vienna now, and I see him once in a while. We were close friends, but I think it was a fairly lonely childhood and I didn't know what my capacities were. There is a part of me that is still surprised when I am asked to go speak somewhere or write something because it is an old archaic complex that is always there. As you know, we don't get rid of those complexes. As Jung pointed out, the best we can do is outgrow them, so I've been spending time outgrowing them for the last few decades.

LTP: Let's discuss further this delicate subject that is important for many people – depression. How did you experience your depression?

JH: I never stopped being productive in the outside world, but I lost the sense of meaning and purpose, and I experienced a loss of energy. I also had significant sleep disturbance. However, I think that the biggest issue was I was living out a false self, but I did not know it at that time. It is as if the psyche, by its autonomous revolt, removed its energy and operated from a false self. Our psyche is actually a self-correcting system but at the time, of course, one does not know that.

LTP: How do you think these early conditions influence our way of working as Jungian analysts? How was it in your case?

JH: I think that all of us, at some level, are first drawn to psychology to understand ourselves better. You would also find a very large percentage of people in the human services professions who came from troubled backgrounds. Sometimes they are a child who was especially sensitive, or maybe neglected, and they attempt to bring their work and life together through their choice of profession. I would go so far as to say, maybe fifty percent of people who are in the health professions, and I am thinking of nursing, medicine, and clergy, and therapy in the broad sense of those terms, perhaps should not be there, because the work continues to link them to their own wounding. This means we must acquire insight and strengthen ourselves, to be able to do this work without being toxified by it. One of the programs I have presented many times here and is called *The Wounded Healer* which addresses the typical family of origin of the professional caregiver. I address the ways in which it creates liabilities and blind spots and some of the ways we can learn to take care of ourselves. When people don't do that, it leads to burnout, ethical lapses, and so forth.

One of the things I find valuable in Jungian psychology is Jung's repeated emphasis that there are two human beings, sharing the same condition, who are trying to address an issue or problem. It is not so much about problem solving as it is about deepening the conversation around the meaning of one's life journey. When the emphasis is on that, we do not ignore whatever the symptoms are that brought the person there, but we begin to include them into a larger framework in which a person has to address their unlived life or address the corrections that their lives are asking of them.

LTP: In what way did your childhood or early adulthood influence the way you treated or educated your children?

JH: I think it was a most positive influence. Jung said, "The greatest burden of the child is to bear the unlived life of the parent." My children saw me go through this process and take these risks, and I think it freed them up – it freed them up professionally, educationally, and emotionally. In fact, my son once said to me, "I am allowed to live my life because I saw you live yours." That is not without cost and sacrifice, which I do not ignore for a moment, but I felt that certainly reframed life. This is one thing I had not received, a sense of permission to live my own journey. It was something that I was required to confront, as I said, by my depression in midlife.

LTP: In addition to this, are there other lessons that you gave your children?

JH: I told them to pay attention to their dreams and that ultimately what was right for them would be found within them. I told them to solicit the opinions of others, but to know there was something always wise and knowing within them. If they could access that knowledge and find the courage to live that, their lives would work for them. Whether or not it fit in someone else's expectations or plan, or not, is beside the point. I also made [it] clear from the beginning that they were here to live their own lives, not to be here to please me or emulate my values.

LTP: The loss of one's own child creates devastating stress in one's life. Can you elaborate on your experience with this?

JH: Yes! My son passed away at age thirty-eight, which was about eight years ago. I would say he was a very close friend. He died from complications of a heart disorder in Santa Fe, New Mexico. His mother and sister and I placed his ashes on top of the mountain where he and I used to go many times to watch the sunset over the mountains. I think about him every day, several times a day. I think of him because we shared values, social and psychological values, and it now gives my work another level of meaning for me. It is as if he is carrying on for me in some way and I for him. I also think that some of the conversations I had with him are among the deepest conversations that I ever had in my entire life, which I think is a rare privilege.

LTP: Your book *Haunting*s is dedicated to your family members but especially to Timothy. Is he a good ghost in your life?

JH: Certainly yes! The body dies but the spirit lingers. It is a painful reminder and is a very strengthening one too. It always reminds me to address the tasks of life. Ironically, I work with the children of other people all the time too, as we all do, and I am very mindful of the fact that I find myself, many times, in a kind of parental transference phenomenon, which sometimes helps people repair their intrapsychic image that was constructed when they were children.

LTP: *Hauntings* was inspired by his case?

JH: No, it wasn't! [A lot] of people think that! By the way, the cover was painted by my wife. I am remarried. I met my wife at the Jung Institute in Zurich, with two weeks left in my training over there. It was meant by the gods, apparently. She happened to be an American living in Zurich, and we had passed all that time and we didn't even know each other. She has been a therapist also, and an artist, and is retired now. She painted that painting about two years before I wrote the book, but they were connected it seemed. It seemed to be an appropriate subject matter for the cover of the book. It was just that *Hauntings* occurred to me as another way of approaching how we don't focus on the past, we focus on the present, but the present is always informed by the past. This work frequently reminds us of the centrality of Jungian complex theory in our work, so I thought a way of personifying complexes or making them feel more palpable was by way of the metaphor of hauntings.

LTP: You have some favorite subjects. For instance, the psychology of men and their way of being able to heal themselves through work, worry, and war. This theme is well portrayed in *Under Saturn's Shadow*. Do you think that books like *What Matters Most?* or *Why Good People Do Bad Things* or *Finding Meaning in the Second Half of Life* are more commercial type of books?

JH: In addition to practicing as an analyst and as a teacher, my other work has been trying to bring the concepts of analytical psychology to a larger public. For that reason, after publishing with a smaller press, I approached some of the larger publishers, and certainly those books are in a more popular tone. I don't think of them as self-help books, but they are certainly trying to reach more people. Through the years, the total sale of these books is nearing 300,000 copies, which is a lot for psychological books these days, especially in a time when books are in decline. Most people are getting their information from the websites, so we are in the middle of a large paradigm shift. The book is not disappearing, but it is certainly declining as a means by which people access information and perspectives. I have always considered the books simply extended classrooms. They are teaching devices.

LTP: I like your writing style! It is, apart from being didactic, clear, sharp, and concise; you also have a lot of substance. Hearing you for eight hours in London, it was like reading ten books; it was very condensed.

JH: (laughing) Yes, that is true! A teacher always has the job of deciding, "How do I move between the complexity of the material and the situation of the learner?" or "How do I explain that?" or "How do I make that understandable?" For me, that has always been stating a principle in a condensed way and giving illustrations of it. That is what every teacher tries to do in every classroom, so that is why I said, "I think of each book as a different kind of classroom."

LTP: You mentioned sports, but you didn't mention anything about music. Do you have anything to do with music?

JH: I have always loved music! I just have no musical talent. I'm always envious of two kinds of people in the world. They are both artists: those who make music and those who make paintings. I have no talent for either one of them, but I admire those who have that. Someone asked me a question a couple of years ago, kind of a cliché question, "If you left a time capsule for another species, from another planet, to let them know what we humans are about, and it had to be one object, what would it be?" I decided what I would leave is a record of the blues. The blues represents something that rose from the earth, from the people, and it speaks of human longing, loss, and suffering, and at the same time transforms it into music. This is a species that suffered and yet also had a spirit that transformed that suffering into something that is meaningful to all of us. I think that the blues somehow summarizes our experience.

LTP: I am glad you told us about this even if it was a cliché question, the answer is still beautiful. After seventeen books, with almost 300,000 copies sold, and a quite accomplished life as an analyst and author, how do you manage to remain modest?

JH: Well, if I am, I would say for two reasons . . .

LTP: You are not?

JH: I would say if I am, I would say for two reasons: one would be because of my whole conditioning of my childhood was about modesty, being quiet, and not noticed. But I think the more important reason and the more mature one is that I know too much about myself not to be modest. As Dostoevsky says in *Notes from Underground*, "How can anybody of any consciousness have any self-respect?" That is overstating a bit, but I certainly understood what he was talking about. I think when one tries to look at himself, he realizes there is much here about which to be modest about. I will never forget that.

LTP: I'll try not to turn my next question into a cliché question. Can you share with us something of your very intimate, secret nature of your true self?

JH: It is a difficult question! It requires me to think. From childhood to the present, I felt that life has to have meaning, because I saw too much suffering around me, or I was aware of so much going on around me. I have always felt that meaning is more important than happiness, more important than peace, more important than comfort, and more important than security. It took me a while to start living that, but I try to live it today. That is a thread that goes back to earliest childhood. I'll tell you something strange, maybe I talked about this in a book; when I was a child between five and seven years, there were times I [would] go out by myself and sing a song that was popular at the time: "Now is the hour when we must say goodbye / Soon you will be sailing far across the sea / While you're away / Oh, please remember me."

I was aware of people that were leaving and not coming back from the war and I would weep for them. I never told anybody that, but I look upon that and think, "What was going on in that child's mind?" The only thing I could say was compassion. It was compassion for the human condition, and I have always had that.

To read the newspaper nowadays, to see what is happening in the world around us, is to be quickly reminded of suffering, even though I know that it is through human suffering that we can all come to our deeper layers of meaning. That is the paradox present, maybe in all of us, but certainly present in my life all these years.

LTP: Maybe I am biased in some way, but somehow, I feel that your sins seem to be hidden.

JH: Yes, I think that is true, but I am very present to them and very mindful of them, and that contributes to that reserve that you sense. I have said in many, many lectures the best thing ever said about humanity was from the Latin playwright Terence, more than 2,000 years ago, "Nothing human is alien to me." Greed, fear, avarice, violence, all of these things are in me, like in everybody else, and I'm mindful of them.

LTP: You are mindful of them in you. What do you love in a woman?

JH: Well, what I love about my wife is that she has a completely different way of seeing and experiencing the world. I learned so much from that. I think as a young person, I was not strong enough to handle that. When we [are] young, we want the other to conform to our way of seeing and valuing things. Today, I realize that a healthy relationship is a dialectical one, where we both inform each other, we care for each other, we support each other, but we are very individual people. When I met her in Zurich, she was an independent person with two children, having also gone through a divorce. She was living on her own in Switzerland and had no intention of ever returning to America. She was a person who had her own analysis. I don't think there is any kind of conversation that we can't have.

LTP: That's why you started to love the otherness of the other.

LH: Exactly, right!

LTP: Thank you so much Dr. Hollis, it was a pleasure and an honor for me!

JH: Thank you! It was a thoughtful interview. I wish you well!

[Editor's Note] Prior to the publication of the interview, we received the following update from Dr. Hollis: "In the last sixteen months I have been in intensive medical treatment for two cancers, have had two surgeries, many tests and injections, multiple chemo infusions, and forty radiation sessions, during which time I worked full time and started the eighteenth book. Work is not a burden if it is meaningful, and I consider myself so blessed that my work is well received. At present the telemetry tells us the cancer is checked, but not gone as we know, and we will continue to monitor its activity from here on out. Turning eighty-one shortly, I plan to keep working for some time yet."

Chapter 10

Afraid But Also Thrilled

Donald Kalsched
INTERVIEWED BY LAVINIA ȚÂNCULESCU-POPA
APRIL 2, 2017 – LONDON

Donald Kalsched, PhD, is a clinical psychologist and Jungian psychoanalyst in private practice in Santa Fe, New Mexico. He is the author of many journal articles and book chapters as well as two significant books in analytical psychology, The Inner World of Trauma *(1996) and* Trauma and the Soul *(2013), both of which have been translated into many languages. He is a member of the C.G. Jung Institute of Santa Fe, a training analyst with the Inter-Regional Society of Jungian Analysts, and an adjunct assistant professor in the Department of Psychiatry and Behavioral Sciences at the University of New Mexico School of Medicine. He teaches and lectures nationally and internationally on early trauma and its treatment.*

LTP: My first question is, what is your earliest memory?

DK: The very first memory?

LTP: Or one of them . . .

DK: It's hard to say; that question came up when I started my analysis with Edward Edinger, back in the 60s. In the autobiography I wrote for him, I reported a very early memory: I must have been two or three years old. I was out with my grandfather searching for pinecones. This was at a resort, where we used to go for summer vacations. My grandparents on my father's side were very important to me. I grew up in a small town called Marshfield in the state of Wisconsin where my parents had settled. My grandfather was from Marshfield, and his father was from Marshfield, and his father was from Marshfield, having immigrated from Germany, so there was a Kalsched lineage going way back. They were lumbermen, farmers, plumbers, and so on. My father was part of that lineage. He moved back to Marshfield, after he went to dental school. In any case, we were away at this resort in northern Wisconsin, and I was out hunting for pinecones with my grandfather. I remember seeing a very large pinecone underneath the porch of the cabin where we were staying. I decided to crawl underneath this cabin, through all the refuse and so

DOI:10.4324/9781003148937-11

forth, and heroically retrieved this pinecone and brought it back very proudly to my grandfather. This is probably my earliest memory, because I don't think I was any older than two or three years old.

LTP: Was your grandfather a hero for you?

DK: Well, he may have been a hero when I was very little, but I don't remember idealizing him later. As I grew up, he was more a companion and my fishing buddy. He was clearly very fond of me and interested in my mind and gave me a kind of parental bond without the usual disciplinary anxiety that so many parents have for their kids. We had fun together. He was an educated man – an engineer, one of the first graduates in our family from the University of Wisconsin Engineering School. He often quoted Shakespeare and loved classical literature. He went to Detroit and made a lot of money designing commercial buildings and he retired back to Marshfield, Wisconsin, the town he grew up in, when he was in his fifties. So, he had a lot of time to spend with me while my father worked all day in his professional office as a dentist. My grandfather built a small cabin on a lake in northern Wisconsin, and I got to help in the construction. Later this cabin became a weekend refuge for me, and it's where I spent every weekend of my boyhood with my grandfather and grandmother.

The cabin was situated on a beautiful lake, full of all kinds of fish, wall-eyed pike, perch, bass, crappies, blue gills, and then another much larger fish you probably never heard of. It was what we call the "apex predator" in this lake and essentially ate all the other fish. It was like the lion in the jungle of this lake, and it was called the *muskellunge,* or "muskies" as we called them. They grow to enormous proportions, and the big ones look rather like alligators. Some of them are six feet long and have huge mouthfuls of teeth. If you happen to get such a fish on your line, it is very exciting and very scary. They are hard to catch so this rarely happens, but whenever you went out on the lake, you knew these fish were down there and that was enough to set the imagination of a young boy aflame. There were even mythologies about these fish told by fishermen on the lake. There was an island, and supposedly under this island were caves and some of the biggest muskies were said to live in this cave. Scuba divers had seen them, or so the story went.

LTP: Was it just a legend?

DK: It's a story of legendary proportions, shall we say, because I doubt there were fish as big as they claimed. But this was my first introduction to mythology, to the story of the Leviathan. And when you're a boy and you're living there, it's not just mythology. I'd be out on the lake at night under a full moon, fishing for the smaller fish that we ate. I'd hear this huge splash in the shallows, and I knew what it was, a muskellunge! He came up and devoured the fish. So, it wasn't just mythology, it was happening right there. It was two worlds mixed together; the imaginal and the real, the archetypal and the personal. Living in between these two worlds was a very exciting place to live as a boy.

LTP: I saw you on the internet in a picture on a lake.

DK: Yes, it's a picture of me in a boat, right?

LTP: Yes.

DK: It's me in Canada, where my wife and I have a home in Newfoundland right on the Atlantic Ocean. There the myth continues because under the surface of that water there are huge fish you can catch, bigger than muskellunge. Sometimes even whales will come up right next to your small boat.

LTP: Aren't you afraid?

DK: Yes, but I'm also thrilled. Being on the water takes me back to my boyhood. I think that being near the water, growing up on that lake in northern Wisconsin was one of the most important shaping influences on my boyhood. It became a sacred place . . . it was a place where I had access to nature, and I was captain of my own little world. I had my own boat, my own little motor. I could fish to my heart's content, and I was free from my father's worry. My father was a great worrier. He was someone who grew up with asthma and various other ailments that made him very afraid of getting sick again, of the dangers of contamination, the dangers in the world, and so on. So, when I was around him, he was very controlling and anxious, hovering around me with all his worries. Not all the time, mind you. There were other times when we could play together, and I could relax in his presence. But when I was with my grandfather, I had freedom that really set me free to explore the world. So, it was just a wonderful opportunity and I'd take every weekend to go up there with them. With my grandmother and my grandfather.

LTP: Were you the only child?

DK: No, I have a sister, two years younger. Sometimes my sister would come with us to the lake, but not so often; she was less interested in fishing. So, she'd stay home with my mother and her girlfriends, and I would get to go with my grandfather. Sometimes my parents would come up too, and the whole family would be together.

LTP: Let's go back to the atmosphere of the first years. What years were those?

DK: I started going to the lake on weekends when I was five to seven years old. I was born in 1943, so it would have been around 1948 to 1950, right after the war. My father was establishing his dental practice in town. They bought a small house and lived there for seventy-five years! My parents were wonderful parents, in the sense that they had a deep love for each other and established a stable home for myself and my sister. They met in Milwaukee, Wisconsin, while my father was in dental school at Marquette University. My mother was a farm girl who was enrolled in business school, and she met my father at the lunch counter and then they went dancing at a nightclub. This was right before I was born – the war had been declared. Everybody was signing up and enlisting, and my father wanted to enlist too, but he had asthma and flat feet so they wouldn't take him in the Army. He had to stay home, but that meant that he could be a father to me during those years when a lot of other fathers had to go to war and when other kids had lost their fathers in the war.

LTP: Did he have any signs of guilt?

DK: I don't know whether he felt guilt, but I do believe he felt incomplete about his life in the sense that he really hadn't been a man the way other men had, serving in the military. When the Korean War began in 1953, he signed up and they accepted him in the Air Force. By that time, he was a distinguished practitioner in dentistry, so they wanted him in the Air Force. He went through basic training, and he was a captain when he began his active duty. He was very proud of his service. That was a lovely time in my life also, because I was ten and he was stationed in Texas at a jet-training base [. . .], and I got to meet fighter pilots and sit in the cockpits of jet trainers on the Air Force base where he worked. This was the beginning of another "mythology" I suppose. Jet planes and their pilots were numinous to me as a ten-year-old boy. It was a magical other world, and I had contact with it through these pilots and their planes on the base. I imagined myself as a pilot and started building model airplanes and eventually built models with small gas engines that could fly. The two years in Texas were another expansive and positive time in my development.

But, to go back to my parents – you know this was a very special time in the history of the country. We had just won the war; the country was full of enthusiasm and hope and the soldiers were returning. There were new jobs, new opportunities, and everybody was having babies. We didn't have the problems, societally, that we have now, drugs and addictions. . . . So, I grew up in a small town where my parents were well-known because my father was a well-respected dentist in town and my mother was a businesswoman, an executive. She helped my father run the office, and they were very close and had a wonderful life together. They participated in the optimism in the country at that time. My sister and I were very fortunate in that respect. There was no war, no poverty, no deprivation. I knew where I was, where I belonged, I knew my father was esteemed in town, my mother was his beloved, beautiful wife, and the two of them were loving parents to us.

Of course, underneath this lovely surface there were "issues," shall we say . . . conflicts that I did not really know about as a boy but became more conscious of as I grew up. One such problem was the difficult relationship between my father and his father (the grandfather who was my fishing buddy). My father never felt really accepted by him. My father grew up as an only child, but he was sickly as a boy with serious asthma, allergies, and other issues. My grandfather, by contrast, had grown up as a kind of ruffian . . . a very strong young man who worked for his father, a lumberman, and a plumber. And he wanted a son who was rough and tough like him. But my father was a frail child with asthma, and his mother (my grandmother) doted on him and protected him. She formed a relationship with him that was very close, and she nursed him through all his asthma attacks and became very solicitous and close to him and I think my grandfather felt excluded. . . . So, I think there was a deep resentment in my grandfather that spilled over into a lot of irritation towards my father. I was sometimes witness to this in the fishing boat: huge tirades and anger between my grandfather and my father, which terrified and confused me.

LTP: Do you think your grandfather got back at your father, so to speak, through excluding him from the relationship he had with you?

DK: Well, I think it's more complicated than that. My father once confided in me that he relished the fact that there was a special relationship between me and my grandfather. It was almost as if, I think, he could see my grandfather's delight in me, which was a delight that he wanted to see in the eyes of his father. He told me that on the one hand it was difficult for him, because that was happening with me and not with him, but on the other hand he claimed he felt a vicarious sense of pleasure watching the connection between me and my grandfather. I don't doubt that. I never was conscious of any of this as a boy, of course, all this came up in my analysis to be explored, partly because my grandfather had died only a couple of years before my analysis began.

LTP: Is your father still alive?

DK: No, he died about three years ago.

LTP: Which of these deaths affected you most?

DK: I think that if I had allowed myself to really feel what I felt, my grandfather's death would have been the one to affect me much more. My grandfather died at seventy-five years of age, while I was in graduate school at Union Theological Seminary in New York, and I didn't go home to attend the funeral. I've always regretted that. When he died, my parents said, "You don't need to come home. You don't have to fly all the way from New York back to Wisconsin." So, they talked me out of it. I never really grieved the loss of my great friend. During my analysis with Edinger a few years later, my failure to grieve his loss came up in a dramatic dream; a nightmare really. The dream setting was at night on the University of Wisconsin campus, and I was visiting my grandfather in the engineering building where he studied many years earlier. He was ill and kept saying to me, "Oh Donnie, I just want to die" (which is what he often said during the prior summer when I would visit him in the hospital). In the dream I tried to cheer him up, to reassure him that he wasn't going to die. Then I left the building and started across the campus in the moon-lit darkness. Suddenly a huge black dog lunged at me from the shadows and grabbed me by the throat. As I toppled over backwards with this dog at my throat, I realized I somehow knew this dog and that perhaps he would recognize me and let me go.

Dr. Edinger pointed out the universal connections between the black dog and death. What I came to realize through the analysis was that if I didn't honor my deep feelings about the loss of my grandfather, the psyche would let me know its displeasure, and it certainly did in that dream. My love for him and grief at his loss then became a major focus of that part of my analysis.

But you asked which of the deaths affected me the most. As I told you, my father died at the age of ninety-seven only three years ago, so when I was seventy-one years old. It is very different to lose a parent or grandparent at the age of twenty-two than it is at the age of seventy-one. Also, I was much more ambivalent about my father, than I was my grandfather, partly because of his constant controlling worry and the fact that he was completely preoccupied with himself. He was also very conservative politically and this led to many passionate arguments during my young adult years. I had to separate myself from him early on because we almost came to blows a couple of times over political issues. During the Vietnam War he was an ardent patriot and gun-toting member of the John Birch Society (a right-wing political group) and, of course, I was against the war. He would accuse me of having "communist" sympathies which made my blood boil.

LTP: What about your mother's influence in your life? Did you inherit anything from her?

DK: That's a good question. One of the things I inherited from her is the realization that if I applied myself, I could succeed at almost anything. . . . Her favorite phrase was, "the world is your oyster." Do you know what that means? It means, "The world is yours to have, you are welcome to it."

LTP: Was that a kind of omnipotence?

DK: Not really. What she meant was: "I was a poor farm girl from very modest beginnings, and I went to business school and became a businessperson and if I could do it then you can do it too." I'm very grateful to her for that optimistic attitude. She was proud of herself, and she had a right to be. Of the six children on the farm where she grew up, she was the only one to go to college. She had a huge belief in education. I remember one time, I was in grade school and there was a publication called, "The Weekly Reader," which published scientific discoveries being made at the time. It had devoted a whole issue to atomic energy and what was being discovered about the atom and how these atomic discoveries [led] to discoveries of nuclear fission and eventually the atom bomb. My mother said, "Okay now, Donnie – we're going to understand this." I was only about seven or eight, and the article was written for high school kids, so it was far beyond me. But she went through the whole article with me, paragraph by paragraph. Finally I got it. By the end of that evening, I understood atomic energy. I was so proud, you couldn't shut me up. I told my grandparents, my teachers . . . anyone who would listen. I think that was one of my first experiences of the pure pleasure of intellectual mastery.

LTP: So, you had a very ambitious mother . . .

DK: I did. She was very ambitious, but she was also very loving. She didn't have to do that. She didn't just give me the publication and tell me, "Go read it." She said, "We are going to understand this," I knew somebody was sitting down with me, helping me do that.

LTP: With your sister. . . . Did you feel the two-year age difference?

DK: Yes. We were always playmates when I was younger until I got pulled into the hunting-fishing scene at around nine or ten years old, with my grandfather, his brother, my great-uncle, and my father. In the fall, the four of us were together almost every weekend hunting for partridge, pheasants, rabbits, and squirrels. So, I "lost" my sister during those years of adolescence. But we were close playmates in the early years. I don't remember any of the common stories about sibling rivalry. There is one famous story from when my mother first brought my sister home from the hospital. I looked at her in the crib and asked, "Where is her neck?"

LTP: Oh, my God! (smiling) Were you an introvert or an extrovert when you were a child?

DK: Extroverted.

LTP: From the start?

DK: I think so. I was very actively engaged in the outer world. I had an imaginative inner life connected to the outer world, but it had to do with nature, like what fish live under that lake's surface or what worlds would open if I could fly airplanes. I was also a great collector: insects, butterflies, moths, stones, arrowheads while we were in Texas, and model airplanes. I did taxidermy with birds and small mammals. I had a lot of friends and was reasonably popular in school. I was good at sports but not good enough to play for the school sports teams.

LTP: I have three questions I'd like to ask. The first question, how did you receive the scar on your face?

DK: I believe it's from an accident I had running down a hill as a kid. I ran into an unseen wire stretched between two trees and the wire hit me right in the mouth. It chipped my two front teeth, just after my adult teeth had come in. Being a dentist, I think the accident was more traumatic for my father than it was for me!

LTP: You mentioned the theological seminary, do you have a religious inclination?

DK: If by "religion" we mean a religious or spiritual sensibility, I think it came from mystical experiences in nature, in my various times in the outdoors, whether it was on the lake or hunting. I remember one time, around eleven years of age, I was returning to the house and looking up into the beautiful blue sky. This was in Texas during the time my father was in the Air Force. It was a beautiful afternoon, and I was suddenly overcome by a feeling of immense gratitude for being alive and a sense of the mystery and beauty and the unity of all things and I was in tears. I didn't know why. I didn't know what that was.

LTP: Did you have anyone to share this feeling with?

DK: No. I shared it later, but not at the time. It was very intense, very powerful. It's interesting that many people report such mystical experiences at around eleven years of age. I believe Jung had one also. I wouldn't describe it as religious, but as Jung and William James have shown us, this kind of mystical, spiritual experience is the root of all religion. I always had a spiritual sense of reality, and when I started to read the British romantic poets, Wordsworth, Shelley, and Keats, for example, I found an echo of those experiences. They felt kindred with mine. And later, the American writers, Thoreau and

Emerson. As you may know, Emerson went to divinity school, and I remember his famous divinity school address. Those writers were all about the mysterious and miraculous dimension we experience in nature. I never connected those experiences of mine to the religious dogma I was learning on Sundays in church. However, when I went to the University of Wisconsin as a seventeen-year-old, I met a young man there, Charles, who was a scholar in the sense that he was a dedicated Christian who aspired to be in ministry. He had been deeply influenced by a certain clergyman in his life and he read the New Testament every day and knew the Bible thoroughly. The Christian story was alive for him in ways it had never been for me. He and I became very close, and he was a great influence in my life in the sense that he challenged my ignorance about religion and made me feel like I needed to give these religious questions greater attention. We had many animated late-night conversations. We both decided to apply to Union Theological Seminary after we graduated from university, and Union was perhaps the most transformative institution I have ever attended.

Charles and I were also studying philosophy and the philosophy of religion, so our questions were framed by our growing studies. I remember the big question for us both at that time was: Jesus Christ – myth or reality? Albert Schweitzer's *Quest for the Historical Jesus* was important to me. There was historical evidence that this figure "Jesus" was a real historical figure, but the myth that had grown up around him, including the virgin birth, the resurrection, etc. These were impossible for me to believe literally. I became interested in the fact that these "mythological" elements also appeared in other religious narratives about their particular "heroes." So the question "Jesus Christ – myth or reality?" became the great question of my philosophical life during my college years, and it was never resolved for me until I read Jung. At the end of my first year of seminary, I had signed up for a summer of clinical pastoral education where young seminarians were placed in psychiatric hospitals to work with staff and patients. I was sitting every day with psychotic patients and then at the end of the day, we'd meet with six other college chaplains and the psychiatrist of the ward and we'd process our experiences. We were also reading things that were relevant to our struggles and understanding. One of them was Jung's essay *Introduction to Psychology and Alchemy*. In that essay, he addresses the question of the truth or falsity of religious creeds and dogmas. He says we've been far too concerned for far too long about the questions of truth or falsity of religious tenets. He said that we don't need to spend more time on things such as "the virgin birth" or "the resurrection." These "truths" would not have lasted for 2,000 years and become the central narratives of religious congregations if they weren't "true" psychologically. The idea began to dawn on me, between myth and concrete reality, there was an intermediate realm that Jung called the psyche. This opened the symbolic dimension to me for the first time. It completely changed the course of my life. It led me into Jungian training and the rest is history.

LTP: What do you think of the BBC interview with Jung, where he says, "I don't believe, I know"?

DK: Well, what he was saying is, this is about experience, not about belief. Belief is about history, about science, and about the rational categories of thought. Experience brings in the heart and the imagination and feelings in the body . . . the psychological . . . the logos of the soul. So, I knew what Jung meant when he said these things would not have been remembered and celebrated for 2,000 years if they were not true in the psyche. Of course, at the time I didn't yet know what he meant by "true in the psyche," but what he was saying is that there's another dimension of being, in between literal reality and the magical or mythic. That dimension is psychological reality.

LTP: And the third question, where did your trauma orientation begin? How did you arrive at your ideas?

DK: Well, you know, that's a very important question and the answer is complicated. Lots of people want to know whether my interest in early trauma comes from my own trauma history.

LTP: I don't think you have a real major trauma history.

DK: Well, I don't think so, either. Although, of course, life is traumatic for everyone to varying degrees. We're all given more to experience in this life than we can bear to experience consciously, some of us are given more "unbearable" experience than others. I don't think I have a major trauma history, although I have some microtraumas.

LTP: Yes, everyone does . . . as you said.

DK: I think one of the microtraumas that I suffered as a boy was being pulled into the male cult of hunting and killing animals too soon. I became a hunting partner to my father and grandfather in hunting and killing animals and birds with guns when I was five or six. It was too early because (although I didn't know it then) I was still identifying with these animals. I think one of the reasons I am so concerned and interested in the issue of innocence in childhood is because my own innocence was somehow violated or . . .

LTP: Stolen?

DK: Well, I don't think it was stolen exactly but exposed to adult experience too soon. In the usual course of a child's development something we call "innocence" must acquire experience slowly. Disillusionment from that pristine, open-hearted core state must not happen too fast or too violently. I think for me, to be given a twenty-two-caliber rifle and sent out to kill rabbits and squirrels at the age of five to provide my father with an adoring hunting partner was a violation, not a malicious one, but a violation, nonetheless. I wouldn't have been able to report this two or three years ago, but I had an experience recently, of all places, in a movie, that brought all this into focus. It happened as my wife and I were watching a film called *War Horse*. It's a wonderful story about a boy's love for this horse. Both he and the horse are drafted into WWI together, and the horse and the boy become separated in the war and then they are reunited toward the end of the war in the trenches of

France. At one point the horse charges off into no man's land, and falls badly wounded, tangled in barbed wire. As the soldiers try to free him, the camera focuses on his eyes. Suddenly, in the eyes of that horse, I saw something that broke my heart. I realized that all the animals that I had killed had these same eyes; struggling for life, fearing death, but still alive to the beauties of life . . . and I had been the executioner of so many of them in that same struggle for life. In the film, I started crying and couldn't stop. It was as though a whole pocket of dissociated grief and sadness had erupted into consciousness. I had been completely defended against these feelings until that moment.

LTP: You were in the role of perpetrator, not victim.

DK: In a sense, yes. So that was a major microtrauma and resulted in a significant micro-dissociation. The dreams that followed confirmed the importance of this discovery. Overall, my experience in *War Horse* was a remarkable illustration of how a film can unearth something that fifteen years of analysis had never touched. I think it's important for people to recognize that these traumatic experiences can be wrapped in oneself like a cyst in the musculature of the body and exist for seventy years without becoming conscious. Then something lances it, and it toxifies the whole body for a short time until it is digested, and that was my experience with *War Horse*. I have written about this experience at greater length in a book called *The Routledge International Handbook of Jungian Film Studies*, edited by Luke Hockley, to be published next year (2018). My chapter is called "Getting Your Own Pain: A Personal Account of Healing Dissociation with Help from the Film *War Horse*."

But your earlier question about the origins of my interest in trauma goes back to my experience in the 1980s of trauma in psychoanalytic training. I was an active member of the C.G. Jung Institute of New York during this time and was a popular supervisor and teacher. So, my caseload had a lot of the training candidates in it. It happened that there was a major sea-change in the culture of the training institute during that time, and a number of candidates in training were found to be inadequate and asked to leave. Five or six of these candidates were in analysis with me, and they were, of course, devastated, as was I. I was also outraged on their behalf (which is not an analytic attitude!) and I protested vigorously but to no avail. Finally, I had to leave all my positions within the training program, just concentrating on the analytic process with these individuals. What I kept finding in their material was a huge amount of self-attack, self-abuse, violence, and shame toward themselves after these events. It was tempting to see the violent tyrannical figures in their dreams as representations of the rejecting analysts who had thrown them out, but the attacking figures were *daimonic*, archetypal, mythic, and so I came to realize that these inner figures were defenses against the very vulnerability that they were feeling. They were being attacked from within. The outer trauma in training had triggered their retraumatization from within. I realized this wouldn't be happening if they hadn't had their own early trauma history which began to appear in dreams. So, my first book, *The Inner World of Trauma*, was born out of this struggle.

LTP: But why were they kicked out?

DK: Because of different perceptions by different people. At the time there was an especially high-minded ideal out there in the professional culture of what it took to be an analyst. This ideal was promulgated by the theories of Robert Langs. I could say more about this, but it's not relevant. These people fell short of it according to colleagues of mine who evaluated them. Who's to say if they were right or wrong? But I was the analyst of these people, and I was holding the shattered remains of their dreams to be Jungian analysts. As you know, this dream is often a big thing. The point is that these people, as children, had already been shattered in ways they didn't know about . . . and that I didn't know about. The defenses they developed to cope with that early shattering were now being triggered by this late shattering in training. As a result, these people were "freezing" in their exams, falling into a dissociated state, into complexes. My colleagues picked this up as "lack of analytic capacity" and acted accordingly.

LTP: Were you an outcast?

DK: Yes. I was an outcast. I also cast myself out. It was a traumatic time for me . . . the loss of my own innocence in a way. But I was very fortunate. I had the chance to form a special program at a conference center called Wainwright House. I called it the Professional Enrichment Program in Jungian Theory and Practice. With several other analysts and psychotherapists in the field, we brought in thirty-five people to study with us. Over a seven-year period, we provided quality Jungian education to this group. But we couldn't call it training. We called it Jungian studies. So, it was in that context that I started to give the lectures that became my first book. It's a book about the dissociative defenses that come to the rescue of what I called the "imperishable personal spirit" or soul of the individual.

LTP: Talking about dissociation, what is your relationship with Dis?

DK: Well, just so our readers understand, "Dis" is the name Dante gave to the archetype of evil in his famous *Comedia*. Dis was his name for the Devil or Lucifer, who ruled over the ninth level of the Inferno, and Dante's descent into his own unremembered pain in the book takes him to an encounter with this monster named Dis, surrounded by fire and ice. When I first discovered this, I was thrilled, because this is the root of all our words for splitting . . . including dissociation. So, Dis is the "Lord" of dissociation in the traumatized psyche. Back to your question, I think I have a greater and greater appreciation for Dis's role in the creation of what I call the self-care system and the role of anger and how important it is to be able to feel and express anger in your relationships. Because my trauma patients have terrible difficulty with the expression of anger. They can't get angry in a related way. They are pathologically accommodating to other people's needs and demands. In their minds they're the victims of evil perpetrators, but if they face them, they can't say "I'm angry, I don't like you, I resent you." They can't get in touch with and express their anger.

LTP: Or they cannot act upon hating.

DK: They can't even feel it. So, I've become sympathetic to the fact that Dis, who represents that anger, is a very important component of our psychological life and he needs to be taken seriously and he needs an avenue for expression, expression of the whole personality, but if he gets turned back inside, attacking the person as he does when recruited for defensive purposes, then he becomes a monster.

LTP: Is he a demon or the devil?

DK: Both. The devil is a demon.

LTP: That's why I asked you. Do you think he's part of the self-care system?

DK: Yes, absolutely. He's the other side of the bright angel who represents Lucifer in his prefallen condition. Together they operate as part of the dissociative defense to protect the orphaned, injured, and innocent child who has escaped from the world and is locked up in the inner sanctum. That is what the light and dark angels are about, because the innocence of the child carries something sacred.

LTP: I hope one day I'll have enough power and courage and knowledge to contradict you.

DK: Contradict me?

LTP: Yes.

DK: Okay. I hope so too. What would the contradiction be?

LTP: The fact that those angels are not opposites, they're not different facets of the same thing . . .

DK: Okay. How do you see them?

LTP: They don't contribute to saving the individual, but in the short run, the dark one can give the sensation that he saves, but then in the long run he wants to destroy.

DK: In the long run he does destroy . . . at least he destroys any hope.

LTP: But he doesn't introduce himself as evil. He's like the Mafia. I'm going to give you something good now, and you are going to pay me later. It's good now . . . but the small good doesn't even count in the long run.

DK: OK, I think I follow you. But the way I see it, this figure doesn't start out as a Mafioso.

LTP: Oh, he doesn't? What I mean is that Dis wants to destroy the individual.

DK: As I see it the self-attacking anger we know as Dis is not really attacking "you" – he is attacking the structure of your experience to leave you dissociated. He doesn't want you to feel your feelings (especially that vulnerable child inside) so he attacks all the connections among the various components of experience. So, you end up dissociated. In other words, he's trying to help regulate you when you confront feelings that are too painful to bear. His intention is to chop up your experience into fragments so you can go on living in pieces. He doesn't want to destroy "you." He's completely dependent on "you" staying in life. I think you have a theory about Dis's total evil and destructiveness that comes from your own experience.

LTP: Yes. That's why he cannot contribute to self-caring. Cannot save.

DK: OK, I think perhaps you have some of your own views in mind here.

LTP: As a colleague I may have to write a paper about these ideas; I don't know if anyone will publish it, but I'll send it to you.

DK: Yes, do that, because I don't disagree with you in terms of phenomenology, the way we experience these things. The dark forces, the negative forces, the nihilistic forces, the ones saying "no, never, bad, awful," they are a reality. We are formed of that . . . these dark forces are part of the fundaments of the archetypal psyche, both the life forces and the death forces. But if an ego can be formed and can tolerate the feelings of both sides, the love and the hate, and carry forward in a life where love is stronger than hate, and live that life with full recognition of the dark side and the light, then you have what Jung calls individuation, right?

LTP: Right.

DK: But Jung was very clear, and I am clear also, that the darkness, the evil is real.

LTP: Right.

DK: But it's an archetypal reality. It doesn't belong to the human realm. Or to put it another way, we are always trying to transform archetypal emotion into human feeling. In the process, we must respect the titanic power of the darkness.

LTP: That's why it's a foolish thing for a person to try to fight with it. I agree with you. If Jung said this, I can also tell you what one of the wisest fathers in our church once said, when asked, "Father, what are you going to do with the Devil? Because he's increasingly bad." And the priest, very wisely said, "What are we going to do without it? Because, as he is increasingly evil, we're meant to be better and better." Individuation.

DK: To challenge that undertone of negation and desperation with life energies. I mean it's happening now in America. After Trump got in, suddenly everybody was finding their voice for democracy, women's rights. Everybody was asleep.

LTP: If the bad thing comes into play, something must be awakened.

DK: That's right.

LTP: My last question: In fifty years, what would you like to be remembered for?

DK: Well, that's a very complicated question. I'm not sure I can answer now, but the first thing that occurs to me in light of our current conversation, is that I would like to be remembered as a man who was troubled by the perennial struggle between the darkness and the light in the world, and who arrived at an understanding of how the darkness gets "in" to the human personality through trauma and how it can be transformed there through a psychological process we call psychoanalysis. I believe that one of the greatest sources of darkness in human life is in the defenses that are erected by the traumatized psyche to go on living and how these impede the healing process and destroy feeling capacity or affective competence. I don't believe that Jung acknowledged this explicitly enough, although an understanding of defenses is implicit in his theory of complexes. The reality of these defenses, their archetypal nature and background, and the way they organize themselves into a "self-care system," which is a kind of core complex of dissociation – these ideas, together with the paradoxical reality that these defenses come into being to protect a sacred, never-to-be-violated core of the personality – these are the contributions I have tried to make that I think have the most practical implications for our actual clinical work with the survivors of early trauma. I am very gratified to know that these ideas have already been helpful to people. Some people have written me things like, "I've read your book and it has saved my life, I now know where I stand." That is very gratifying. So, I keep writing and sharing my insights into these fascinating inner and outer processes. I'd like to just continue that as long as I can.

LTP: Thank you very much. It has been a pleasure.

DK: You're welcome. I have enjoyed our dialogue very much.

Chapter 11

The Short Pants

Samuel (Sam) Kimbles
INTERVIEWED BY LAVINIA ȚĂNCULESCU-POPA
(DECEMBER 10, 2021 – VIA ZOOM)

Dr. Sam Kimbles is a clinical psychologist, Jungian analyst, member of the C.G. Jung Institute of San Francisco, and a clinical professor (VCF) in the Department of Family and Community Medicine, University of California, San Francisco. He has served as president of the C.G. Jung Institute of San Francisco. He has lectured and presented papers on topics related to the theory and practical applications of analytical psychology nationally and internationally. He is a clinical consultant and has taught at the C.G. Jung Institute of San Francisco, colleges, and universities, as well as trained mental health and analytic professionals. His published work on cultural complexes is a significant contribution to the application of analytical psychology to the study of groups and society. His previous books, The Cultural Complex *(Singer and Kimbles, eds.),* Phantom Narratives, *and his recent book,* Intergenerational Complexes in Analytical Psychology, *explore the themes of psyche in groups and society. Dr. Kimbles is a long-time practitioner of Buddhist meditation and has a long-standing interest in the intersection of shamanism and analytical psychology. He has a private practice in Santa Rosa, California.*

LTP: I am going to start with the beginning. What do you remember from the first years of your life? What would be one of the first memories that you had?

SK: Well, I don't know if I had this as a memory or a strong image I acquired as a young person. I was born in my family's home, and we had a midwife who came to deliver me. I have felt for a long time that I was present (aware). My consciousness was above my body during the delivery process. I saw myself being brought into this world. So, that is my oldest and most profound pre-childhood memory. I also remember a neighbor, kind of a neighborhood nurse, who helped folks with everything. She lived next door to our house so she was obviously called into service at the time of my birth. I remember the experience as very real and I did not feel the need to reduce it by trying to determine whether it happened or not. I did ask my mother about it. She said,

DOI:10.4324/9781003148937-12

"You are right; your birth did take place right in this bedroom. The nurse was there." I remember her as wearing a white nursing outfit, but I don't know if she did.

LTP: A white nursing uniform! Okay!

SK: My mother wasn't sure what the nurse was wearing but she confirmed she was there, "So that part of you, you were seeing correctly." So, that beginning became a jumping-off point for me into a lot of different things. I remember, as a little guy, being very curious about sexuality. I remember asking my mother about where babies come from and wondering, "What's the difference between what you have and what I have?" My mother said, "That's not something you need to know anything about right now." I kept that as her response to something that remained a mystery to me. My mother's response is what I remember very clearly, I was conscious of asking and conscious of her response to me.

However, I am not quite sure how another experience came into my life as a young boy, around age seven. A package came to our home, and I opened it up. There was a red vinyl record and it was an instructional about how to do self-hypnosis. I did not know what that meant but it basically gave instructions on how to close your eyes, relax, and see. I don't know if the appropriate word is visions or images, but how to see things that were happening inside of you. So, once I heard that, I could do that without listening to the instructions, I just knew how to do it. That was my earliest experience of having some sense that there was an internal world that I could make contact with, even though I did not know what that meant at the time, but I was drawn to doing it. I didn't affirm it outwardly, I would wait until my parents were out of the house, or not nearby. I would sit in a chair, close my eyes, focus on my breathing, and I would find myself in this altered world.

LTP: Who ordered the record, your mother or your father?

SK: I have no idea. I have no idea who ordered it.

LTP: Maybe unconsciously you did.

SK: That could be. But [whoever] ordered it, I never spoke to my parents about my experience. The record was there, they could see it, they knew quite well, but not about my experiences with it. So, it was all a personal experience, of an internal world that felt to me like another world which I was in. I could see outside, through the images I was having. This was a totally different world than I had ever been in my own life.

LTP: How was it there, in this other world?

SK: It was not frightening. It was soothing; it was comforting. I was about seven then. I was in a neighborhood where I had several friends, four young boys, and we learned to play together, compete, and sometimes get into fights with each other. One friend lived right next door to me, and the other two became lifelong friends. This is in the southern part of the United States. At some point, I offered to make up a story that would include all of us. I would spontaneously generate action stories in which we all played a part.

They seemed to be cool with that. Something was providing access to an internal world that could accommodate my friends in that world. It was a funny experience. It's hard to know where my storytelling at that age was coming from. It's not as if I made up the story in advance and then decided to tell them. I just sat down and spoke what appeared to me, something like mutual active imagination with a patient. So, my friends would sit down and share a dream, and I would react to the dream in some way. Certainly, we both are elaborating on that experience of a common experience of an image; my storytelling was somewhat like that. So, my friends began asking for stories, and so forth. I was just sort of in seventh heaven with that. All I know is I had a comfort level, flowing from one experience to another in this other world. Sometimes it did lead me into awkward, strange places. For instance, the woman who was the midwife and lived next door to my family with her daughter who was in her thirties. At one point, I grew concerned. I wanted to see what happened in their house because this woman who delivered me seemed strange in my imagination. I would find ways to peek into her house to see what she did in that house. So that became part of my home too. You can hear very much a kind of a curiosity related to something I could work with externally and act on it in some way without negative consequences.

LTP: You were literally "traveling" between these worlds . . .

SK: I could enter that world and share, talk, and play, and so forth. The odd thing is that I was not a daydreaming kid, just sitting and staring into space. But I was very sensitive to perceptions that people made of each other. There was a newspaper man who would deliver the newspaper to our house. I would happily retrieve it to give it to my father. He would sit on the porch, read the paper, and I would have completed my task. One day, I was waiting for the newspaper man to come. When he came and threw the paper, I caught it. The newspaper delivery man said, "Sam, Sam, god damn Sam!" He said it with such energy. There was something from his excitement that went into me and I asked myself, "Wow! Whoa! What was that?"

LTP: He called your name.

SK: He called my name with a sense of emphasis. "Damn, damn, god damn Sam!" I just thought it was like a verbal "Hi Five!" It was a wonderful moment. It was about that time that my mother said that she wanted me to start going to Sunday school at the church in our neighborhood, which was not far from our house.

LTP: That was also around seven years?

SK: Well, I'd say six. Maybe a little earlier than that, five and a half, somewhere around that latency age period, you know. She wanted me to go to church but I didn't quite know what church meant. My family was not a particularly religious family at all. My mother said, "You need to go because you're going to be a minister one day." And I asked, "A minister? I don't know what a minister is." She said, "No, that's why you're going." So, I dutifully said yes. She got me some special clothes, a little hat, some short pants, and a white shirt. I used to have a photo . . .

LTP: Do you still have it?

SK: No. Three and a half years ago our house burned down in Northern California. Sadly, my photos went with it. That was one of my favorites. I also liked it because I didn't recognize this young boy. It was so formal, you know. It was so unlike my internal world. I also had one in a frame of my mother holding me as a baby. So that was an important photo.

LTP: Which was very playful, colorful, not that formal . . .

SK: Yes, it was all of that. I just didn't recognize myself in the photo; only later as I reflected back on it. You spoke about the persona. My mother wanted me to acquire a persona to relate to the world outside, from a certain position of integrity, something like that. I've made sense of that. I'm the oldest of six and the only one that was asked to go to church.

LTP: Yes, that was my next question. You just took it from my mouth.

SK: I'm the oldest child. At that point, I had two siblings . . . I had a younger brother and a younger sister.

LTP: Okay, so you had five brothers and sisters in all?

SK: Well, you know, it's now years later and two have died.

LTP: I'm sorry. So, you were the oldest.

SK: I was the oldest. I was the only one asked to go to church because my mother had this projection onto me that I was going to be a minister, which obviously meant something very special to her. You don't know much about the black church, but then they had something called Bible school, which meant you go to church, sit with the other youths, and you read stories from the Bible. You talk about the stories and what they mean. So that's what I would do on Sunday morning.

LTP: Is this like catechism? Catechism is like a Sunday school for us [Eastern Orthodox].

SK: Yes, this would be it.

LTP: But this is after the service. So, Sunday morning you would go to the service, and afterwards the children stayed over for Bible school?

SK: Yes, but in the African American church, the order was the other way around. We would go to Bible school first, then some children left before the service, and some of them stayed. I always went back home.

LTP: Okay.

SK: So, it's interesting, my mother was very proud. She thought it was wonderful. I must say, I still didn't know what it meant.

LTP: But her projection onto you never came true; she wanted you to become a minister, but you never did?

SK: Well, what's odd about it is that I have received that projection throughout most of my life. I've spent a lot of time reflecting on spirituality and spiritual things. I realize now, her projection opened me up to another realm of reality. As I began to make sense of the early experiences I had with the self-hypnosis, I realized it was all one piece of the whole cloth. Fast forward just a couple of years, there was something in the black community at that time called "revival." It's a time when itinerant visiting pastors come through to preach special services. They would preach for two weeks to anybody who came in. Typically, the community comes and there are loud things happening there. If they're a good revival minister, they really have a way of energizing the congregation with words, songs, and music.

LTP: Lifting people up?

SK: Yes, getting people up. So, on one night, my mother says to me, "This revival is happening tonight at church, and I want you to go." I said, "I don't want to go! I really don't want to go to this." She said, "I want you to go." My father sat there and said nothing. He just sat there and watched. I went to the church and a most remarkable thing happened.

LTP: What?

SK: So, in the black church at that time, along with the music, the preacher starts and slowly, elaborately opens the story. Then they get more intense and emotional along the way. Suddenly the congregation is moving, clapping, and singing beautifully. So, it was happening in that way on this night, and the minister was really generating energy. At that point, the choir began to sing, with the music in the background. Women got up like they were possessed. They were making all kinds of sounds and screaming. I had never seen anything like that in my life. I thought, "Oh, my goodness, what is this?" So, the way it goes, the minister brings up chairs in front of the pulpit. Members of the congregation have a chance to become sort of possessed, taken over. Then the minister brings the energy down. Then, to intensify the evening, he suddenly asks a question, "How many of you have been moved tonight? Put chairs out front for anyone who has been moved to such an extent that he or she wants to join church, to be baptized another time." So, they set down about three or four chairs and the people begin to hum in the background. Then the minister calls out, "Is there anyone who would join the fellowship?" I got up, walked forward, and sat down on one of the chairs. I must say that it was not a choice I made. I was lifted to go there. The music and everything else there lifted me. I was there.

LTP: How old were you?

SK: About seven and a half or eight?

LTP: Okay, so still a boy.

SK: Still a boy. Oh, these things all happened before I was ten.

LTP: Oh, my God!

SK: Yeah. It was a rich period of life, the latency period from birth until latency, a very rich period. So, I joined the church that night. I came back home, I told my mother, and she was so happy she gave me a big hug. My father said, "Wait, you did what? You're out of your mind to have done that!" What was I supposed to do? Clearly, he was saying, "I would never do that in a hundred years. I wouldn't ask you to do that. It's your mother." So, there it was, I had done it!

LTP: What you're saying is very interesting, because normally the father has the role of putting the child into the world, and so on. You've mentioned very little about your father. Your mother was very present until this moment. What about your father?

SK: Oh, my father would do fatherly things. We would go fishing and hunting. He bought me a BB gun. He would tell me stories about his life. He had been in the Navy during the Second World War, so he had his way of relating. So, I got to hang out with him and ask him and wait. On the other hand, his talking with me was very much of a story to teach about character and about perceptions. One perception he gave me was that at that point in the South, we lived in a segregated community.

LTP: Yes, I was going to ask you what year that was? You were born in . . . ?

SK: 1944.

LTP: Oh, so right after the war.

SK: Yes, after the war.

LTP: And how was the atmosphere in the South?

SK: The Southern atmosphere was very segregated. Blacks in one place, whites in the another. I must say that I became aware of segregation in an odd kind of way. It was difficult, because there is an unmarked boundary between the black community and the white community. So, what that meant was that me and my friends could play with the white kids.

LTP: You were playing with the white children?

SK: Yes, we would play with each other.

LTP: So, it was not that segregated, at least not between children.

SK: Not between children at that point. What happened is that my father, this is my father's way of observing and teaching things, called me aside one time after he saw us playing together. He said, "Boy," that's how he talked to me when he had something serious to say, "I see that you are having lots of fun with those children, but I want you to know you should never believe anything that they tell you about who you are. Only listen to us and the people who know you." And I thought, "I'm not sure what that means." But I knew he was saying something important to me. It took me a while to understand what he was saying. I didn't know I had been protected from the reality of racism in my community, because it was an all-black community, we knew each other, we knew our area. I loved oatmeal cookies and apple pie and sometimes I would go into town to the shops, but I was totally unconscious of racialized structures. My father wanted me to keep in mind that people would tell me things about me, but that it's not me and I shouldn't believe what they said to me. He was saying I should listen to my parents, my immediate family, my extended family, my neighbors, my friends. These are the people who really knew who I was.

LTP: So, this is a very protective attitude of the father!

SK: Oh, yes! He was very protective. So, I will just fast forward to when I was about eleven. I did the same thing with the newspaper. I was always happy to get the newspaper for my father. I'd get to spend a little time with him sitting on the front porch. He would tell me stories and I would make up stories to tell him stories. Sometimes we had time to play checkers or another game, and we had a small black and white TV with a little antenna.

LTP: The little antennas!

SK: Yes! So, he was very related in that way, talking about life and its meaning. His mother, my grandmother, would come over and she would always bring us children a silver dollar bill. So, he had his ways, but it was definitely my mother . . .

LTP: Yes, I could guess!

SK: Yes, this too is a fast forward, but it is a very important point in my childhood life. On this day, I picked up the newspaper and I took it to my father. As I gave it to him, I looked at the headline and it said a black boy has been murdered and his name was Emmett Till. As I am giving the paper to my father, I asked, "What is this? What is going on with this? I don't understand!" He said, "Come with me." So, he took me into a closet, and he showed me that he had guns.

LTP: Guns?

SK: Guns! He said, "Son, they will never fuck with you!" I just said, "Oh!" First of all, I did not have a picture of who the "they" were and that "they" were potentially dangerous, enough so that my father had guns to protect me, all of us, from "them." That was a huge step, a very huge step. I was just beginning to see that there was a racial world structure that was very dangerous for me as a black person and, by extension, my black community. But it was not spelled out or articulated in church or. . . . In school, throughout that time, beginning in elementary school and going through high school, we had something called "Black History Week," where we studied literature written by blacks about black experience. So, about that time is when I saw that this young boy, Emmett Till, had been murdered [Ed. – August 28, 1955].

LTP: Emmett Till?

SK: Yes, it's one of the pivotal stories in American culture because he was a boy from Chicago. He had come down from Chicago to be with his family in Mississippi. During that time, he had been told by his mother, "You are going to a world where the rules are very different, so be aware of that." That is a version of the talk that people of color in America would give to their children, in the South especially. Even now, there is a disproportionate number of young boys and men of color being shot by police officers. Parents are obliged to give their children, their sons especially, a cautionary talk, "Look, they don't see you as we see you. They have pictures of you and those pictures make you dangerous to them."

LTP: Pictures?

SK: Fantasies. They have fantasies of you. And those fantasies make you seem dangerous to them and they will become triggered towards you. They are blinded by all sorts of things. That's the talk given by parents of color to their children in America.

LTP: The scapegoat effect.

SK: Yes and the parents' job is to help children understand the phenomenon as a survival strategy.

LTP: As a survival strategy, yes. But if we can come back for a small clarification. What town was that? Where were you born or where did you live?

SK: Jackson, Mississippi.

LTP: You said there was segregation, but the black community was the majority or just a part?

SK: We are a segregated community. There are segregated communities in most of the big cities of America. You know, where you have people of color in a segregated community. Asians are in a segregated community, multiethnic Europeans lived in certain parts of New York, so there are always boundaries. The black community was a part.

LTP: Ah, okay. So, the boundaries were quite fluid.

SK: No, boundaries are not fluid when you consider scapegoating and racialized violence, you have to be aware that when you find yourself on one side of the boundary, you are at risk of being randomly attacked in some way. So that is why there is the talk. The talk is to let your children know about those dangers, so they can protect themselves and learn how to read the nonverbal signals.

LTP: Gestures?

SK: Yes. You learn about this stuff. So, that piece of acculturation has been a part of African American life forever in America, for all people of color. You must know that because the rest of the world does not necessarily see you as a person. They will turn you into something else, like an object. But African American people can see that, just look at the history of violence towards blacks in America, terrible violence, mostly against blacks, even after World War II. Emmett Till's father was in the military service, and he had been murdered. He was accused of having some sort of secret relationship with a white woman [Ed. – Louis Till was executed by hanging by the US Army in 1945 after being accused of sexually assaulting two white women in Italy and murdering a third. The accuracy of those charges and his conviction have since been called into question by several legal scholars and historians.] His son, Emmett Till, was a fourteen-year-old boy who was accused of whistling and making advances at a white woman in a store. It was her husband and another man that came in the middle of the night, grabbed him from his home, hung him, and threw him in the Tallahatchie River [Ed. – Emmett Till died after being tortured and shot in the head by his abductors.] It took days before he was found. I am elaborating on this story, but I want you to have some sense of the horror I've carried since I was a young boy.

LTP: Horror?

SK: Horror, yes. Absolute horror. This is what I realized my father was trying to tell me about. It took this experience with Emmett's murder to open the depths, for me to think, "I see what you are saying. That is out there." So, to connect Emmett's murder to the present, George Floyd was murdered recently [Ed. – George Floyd was a black man murdered in Minneapolis, Minnesota, on May 25, 2020, by a white police officer while in police custody.] It's a very interesting connection because Emmett Till's body was brought back to Chicago. His family did not want him to be buried in the South. He was so disfigured that his mother could not recognize his head. He was swollen, he had been in the river, after being beaten and killed. So, what did his mother do? This was genius on her part! She said, "I want to have an open casket in the Central Square of Chicago. I want the whole world to see what this murderous racism looks like." Looking back on this, I thought, "Oh, my goodness!" So, they did just that! They set a place in the center of the city with an open casket so that everyone could see his body. People from all over the world took photographs and they could see the result, the face of murderous racism in the presentation of this young boy. At that point, I got it. I got what my father had been telling me.

LTP: Oh! This is the terrorism you were trying to tell me about, in your gentle way, because it is horrific!

SK: So, it was important that his mother wanted to expose Emmett's body to the world to see the face of racism in America. Now I fast-forward to George Floyd. The racism now is just as brutal; what happened to Emmett also happened to George Floyd. The only thing that is different now is that we saw it happening in real time. We all got to see the face of white terrorism and racism in America. It changed everything! That really impacted the world, especially Americans, who, because of Barack Obama, thought that we had passed beyond racism, that we lived in a postracial world. Then they saw the George Floyd murder as it was happening. Oh, no! The face of racism is still here!

LTP: It's still here!

SK: The monster is still here! So, though the monster is still here in plain sight, and we must face that monster. The reason that we don't always see the monster is that whites are protected by privilege and power. That is why exposing the deaths of Emmett and George was a way to break through the denial and show the American shadow in its rawest and most violent form.

LTP: In your opinion, do you think it's also sometimes about racism from the black population towards whites as well?

SK: Well, . . . after 400 years of slavery and postslavery violence of whites towards blacks, we have to see and answer those kinds of questions within the racialized social structures of power (perpetrator, victim, and as important bystanders). We are all implicated in what is happening racially. We need to confront the denial, the myopia, and the presumption of innocence.

LTP: Isn't it about the other one's shadow? Because you're black, you are my shadow, and because I'm white, I'm your shadow? Because something from my shadow bothers me and I project something onto you?

SK: Well, this is an interesting question because when you think about slavery, the shadow would have started very early on. The 1619 Project was just completed a couple of years ago, with the 400th anniversary of slaves being brought to America [Ed. – Initiated by *The New York Times*, the 1619 Project is a historical review and reframing of the impact of slavery on America with an emphasis on recognizing the contributions of black Americans to the American narrative.] Now, that whole experience is rife with shadow. In fact, some of us have referred to it as "America's original sin." It is an original sin that has not been acknowledged in its entirety. Instead, between 1619 and now, people of color have continued to carry the shadow of America. So, white people carry some of this shadow, but in a way, they have earned it. It's not like we came about this interpretation without some basis; it's not fantasy projection. It's real stuff. For example, if you look at the racial disparities in terms of who is showing up with COVID. Ideally, we should see that we are all vulnerable. It should be possible to become one great family because we're all exposed to the virus, it's an equal opportunity virus. It gets anyone! But that has not happened! Instead, what we saw was that the people most likely to get the virus and die from the virus are people of color. Why? Well, because of disparities in access to healthcare and access to quality food and education, as well as living in substandard housing. The residual effects of racism continue to make people of color more vulnerable to something like a virus. What we saw, though, and I think a lot of young people had an opportunity to see, was that racism is there all the time, but often we can't see because it is structural racism. It has to do with the setup. Once you are operating in a structural racism environment, white people can portray themselves as nonracist, "It's not me. It must have been those guys who have the ropes. I am not the racist." But the point is that if you benefit from the structure, the setup, the structural racism, you are implicated. You're an implicated subject. So, structural racism allows us to see that we are all implicated in this. Structural racism can only operate if those "other" people participate in it and close their eyes to it. That's the only way it can continue to work. I don't think we have enough time, but I wanted you to see how that all came into that moment when I was about eleven years old. My whole childhood world was fleshed out with the darkness and evil that were present.

LTP: But after you joined the church during that revival, were you inspired to continue going there? Did your life change in any way?

SK: I think the way it changed was that I no longer had to believe in God. I no longer had to believe in the Spirit, I knew the Spirit. I didn't have to believe, I knew.

LTP: You were a little bit younger than Jung when you said it. Jung said that later in his life, but you were a prodigy from this perspective.

SK: I tell you, some things are just that real. I don't know if you know of a black blues singer, Ray Charles?

LTP: Of course, I've heard about Ray Charles!

SK: So, Ray Charles was asked at one point, "How would you define soul?" He said, "I don't know how to define it for you, but I can tell you if it is present or not." I don't want to try to define Spirit for you, but I can tell you if a person is genuine, if they have integrity, and it's connected to something transpersonal that's real. I can tell that of a person. So, that's what I received. That's what the church gave to me. That's what my mother gave to me. As a grownup, other people said you don't need to become a preacher because becoming an analyst is like being a preacher.

LTP: It is similar; it's very much the same. I want to back up a bit and ask two questions. You told me about a red vinyl record that came to your house, but I also see the *Red Book* behind you in your room.

SK: Oh, yes.

LTP: Did that book also help you in any way to continue your active imagination experience? Do you have a regular practice of this? How do you integrate it in your life?

SK: You mean how do I make use of the *Red Book*?

LTP: Yes! If you use it? If yes, how did you benefit from the publishing of the *Red Book*?

SK: Well, I was president of the C.G. Jung Institute of San Francisco at the time the *Red Book* was published, and I remember the members were asked to declare if they wanted a copy of the *Red Book* at a dinner meeting.

LTP: A dinner meeting?

SK: Yes. We would have dinner meetings once a month, and I will never forget that evening when the *Red Books* were delivered by a truck. They were bringing in the boxes, stacking them up. I said, "Oh, my God! I didn't realize that it was so big. And so many of them." So, I remember not just the size of them, but also the number of books. When the meeting was over, people came up to get their books and I was walking up behind them. Some of them had two books, one in each arm, and I thought, "What a sight! It's like they got the Bible!" They were happy to take it with them, it was one of those wonderful moments of joy. So, I've taught a number of seminars on the *Red Book*, some for the public and some with the institute. In fact, I am scheduled to do something early next year with our candidates. There's a lot in the *Red Book*, and it is a wonderful way to open candidates, or anyone, up to the mythopoetic attitude where they can have some sort of access to the imagination and the psyche. I think that the problem that we have in today's world, especially in our psychologies, is that the psyche has become identical with the mind. So, you do things to impress the mind, to educate the mind, to connect the mind with the body. Jung's attitude was oriented towards the phenomenology of the psyche, that is the spontaneous, autonomous manifestation of the life of the psyche. That's what we are trying to get at. That's not the mind. The *Red Book* documents Jung's approach to the psyche.

LTP: Or at least not only the mind!

SK: It's not only the mind, not only the body, not only the Spirit, not only this world, not only that world, it's autonomous. To get that principle across, there is nothing better than the *Red Book*, but you must know how to talk about it, so people can have their imagination opened again to a way of being, an experience of psyche, that would make the *Red Book* accessible to them. So, that's the challenge, sort of like my mother and father. My father taught me about racism, my mother tried to put me in touch with the Spirit. You can talk about something until the cows come home, but the point is that if I had not gone to the church revival meeting, it would have all been intellectual. I would know the stories, but something had to happen. So, something, a spiritual sensibility or sensitivity, had to have been in me to be activated by that experience which said, "You are now home! You know what home looks like." When we are teaching the *Red Book*, the trick is how to open them up to it. There is a book that you may have read, an exchange between James Hillman and Sonu Shamdasani – *Lament of the Dead*. I think it is Hillman who said that he thinks the *Red Book* is opening the mouth of the dead so they can speak.

LTP: The dead inside of us, right?

SK: Well, it's not so clear whether they're inside of us. They come through us. They're not personal. That's the other piece that is interesting with the *Red Book*. Jung never claimed his figures as personal. He made use of them to access aspects of himself that we would not have accessed by looking at them personally. Because the moment you look at them personally, you have reduced them down to your size. God is not personal. You can have a personal relationship with God, it could be like Saint Francis in his prayer hut which he called *Conversaciones Con Dios* [Conversations with God], "I am talking with God now and he is going to listen to me." And then there's an old saying, "May you not find yourself in the hands of a living God." In other words, it is like a type of energy, but it's not exactly a *kumbaya* [meaning "come by here" – coming together as people in our essential goodness]. So, in the *Red Book*, Jung shows us a way of developing relationships with these other manifestations of psyche that are unique to our own soul. In encountering and working with these manifestations, we have an opportunity to discover aspects of ourselves that would not have been accessible to us otherwise. If you can do that, your attitude must be phenomenological, it's not a thinking thing. It's not regular psychotherapy. It's something like active imagination but it's different also. So, for me, that's the biggest doorway we must open to teach the *Red Book*; otherwise, it remains just pictures and interesting things. As you know, most of the people who bought initial copies of the book put them on their coffee tables and they stayed on their coffee tables. Now they are on the lower shelf of their coffee tables because they don't know what to do with them!

LTP: Yes, it's a heavy book from many points of view, so to speak.

SK: Many, many points of view. Anyway, when I can, I go back to it and connect to it on my own. But most of the time it's when I'm teaching, or in a case when I encounter someone who says something that refers to something in the *Red Book*, I go find it and talk about it. I want to tell you something else, but it's not about my childhood. It's much further along, which is how I got to Jung.

LTP: That was my next question. How did you get to Jung, especially considering Jung's past?

SK: Well, I was in a graduate program in psychology and the program included working in groups. So, we all had to watch groups and participate in groups, even marathon groups. The man who was over the program was a very charismatic psychologist. I said to him at one point, "I'd like to see you for therapy." He agreed and we set up some meetings. About two months into it he said, "Sam, I have to tell you this, you have lots of dreams. I don't work with dreams! But I want you to go see my analyst who does work with dreams." So his analyst become my first analyst.

LTP: Someone we may know?

SK: Yes, you may know. His name is J. Marvin Spiegelman from Southern California. And he was the right medicine for my dream world. Shortly after I met him, I had a dream in which there was this beautiful, tall, lovely, blonde woman.

LTP: Blonde?

SK: Blonde. She appeared in my dream, coming out of the forest. She looked at me and she said, "Come with me!"

LTP: *Anima*!

SK: So, I did! Ultimately she became my wife. But I also got her into Jungian analysis. It turned out that her analyst, my analyst, and James Hillman were all at the Jung Institute in Zurich at the same time.

LTP: Oh my God!

SK: Her analyst and my analyst were close friends. They were called the Three Musketeers or something; they were close friends. At some point, I said to my analyst, "I think I want to go to Zurich to get in and study Jungian analysis." My analyst said, "Well, you could do that. Or you can just apply here in Los Angeles, and I think you'll have no trouble getting in." I said, "No, I need to go to Jung." So, I went to Zurich for one year and I met with James Hillman, and Hillman talked about the Jung Institute; its problems and challenges, and so on. He said, "You probably need to get a job, as it is very expensive here." So, I applied for a position with the Army base, to be a psychologist at the base. They said, "We can give you a job, but you have to stay six months in Europe." I thought, "Oh, my God, another six months. I am not prepared to do that." So, we decided to come back home. I did not go back to

Southern California. Instead, we went to Northern California. That was significant because when we were in Europe we met a number of Jungian candidates who had become Jungian analysts. One of them called me once we got
back to California to invite me to come to talk at the Inter-Regional Society
[IRSJA] conference that was being held in Alabama on the contributions of
African Americans and Native Americans in psychology. I said, "Why do
you want me to come?" He said, "Sam, they are doing this conference, but
they have no black person, they have no Native American to present!" Oh my
God! That's what they didn't tell me.

LTP: You were the spot of color!

SK: I said, "I don't want to do it!" He said, "Oh, yes, you should do it! Just show
up and say something. I just want to make all of us honest about what we are
doing here." I said, "Okay, all right!" So, I did. James Hillman was there; he
gave a talk on whiteness. So, after that conference, an analyst from Texas,
David Rosen, who used to be in San Francisco, said to me, "When you go
back to San Francisco you should meet my close friend, Renaldo Maduro,
who is a Puerto Rican Jungian analyst. I think you two have a lot in common."
So, I did meet with Renaldo, and I asked him, "What's the San Francisco Jung
Institute like? How about the racial thing?" He said, "Sam, if I were to tell
you how many times I've heard a micro-aggression, I would be speaking all
the time." I said, "Oh, why the hell would I want to be there?" He said, "But
if you'll call them on it, tell them what they just did, then they'll listen to
you." I replied, "Wow, what an incredible train of thought! I've got to call
them on it. They are not conscious!" He said, "Let's work it out. You can go
into analysis with me, get those analytic hours you need, and then you can go
ahead and apply." I did and about three months into it he fell against the wall,
and I asked, "Are you okay?" He replied, "I'm just dizzy." So, I said, "Well,
have a seat and I will see you next time." Then I got a call from one of the
San Francisco analysts and he said, "Renaldo will not be coming back to you,
he is in a coma in the hospital." What was happening is that he had AIDS and
he hadn't told me about that. He probably hadn't told most of the institute
members about it. But that opened up a bunch of things about shadow, his
shadow, the institute's shadow, and so forth. But I did apply, and I did get in.
Then I started my own journey through the Jungian world. I began to search
for language to talk about the kind of experiences I shared with you from earlier in my life; some of the things I spoke about around my consciousness of
racism and the racial signs. I began to become aware [of] how a lot of things
are passed on through cultural complexes, phantom narratives, and intergenerational cultural complexes. But our analytic world has so separated the individual psyche from culture and context that I am afraid analytical psychology
will continue to be seen as occupying a narrow little space in the world. Until
we can open up and include the cultural context and political processes as
part of how we think about how subjectivity is shaped, it will remain narrow.
It is not just shaped by our relationship to our archetypal psyche, or to our

personal psyche; the culture is also an important part of the context of the waters that we swim in. So, all of my work has been about that, and that work has been necessary because of those early experiences that I had. There was no way I could avoid dealing with these kinds of issues. White folks can have the privilege of not having to deal with this issue; people of color cannot. We must do it. If you look at the writings of some of the earlier authors: Richard Wright, Ralph Ellison, James Baldwin, or Toni Morrison, these authors are writing about these experiences in their own language. They're doing what I'm doing from a psychological perspective, which is that you must find some way to reimagine the past in a way that you can work it, so you can experience it in the present, and integrate it in some way. So, that is the kind of work I am doing and others are doing. It's small little steps along the way, not big steps. But I think it was necessary that the world has been so impacted by climate change, along with COVID and the disparities it has revealed, the movement towards autocracy and fascism, and the impact of social media. These are monsters. We will not be able to deal with these monsters if we don't make them part of how we think about what psyche is doing.

LTP: Let's come back to your sexuality at a very early stage. How old were you?

SK: When I asked my mother?

LTP: Yes.

SK: I must have been about four.

LTP: And how did this come into your mind?

SK: I think it probably came to mind because I heard my parents having sex.

LTP: What was that experience like for you?

SK: It came in through hearing something and I was thinking, "What was that?" I was really asking her about that. She could probably hear and know that I was curious about what was happening sexually between she and my father, but she did not want to go there, because how could she explain it to a four-year-old?

LTP: Later, you said you met with your wife by seeing her in a vision, she came out of the woods, and so on. Are you married to a white woman?

SK: Yes, I am.

LTP: How was it between the two of you; the putting together of the opposites?

SK: You know, I didn't feel the reality of the opposites in our initial love, attraction, and connection. It has taken quite a while to flesh out the opposites, because both of us recognized the racial differences through our own subjectivities, which had been shaped by different kinds of forces. But she has been wonderful in bringing me into a broader view of whiteness, where whiteness is not connected so much with racism. And I brought her into the suffering of the African American people and people of color. That is there, but not all of our subjective life is oppressed by racism. We get to dance and have fun. It doesn't reduce us to only racial suffering. She is very sensitive in that area and has recently been doing groups on difficult conversations about race. We invite colleagues, friends, and other people to talk about race and racism. I think that two or three of them are clinicians but most of them are educated people who recognize that they are able to identify racist elements in themselves, but they had never learned how to talk about racism or race.

LTP: How did you and your wife meet?

SK: We met through a colleague of hers who had taught sexual education at UCLA, sexuality courses for adults. About five to six hundred people that took classes. So, my wife was friends with the instructor and said to me, "Let's go to his party," because he was having a party on a particular night. It turned out that he had a very big house and in various rooms he had different sexual activities going on for people who wanted to watch him on the screen or who wanted to participate with their own partners. I thought, "Oh, my God! I've never seen anything like this before." It was kind of like a movie . . .

LTP: What kind of church is this?

SK: (smiles) You know, there's a movie called *Eyes Wide Shut*. Do you know that movie?

LTP: Yes.

SK: That's a similar kind of thing. Of course, it's a metaphor for being unconscious. But that is where we really met, in real time.

LTP: But your vision was prior to meeting her or after meeting her?

SK: The vision was prior to meeting her.

LTP: So, you were, or are, a very intuitive person.

SK: You know, by following her, I followed me. And she followed me and suddenly we had this wonderful life with lots of richness to it. There's a lot more because of her analysis and my analysis. All kinds of things we have freaked out with or been into. It's been there and it's been a wonderful relationship.

LTP: My last question, in a nutshell, what did you take out of your relationship with your father and your relationship with your mother? As well the context of those relationships? What elements stayed with you from your childhood? In terms of psychological attributes, what did you assimilate from your father and your mother?

SK: Well, I think that both are steady, in terms of making commitments and following through, holding structure, providing containment, and that kind of thing. Also, my father was all about safety. He was conscious of safety, let's say, in a very Winnicottian way.

LTP: Winnicottian?

SK: Very Winnicottian. If you have containment, structure, and boundaries, then you have space to become yourself. I think that my parents' focus was to free me up to have access to myself. I think my mother was steadfast in her support too, she really wanted me to understand the persona. So, she saw me as a minister, that's a social role. In a social function you really need to know how to carry that role and be related to the community. I'll tell you one quick little story. At some point we moved to Los Angeles, near my mother's side of the family, but I didn't feel happy in Los Angeles. I wanted to go back to Jackson because I had my friends there. My mother said, "You want to go back to Jackson? Okay, go back to Jackson." So, I went back for my junior year of high school when I was sixteen years old. I reconnected with my two buddies. At that same year, a new teacher came to teach. I had not met him previously. He was a Spanish teacher from Chicago, and he always wore a three-piece suit, the only teacher in the school who wore a three-piece suit. At one point, he said, "I want you, boys (me and my two buddies), to come see me after class." He said, "Now, boys, you are all bright boys and you can go a long way but you are not going to get very far if you act the way you act in my class. So, I want to teach you something. During the next school assembly, I want you to dress up, with a suit and a tie, and wait until the assembly starts and walk in." I said, "I don't have a suit and a tie!" My other friend said, "I don't have a suit and a tie. I have a white shirt." He replied, "You guys come over and you take clothes out of my closet and you wear those." So, we did. The big assembly happened, we waited about ten minutes, and we walked in and the whole assembly response was, "Wow, who are those guys?" And I got it! We got it! That's what a persona can do!

LTP: Yes! He gave you your first persona, so to say!

SK: He had a persona and he said this is what it looks like. My mother said, "You go to church, you learn how to stick to those people, you learn how to carry yourself." My father said, "Be steady, be sharp, stay with structure, you can do it." These are the kinds of things I got. So, they were both teaching me ways of being in the world, through the persona, but also to be steady and listen to people. They also taught me, when you're in trouble, go to other people who are helpers. Mister Rogers [host of a children's television program – *Mr. Roger's Neighborhood*] was a significant figure for American children. One of his teachings was, "When in trouble and you're lost, go towards the helpers. Go around the world and see who's a helper and go to that person." So, it's about learning survival energy. My mother's saying would be, "With the right persona, the right attitude, then you can change things, you can turn heads." Also, that peer time I had with my friends in Jackson. It was a very dynamic period of my life, from childhood until I moved back to Los Angeles after graduating from high school.

LTP: What was your father's profession?

SK: He was a foreman in a warehouse.

LTP: And your mother?

SK: She stayed at home and later she became like a nurse's aide.

LTP: Thank you very much, Sam! Maybe one day you can also give us a lecture in Romania.

SK: I'd be happy to. Just let me know when you're ready. I just did one with a Cantonese group, and I've done a number of talks this past year. With everything going on, you know with COVID, I want to tell you that people are going out of their minds and saying, "Come and say something to us about what's going on."

LTP: Thank you very much for helping us and accepting. Thank you! Have a good day! Goodbye!

Chapter 12

The Needle of Hope

Debora (Dvora) Kutzinski
INTERVIEWED BY LAVINIA ŢÂNCULESCU-POPA
APRIL 23, 2018 – TEL AVIV

Mrs. Debora (Dvora) Kutzinski is a Jewish-Czech born Jungian analyst. She was one of the members of the first Jungian group in Tel Aviv, as well as a friend and supervisee of Dr. Erich Neumann and the analysand of Julie Neumann. Mrs. Kutzinski received the Honorary Member Award during the 2019 IAAP Congress in Vienna. During her award acceptance she said, "My life developed between these poles: Auschwitz and the murder of my whole family and eighteen years of analysis and supervision with Julie and Erich Neumann, for which I am eternally grateful. I am now working for sixty-four years in private practice and hope to go on till the end." Mrs. Kutzinski survived four years in Nazi concentration camps before beginning her journey to become a Jungian analyst. She is not known for her professional writing, but rather for her presence, energy, and insight as an analyst and teacher. When asked about her writing, she commented, "I am sorry, but I am not a writing person. There was nothing published. But since I started the training in our association in 1962, I gave a seminar every year from then on. But I destroyed those manuscripts immediately at the end of the seminar, just so I do not repeat myself."

DK: Before we begin discussing my life, tell me some things about you.

LTP: I am one of the people who started to learn about Jungian analysis in Romania twenty years ago. As part of that, I ended up visiting Küsnacht in 2008. At that time, the routers group was not yet constituted in Romania.

DK: I was in Romania.

LTP: Yes, there were a lot of people in the conference you held.

DK: So, you are now a group of analysts who started the work. Yehuda Abramovich is coming to Romania, am I right?

LTP: Yes, he is our IAAP liaison officer, and he was along with us almost throughout the entire journey. During my trips to Zurich, I went to both the C.G. Jung Institute – Küsnacht and ISAP for open lectures and some seminars. I like the constant study.

DOI:10.4324/9781003148937-13

DK: I studied for eighteen years when I was trained as a Jungian analyst, and I have never regretted it one minute. I would have gone on, but they both died, Julie and Erich Neumann, so I stopped.

LTP: Yes, I know how important central figures are in our lives and training. One of the first meetings I had was back in 2009 with Jung's younger daughter, Mrs. van Hoerni.

DK: Why did you want to interview me?

LTP: I was exposed to a lot of people in all these years, but the ones who captivated me in a way with their life stories, I wanted to go much deeper with. I was already thinking of you after the conference in Bucharest, and Yehuda emphasized that you were quite a significant figure in the Jungian landscape, not just in Israeli psychology, but the whole Jungian world.

DK: Has Neumann been already translated into Romanian?

LTP: Yes, some of his works.

DK: It is quite difficult to read and to translate.

LTP: Yes, it is indeed, but we also read part of his work in English – *The Great Mother, The Origins of Consciousness*, and *Depth Psychology and a New Ethic*.

DK: You should read *The Fear of the Feminine*.

LTP: *The Fear of the Feminine* was one of the subjects I want to discuss.

DK: Ok, now I know who you are. What would you like to do with the interview?

LTP: Actually, I am developing a book about the early life of senior Jungian analysts. The theme is unique because all the interviews are with well-established professionals, senior figures with decades of experience. But I want to discuss their childhoods, as the basis of their individuation process.

DK: All right, I will tell you about my childhood.

LTP: The interviews are under the umbrella called *Beyond Persona*. You gave an interview to Henry Abramovic and in that interview, I liked something that you said, that "We should all serve the soul and not the ego." I am interested in deepening this idea in this interview.

DK: Ok, so let's start. I am from Czechoslovakia [now the Czech Republic]. I was born in 1925, so in two months I will be ninety-three. I think I'm one of the oldest Jungians. My parents were both academics. My father, a deeply introverted person, was a professor of Greek and Latin – both dead languages. My mother was a musician, a singer. But she was not allowed to sing, because, back then, a lady of the society was not allowed to sing. Going on stage would be seen as very close to being a prostitute. So, for twenty years she just cultivated her voice. At home, we had music from morning until the evening, which was very fine for me. I had an older brother, three years older. We moved from Brno, which is the second largest city in Czechoslovakia, to Prague. I attended the humanist gymnasium. But as the Nazis entered Czechoslovakia on [March 15] 1939, they threw the Jews out of the schools. Then, the Jews organized a seminar for gymnastics teachers, a two-year seminar. As I had always loved sport, I thought that was the right occupation for me. I was the youngest in the course. I have a diploma certifying that I am a teacher of sports – athletics and gymnastics. Until the Nazis came, I had a very happy childhood. I think this explains why, when I came back after four years of concentration camps, I didn't have a breakdown and why I could develop my personality and go on to pursue my real vocation. I don't know if you have met many people who survived Auschwitz?

LTP: No, not so many.

DK: I admire the human soul which, after such terrible experiences like Auschwitz, which is the most terrible thing you can imagine, can come back and is sane, more or less.

LTP: Do you agree that being sad – not sane – is transmitted to the second and the third generation of the survivors?

DK: I started working with people from the first generation of survivors, as I had the same experiences and I preferred to work with them. Then, many more came from the second generation. Now the third generation entered therapy. They all are damaged. You can differentiate people who are constantly talking about the Holocaust with their children, and people who didn't say a word. I belong to the people who didn't speak about it.

LTP: Why don't you speak about it?

DK: It was too difficult for me to tell the children about it. At the age of eleven in our schools, they have to write down the family tree. This was the first time my son came to me and asked me, "Tell me about your parents, tell me about your grandparents, tell me about your family." I broke down crying. My husband took him away and told him, "Don't ask your mother this." So, he didn't know. My husband supplied our son with whatever he knew. But even he didn't know. There are people who found it easier to talk about it, and there are also people who find it easier to be quiet about it. I belong to the last category.

What else could I tell you? I had a wonderful childhood and education. As the family was bourgeois, one had to play the piano, one had to learn French (back then it wasn't English, but French), one had to know how to cook. I had trouble with my mother because I didn't like cooking and didn't want to learn to cook. Even today I don't like cooking. So, my mother was deeply afraid that if I didn't know how to cook and to manage the household, nobody would want to marry me. This was a real problem in her eyes. She tried to push me into the kitchen, but I didn't want to be in the kitchen. And you know why? Back then, one would buy live chickens and the cook had to cut the chicken's head off. I saw it once and cried and ran out. This was my last time in the kitchen.

LTP: Your last encounter with the kitchen?

DK: So, I heard all the time, "My child, what will happen to you? Nobody will marry you! You will never earn one penny! You will die from hunger." She was very sad and anxious that I was a misfit, that I was not worth anything. This is the prophecy I grew up with.

LTP: That you are not worth anything?

DK: That I couldn't manage a household, I didn't know how to cook. I wanted to have a vocation. From the age of ten, I knew I wouldn't marry until I found my vocation. Do you know why? In the bourgeoisie, the man earns the money, the woman is the lady of the house, there's a maid, there's a *Kinderfräulein*. But my mother "fell from her feet" because she worked so hard to manage the household! My father gave my mother money every week, I think on Wednesday, on pay day. He gave her a very generous amount for the household. We were not poor. But I remember that if on Wednesday she got the money, on next Tuesday she said, "Peter" – this was my father's name – "I have no money anymore." He said, "Already?" So, this one word, "already," made me absolutely decide I wouldn't marry until I earned my living, which I did.

LTP: At the age of thirty?

DK: I didn't want somebody to ask me, "Already?" I found this to be something degrading. I was going out with my future husband for three years and he said, "Let's marry!" After four years, I said, "No, I want to finish my studies at the university" (I got my BA and MA in psychology, philosophy, and pedagogy), and I said, "I can't marry before I earn my living." He said, "But I earn enough, let's marry. We already know each other, we love each other." I replied, "Under no circumstances!" Then the second problem was he didn't want me to be a psychologist. I didn't know why. He told me that I can choose any occupation, any job, whatever I want, that I didn't need to work, "Just don't be a psychologist." He didn't tell me the reason, not even after we married. I started to work and right from the beginning Erich Neumann sent me patients. So, in two months' time, when I could not take one more patient, I said, "Let's marry."

In Prague we lived in a flat near to the famous clock [Ed. – the Orloj clock]. My father had many friends from the academic world; every four weeks there would be a salon. He would invite famous professors and artists. There was always a big shout and debate about spiritual things. One of our visitors was Max Brod. This was in 1939 and he was already internationally famous. Max Brod was a writer and artist very well known as the best friend of Franz Kafka.

LTP: Yes.

DK: Brod is the one who didn't keep his promise to Kafka, who had asked him to burn everything he wrote after his death. Kafka was absolutely neurotic. He was a perfectionist; nothing he wrote was good enough for him. But Max Brod, himself an artist, understood that Kafka's writings were phenomenal, so he published them. Brod was one of the last Jews to leave Czechoslovakia when the Nazis came. He died here in Tel Aviv. So, today I think he is more famous as the publisher of Kafka, than he is for his own writing. He published fifty books and a hundred articles. He was already internationally known when he met Kafka at age eighteen. From this point on, he put himself aside and did everything to bring Kafka to the awareness of the international public. Because of him, Kafka is known as one of the best writers of the 20th century, Dostoevsky and Kafka. As you know, I am preparing a seminar on Kafka for the Jungians. Brod told my father that we lived in the flat of Kafka. We didn't know it because the Nazis didn't want the public to know about Kafka because he was a Jew. Today, downstairs in the same house, there is an exhibition of Kafka. We lived there until February 1942. In 1942 the Nazis began to send the Jews away to camps and the ghetto in Theresienstadt.

LTP: I am going to ask you a very naive question. How did they know that someone was a Jew?

DK: In those years, you declared your origins, so they knew it. They took over the municipality and the archives, it was very easy. Then the Jews were mostly German speakers and had a German culture. One of the mainstays of German culture is discipline. So, the German Jews were very disciplined, you had to declare yourself, and you had to wear the Jewish star. They dutifully went to these places where you got the yellow star and put it on. Only the most clever ones, who weren't German Jews, but more Czech Jews or Jewish Jews went in the resistance, the underground. But most, I would say ninety-five percent, were very disciplined and declared themselves to be Germans with Jewish origins.

LTP: So, your parents did the same?

DK: Gradually, from 1939, every day there were more things forbidden. You couldn't enter a store; you couldn't go to the theater and so on. Then at the beginning of 1942 they started the transports.

LTP: In the beginning, when they told you to go to declare yourselves and to pick up the stars and so on, did they give you a reason why?

DK: No. The reason was that "the Jews were the enemy of the German Reich," but Germany was very poor because of the armistice from 1918. They had to find a scapegoat. You need a scapegoat to establish yourself. Also, in psychological terms, you need an enemy, so you project your shadow onto somebody. When Hitler came to power, the best scapegoat were the Jews. They were very prominent in culture and in finance.

LTP: Yes.

DK: This was reason enough for the Nazis. Not for us, but for the Nazis it was quite enough. Ok, so I'll go on. What do you want to ask me?

LTP: How old were you?

DK: In 1942 I was not yet seventeen, as I was born in July. So, in February I was almost seventeen.

LTP: When did you realize what was happening? Did you ask your parents why?

DK: No, not quite. Don't forget that the Nazis took Austria in 1938. Czechoslovakia is very close to Austria, so we knew what was going on. Then they took the Sudeten. Then, it was Munich. Chamberlain didn't stand up to his promise, nor England or France. They agreed with Hitler that he could take the Sudetenland and there wouldn't be a war. In 1939, Hitler took Czechoslovakia and the Republic stopped existing.

LTP: Maybe it is difficult to answer, but what did you feel inside?

DK: I'll tell you. Youth is optimistic. Youth is not afraid. Youth thinks, "This is like an adventure." We packed up. You could take up to twenty kilos of things with you. You got a number, you wrote the number on the luggage, not yet on the hand. A thousand people were put in wagons and trains, from Prague and you arrived in Theresienstadt. But you were still with your friends. I had belonged to the Jewish youth movement for two years, so I wasn't afraid.

LTP: You also had a brother.

DK: My brother volunteered to go in November in 1941 to Theresienstadt. The SS asked the Jews to mobilize a thousand young men, volunteers, and be sent to Theresienstadt to prepare the ghetto for the arrival of the Jews. So, my brother was already there, he was not yet twenty.

LTP: There were Jews preparing the terrain for other Jews?

DK: This was clever of the Nazis. In Auschwitz they put the Jewish *kapos* in charge of other people [Ed. – Jewish prisoners recruited to oversee other Jewish prisoners]. They spared themselves.

LTP: They cleaned their hands, so to say.

DK: Sure, the heads were the Nazis and under them there were *kapos*. This was the clever trick of the Nazis. The Jewish boys prepared the ghetto, it was not a concentration camp. The most difficult thing was that we were terribly hungry. Not yet the hunger of Auschwitz, but we were terribly hungry. In the beginning, the men and the women lived apart, so I was just there with my mother and grandmother.

LTP: Maternal grandmother?

DK: Yes, my maternal grandmother. We called her "Babicka." By then she must have already been like eighty. At eighty she was still a beautiful woman, like a queen. She had nice curly hair; she was really beautiful. We laughed with her. She died in Theresienstadt. I inherited the energy from her. She was a very energetic, clever woman. But I was also afraid of her, because when I was a little child, she made me eat. Now, I don't have this problem anymore (she laughs).

In Theresienstadt, there were thirty to fifty people in a room like this, there were no beds. They gave us. . . . How do you call it, in English, the thing you lay on?

LTP: A blanket?

DK: A blanket . . . no . . . (she laughs bitterly). A sack that you fill with hay. There were no blankets. We had only one gray, scratchy blanket, like the soldiers get. This was terrible. It was only this small room and, in the night, when you needed to turn, everyone must turn.

LTP: A domino effect.

DK: Theresienstadt was a little town where the Austrian army was stationed. There were big houses where the Austrians had lived. The Austrians were gone and there were rooms for the youths. Also, the Czech population was gone. For the Nazis this was the best place to put thousands of people into. The Nazis later opened the ghetto, which meant that men and women were allowed to live together. The youth got two houses and they moved all of them in. I was in a room with fourteen girls. I was one year older than the other ones by then. They were fifteen and sixteen, so, I was seventeen, I was the *madrikah*. What do you call the *madrikah*?

LTP: The mother, the elder, although you were only a child.

DK: Yes. As we were a Zionist youth organization, my task was to educate them towards Palestine.

LTP: Towards Palestine?

DK: Yes, Palestine. There was no Israel yet. Nobody, not the children, not us, thought about an end solution. We thought that the Germans would lose the war and afterwards, we would go back to Prague. An interesting thing about Theresienstadt, there were cultural activities going on at a high level. There was an orchestra. The Jews smuggled their instruments into the ghetto. There were singers, actors, and philosophy professors. In the evening there were concerts, theatre shows, and excellent philosophy talks by internationally known professors. This activity was forbidden and because of this it started after 9 o'clock under the roofs, in the darkness.

LTP: Do you remember anyone (from there)?

DK: I remember I heard about Spinoza; I heard about Leibnitz. I saw the national Czech opera *The Bartered Bride* five times with wonderful singers [in Czech: *Prodaná nevěsta*, by Bedřich Smetana – *The Sold Bride*]. The Jews organized everything in secret. There were very famous conductors and singers in the choir. They organized Verdi's *Requiem*, which was given several times.

LTP: The Verdi's *Requiem*?

DK: Yes. In 1943, as the Germans started to lose the war, their front in Russia collapsed and they started the retreat. They felt the danger, so they wanted to liquidate Theresienstadt, at least the men. Am I clear?

LTP: Yes.

DK: Have you heard the word *Judenaeltesten*?

LTP: No.

DK: *Judenaeltesten*, in translation, is the older Jews. So, the Germans asked the Jews to organize a kind of government which was called the "Oldest Jews," the "*Judenrat*."

LTP: Like a council.

DK: They had to choose – this was tragic – a thousand men to be sent away. The *Judenrat* knew that it wasn't what the Nazis claimed it would be – "another work camp" – but we didn't know. It was Auschwitz. But the *Judenrat* didn't say, because it would have brought panic. They had to choose by themselves, which means they chose who was going to die. This was the hardest job for them. I always thought what would I have done? I would have killed myself. I would not have been able to choose somebody to be sent to death.

They started the transports. Babichka had died in the meantime. I was by then almost eighteen and I fell in love for the first time. It was with a wonderful boy, also a *Madrich*. *Madrich* is the one who is one or two years older and teaches the youth. I fell in love with his character. But I was not lucky, he went out with the most beautiful girl of the youth organization, a blonde. So, what could I do? I called my best friend, a girlfriend who I knew would talk, she couldn't hold anything back. I made her swear she would not say one word of what I was telling her, knowing very well that tomorrow he would already know. I told her a secret I am very ashamed of, "I am very in love with him, but he is not free, he loves this other girl." And she swore she would not tell a word of it.

LTP: (Laughs)

DK: After three days he came and told me he heard I wanted to take English lessons. He knew English very well, and I said, "Yes." For fourteen days I learned English with him. By the third week we had already kissed. He left this girl, and we were in love. This was a big experience. I loved him very much. After some time, the Germans allowed marriages in the ghetto. He was twenty-two and I was eighteen, and we decided to marry. I said, "You have to go to my father and ask for my hand." I was sure my father would say, "I'm sorry, she's too young." I had a father complex. My father was the ideal person for me. Intelligent, quiet, introverted, and, first of all, had integrity. So, I was sure he wouldn't give me away. Did you hear the name Leo Baeck, the chief Rabbi of Germany?

LTP: Yes.

DK: Leo Baeck was also in Theresienstadt. They didn't kill him because he was internationally known. He was dignity itself. You could feel his dignity from meters away. My boyfriend told me he would very much like Leo Baeck to marry us. So, we went to Leo Baeck.

LTP: Even if without your father's blessing?

DK: I first had to get my father's consent. So, we both went to my parents who, by then, were allowed to live together, in a very small room. My parents had a wonderful marriage. I have never seen a marriage like this. In all these years I think I heard only one time a little fight. They lived in Theresienstadt in a little room. I was expecting the scene: Peterl asks for my hand and my father would say, "I'm very sorry but she is too young" and Peterl would ask again, and my father would again say, "No."

Peterl was very shy, a twenty-two-year-old boy. He said, "Professor Zeckendorf, I ask for the hand of your daughter." My father looks at him and asks, "Do you love her?" He said, "Yes, very much." My father looks at me, "Do you love him?" I said "Yes, very much." My father said, "So, I'm very glad." I started crying like a baby. My mother, my father, and Peterl looked at me and asked me "What are you crying for?" I said, "So easily, you give me away? So easily, you don't want me anymore? How can you do this?" My mother laughed. Father was a clever man. He saw what was coming. That is why I loved him. He was glad that I was not alone, and he was right. We went to Leo Baeck and asked him to fix a date and we were married.

The Chaverim [the boys and girls of the youth organization] stood in a row as Leo Baeck married us very nicely. My mother, a Jewish mother, thought you don't want to give everything at once. . . . Then what would be by night? So, from a bed linen she sewed me a bridal nightgown that was closed from here, till here (laughs, she gestures from the top to the bottom of the dress). Neither me nor Peterl could take it off, so we both "worked" at it for 50 minutes. So, this was the marriage.

From 1943, the transports started, every month. The Jewish executive council had to choose people, and my parents got notice to go. We didn't yet know about Auschwitz. By then it was already the beginning of 1944. The Germans were fleeing from the Eastern Front. The Normandy invasion began in June 1944.

This was around that time. The Germans felt they were losing the war. We knew that they were losing the war and we hoped we would return to Prague. We kissed my parents as we said goodbye. It never occurred to me that we would never see them again. We said, "See you later!" with "later" meaning "Au revoir, we see you in Prague, in three, four months." We were optimistic, we embraced, we kissed, and they went.

One month later, my brother fell into the transport, and he went. So, I stayed with Peterl in Theresienstadt and in two months' time, Peterl got this notice to come to the station where the trains were leaving from. Not me, because they wanted the young girls to stay in Theresienstadt and work for them. So, I said to Peterl, "I am coming with you, I will volunteer." So, we arrived at the train station and there was an SS officer with a pistol who read the names. He reads, "Peterl Karlplus," so my husband stands up, and I stand up and go with him to the SS. The officer says to me, "You go back," and I said to him, "This is my husband, I am asking to volunteer to go with him." He raised his voice and said, "Go back! Zuruck, Zuruck." When you are young you don't think twice. I was not afraid, I had *chutzpah* [Engl.- *courage*]. I said, "I volunteer to go with him, he is my husband," as if it was normal. He raised his voice and shouted. He thought that I would run away. But I said, "If I can't go with my husband, my husband isn't going either."

To this day, I think, "How could I say this?" Then, something happened. The officer was so surprised, which didn't happen often. You don't answer back to an SS officer, not when you are in front of the train going to Auschwitz. It took him two minutes and he said, "Both of you go back!" He was flabbergasted. He didn't know what to say. So, we were saved. The train was leaving, and we went back. We embraced, we laughed, we smiled, we wept, and went home where we lived in the attic of a big house. This is a moment which I treasure.

Then, fifteen days later, there was another notice for Peterl to go. This time, I was not the only one. There were other girls who wanted to go with their parents, with their boyfriends, with their sisters or brothers. This time there were twenty or thirty volunteers. Some German, not an SS, a civilian

German who was overseeing my workplace, saw the scene when I volunteered the first time and called me aside. He told me, "Girl, don't go, you won't stay with him. I am forbidden to tell you, but you'll travel with him for twenty-four hours and after, they will separate you. Don't go!" I didn't believe him, and I said, "Nevertheless, he is my husband, I am going with him." So, I went. After twenty-four hours, the Germans separated us. The Germans were clever like foxes. The trains arrived only by night, in darkness. You don't know where you are. Suddenly, the train stops. There were big lights on you and SS officers shouted, "Out, out!" Far away stood an officer, with his hands in his coat, with a big dog. This was Mengele.

LTP: Mengele? The doctor?

DK: Yes, Doctor Mengele, with his cane. First, they separate men and women. We embraced and said, "Next month, in Prague!" This was already September 1944, after Normandy. The interesting thing is that even in an isolated concentration camp, and also in the ghetto, we received the daily news. I don't know how. We knew every day what was happening on the front, what was happening in the war. I think the Czechs who brought food to the ghetto told us and it spread from one to another.

It was September 1944 and we knew they were losing the war. We embraced, we kissed, and we said, *"I'll see you next month in Prague. Au revoir!"* I never doubted Peterl would come back. In that transport there were 5,600 people, and Mengele shouted, "The men to the right, the women to the left." We were two hundred girls and young women. First, they took us to the showers. We encountered the *kapos* – they are the Jewish overseers, who had been in Auschwitz for months and they knew everything. They told us there may be showers and there may be gas.

We were desperately afraid of the showers. We didn't know what would come out. It was the showers. Most girls cried. I didn't cry. I don't know why. They shaved your head and everywhere else. Then they put Lysol on you, a disinfectant. You are naked before fifteen to twenty SS officers, which you didn't mind, it was not important. Then you waited, like in the Army: you always wait. It was desperately cold. We had to lie down on concrete. I never felt so cold in my life. You had to wait until you were sent to the barracks.

It was all like a moving conveyor belt in a factory. The Germans were perfectly organized, from A to Z. You go and receive clothes. Until 1944 they had these clothes with blue-gray stripes which had been warm. We only got summer clothes from people who were dead, shoes which didn't fit, no underwear, no bra, no slip. It was terribly cold. Then, they pushed us into the barracks. Then the big hunger began. You get two cups of soup, very thin soup and three slices of bread a day. You know what hunger is? Hunger is when you constantly think of food. And your eyes are constantly looking for something to eat. Everybody says this about the concentration camps. You are so hungry; you lose weight immediately. Is this too much for you?

LTP: No. I am very emotional, very touched, but I want to hear this.

DK: I will tell you two interesting things. First, at five o'clock in the morning you have to get out of the barracks, to attention. The counting of the prisoners! If you don't go out, you go to the gas.

LTP: You already understood what was going on.

DK: Yes. Just as Mengele ordered, older people went to the gas. I hoped that my parents died in the gas chamber, so they didn't have to go through this. Regarding my parents, I was sure about this. Since my brother was a sportsman and my husband was a sportsman too, both were very fit, I thought they would be able to go through all this, like me.

I didn't know what depression was. But, on the fifth or sixth day, I decided I wouldn't stand up, I was fed up, I no longer cared about anything. I wanted to be left alone. The girls on my right and left were my friends. My girlfriends from the youth organization took me by force, by my arms. I shouted, "Leave me alone, I don't care anymore!" If they hadn't done this, the SS would have come into the barracks looking to see if anybody was in bed, or ill, and they would have sent me directly to the gas.

One day in October, we were told that if they march you across the train rails – to the crematorium – you are going to die. So, sure enough, there was an order, "Stand up! March!" We knew we were going to die. Nobody cried, nobody shouted, nobody said jokes, it was a moment of black humor. Beside me there was a girl. She was called Magda. She's still alive in Beer Sheva. She suddenly saw something on the earth. It was a needle, shining in the sunlight. I told her, "Magda, where we are going, you won't need it. Throw it away!" But, until this day, I remember what she replied. She said, "You never know!" And she picked it up! The needle served us until the end.

After five minutes, there was an order, "Wait!" And then, twenty minutes later, there was suddenly a new order, "Turn around. March back to the barracks!" The crematorium was so overflowing with people, they couldn't manage. There were so many put to death on that day, that they couldn't manage. We went back to the barracks.

The next morning, we received a new order and we thought, "Again?" No, it was a march to a train. They sent us to another concentration camp, and we were saved from the crematorium. Nobody cried, nobody shouted, nobody sat down. By then, you become lethargic. This was a smaller concentration camp fifteen [kilometers] from Dresden. We were two hundred girls. The Germans needed us as workers, because every German from sixteen to seventy was mobilized. They were losing the war.

In this little town called Öderan bei Dresden, there were factories and we had to work in the factories for the Germans. We made ammunition for anti-aircraft guns. We sabotaged whenever we could. If the SS weren't looking, we would sabotage them. The factory was in operation twenty-four hours per day. So, we worked from 6 am to 2 pm, from 2 pm to 10 pm, or from 10 pm to 6 am.

LTP: In three shifts?

DK: Yes, in shifts. Sometimes I was on the day shift, sometimes in the afternoon, and sometimes on night shift. One day, I was on the night shift and the next morning I was tired, still in bed, when suddenly the top officer, the chief of the camp, came into the room. We were very much afraid of her. She was a blonde woman, who was around thirty-five or forty years old. She saw me there and I stood to attention. She asked me, "Are you fit to work?" You never say, "No," so I said "Yes." She asked, "Can you lift big weights?" I said, "Yes." I didn't know what she wanted, but she said, "Go down to the kitchen and tell the officer there that I sent you."

I went to the kitchen and told the SS officer that I was sent by the chief and I started to work there. In the concentration camp, being ordered to work in the kitchen is like going from being a slave to being an empress. Do you know why? Kitchen workers ate one more serving of soup, which was one hundred percent more. The ratio is one soup and three slices of bread. In the evening you get one more soup, which is what everybody wants, because you are hungry like a dog.

LTP: In the kitchen? If your mother could have seen you . . . (laughs)

DK: Yes, in the kitchen (laughs). This was the revenge of my mother, I was finally cooking. She should have seen me. What am I cooking? Soup, of course. You are right. My destiny caught up with me. I am a woman; I must cook.

One day, I was on the night shift. On night shifts you work alone. You don't need many people and an SS officer supervised you. On the night shift, the SS officer was a beautiful blonde, tall girl. She had a revolver, but she was not looking at me because she already knew me. She was quiet.

Suddenly, I felt a breeze in the room. I went to the windows, but they were closed. She asked me "Do you notice something?" I said, "Yes." We heard a noise which grew louder. It was the night of February 13, 1945. The day is known in every history book. Do you know why? This was the vengeance of Churchill who sent bombers to Dresden to bomb the famous *"Frauenkirche"* church. It took the Germans fifty years to build it anew. People come from all over the world to see it. The Germans had destroyed famous cathedrals in England near London, so Churchill took revenge.

The SS officer heard that the sirens were going off. She shouted at me to turn off the lights and sit down by the window and suddenly her tone changes, she calls me "Vous." "Vous, the lady please, sit beside me." A completely changed tone. I understood that she was afraid, "Sit near me!" I sat near her and we saw that Dresden was burning. For me, it was wonderful. She was shaking and started talking to me in a polite tone. I felt I had the upper hand. She said to me, "War is terrible. We, Germans, didn't want it." I said, "We, the Jewish people, didn't want it, either."

She went on, talking politely to me, "I am only twenty-three." I said, "I am nineteen." And I saw how afraid she was. Then, she said "I am from nearby," she was a girl from the village. I was a bit arrogant thinking, "You couldn't be a maid in our house" (although I didn't tell her this). She didn't speak

German well, even if she was German. She said, "My fiancé stands on the Eastern Front in Russia." I said, "There is no Eastern Front anymore." The Germans were terribly afraid of the Russians. I saw that she was shaking. I wondered what I should do if she wanted to hold my hand. I didn't know what to do. The most important thing was said after she said, "We, the Germans didn't want the war," then she said, "But our *Führer* doesn't know about the concentration camps." She believed it. This was her belief that the *Führer* didn't know. Hitler was like a God for her. I didn't answer.

I still was asking myself, "What am I to do if she wants to hold my hand?" All the time I thought I had the upper hand, and this was my little vengeance regarding the Germans. I was glad that she was distressed. She asked me, "Do you think that we will die?" I said, "This is almost certain, because we don't have a safe place to go." She was even more afraid. Suddenly my mind changed. You know what happens when you are in a small room where you feel that you are in danger? I began to feel the same despair as her. I felt that we were two young girls, and we would die there together. I didn't hate her anymore. You see? It's funny. I was reconsidering this when the alarm stopped. She immediately started to shout, "Turn the light on! *Weitermachen* [Engl.– *Go on*]." I was avoiding her eyes. I was afraid to meet her eyes, perhaps she will be ashamed that she was afraid. I started to work again. At two o'clock she left the kitchen.

LTP: So, later you found out that your parents and your brother died?

DK: In April 1945 they put us onto the trains because they didn't want the camp to fall into Russian hands. They didn't know what to do with us. Germany was in chaos. Everything was destroyed by bombs, the trains didn't work, to make the story short, they returned us to Theresienstadt, which by that time was taken over by the International Red Cross. The Red Cross already knew that thousands of people were coming. They prepared a big quantity of soup. It was a tragic moment: people got soup. They were so hungry, and they started to eat and eat! Because of this, some people died.

LTP: Why?

DK: When you eat too much, after a long time of being hungry, the body cannot manage to digest the food and you die of overeating. They ate five, six, or seven cups of soup which their organism couldn't take. On the night of May 12, I ran away from Theresienstadt. We were in quarantine because there was typhus. I ran away with a friend at night, because we heard that a train would be going to Prague. And Prague meant home.

We didn't look back. The people took us on the train without money and we arrived in the morning of May 13, 1945 in Prague, which was a historic day. On this day Prague was freed.

In the night, the Czechs went out and they placed every SS and functionaries of the Germans into Czech concentration camps. You see, history was turning. At 8 o'clock in the morning all the church bells started to ring. It was fantastic! All the people went out from their houses and started to sing, to dance. This was the feeling of freedom. We stood there and didn't know what to do. We had no home, no money, no clothes, no hair. Somebody told us that the Jews had already organized a house where Jews were welcome. They expected people returning from the camps. We got the address and arrived there. I must tell you that the Jews are fantastic people, when they have to be. If they don't have a need to be like that, they are not. But they are organized. There were Jews from Slovakia who were in the underground and knew that the war was ending. They came to Prague and organized themselves. They knew that the people would come back from the camps, from Auschwitz, and they prepared a list of Germans flats, to give them. So, they asked how many we were. We said, "Two," and we got a two-room flat.

LTP: Two? Who was the second person?

DK: A girlfriend of mine, we came together from Theresienstadt to Prague. We arrived at the house. We talked with the concierge. He opened the flat, which was on the seventh floor. The flat was evidently left in a hurry by an SS officer because there were boots and uniforms. There were some toys of a small child, a young couple it seems. We cleaned the flat and that was it. What was the first thing which we did?

LTP: Eat?

DK: There was nothing to eat in the house. No, you take a shower or a bath. I was dying for a bath. And there was a bathroom, with warm water. My friend was the first to take a bath and I thought she would be nice enough to leave me some water. She did. And then, we started our life. That's it!

LTP: What was going on inside of you?

DK: I'll tell you. First, I was waiting because I didn't know anything about my brother, I didn't know anything about my husband. I was sure that they would come back. After the war, Call Europe was a radio center. There was no television then. The radio transmissions were just messages, "Who knows this? Who was there? Who has been seen?" because everybody was looking for somebody. So, I waited and waited. After one month I heard that my brother died on the last day of the war. He was shot on the last day, twenty-two years old.

I didn't hear about my husband for months. Then somebody put a little note in our mailbox that said Peterl had died in his camp. In his camp there were only three survivors. All others died because of hunger. They worked in stone quarries, and all died. So, that was it. Only a few came back.

When I heard that I had no family anymore, I just wanted to get away from Europe. Suddenly, I got a letter from the parents of Peterl who were already in Palestine. He didn't want to go with them because he was a leader in the youth movement and said that he would go one year later with his group. In the meantime, the war broke out. I don't know how they heard that he had married, or how they heard about me and contacted me. The father wrote to me and sent me pictures so I could see them. They asked me if I wanted to come to Palestine. He was a high officer in the British mandate, and he would try to get a certificate for me. I said, "Yes." He sent the certificate, and in March 1946 I came to Israel, then Palestine.

LTP: In all those experiences, from 1942 until 1945, in those terrible years when you stayed in the concentration camps, did you have a constant discussion with someone above you? I'm talking about being in contact with the soul and not necessarily with the ego.

DK: No, not at all because I am not from a religious family. I came from a completely assimilated family until Hitler came. I didn't even know that I was a Jew. My father was a German Social Democrat. One night, after the Nazis crossed the border to Czechoslovakia on March 15, 1939, our telephone rang. My father answered and after the end of the telephone conversation, my mother asked, "Who was there?" He said, "A crazy person" who said, "Take your family and run and cross the Polish border." It was the right advice, but my father said, "A good German doesn't flee." They killed him like a cockroach. In Theresienstadt, he looked terrible. He said, "I served the wrong god and goal!"

LTP: There is a thing that I am interested in, about Neumann. I've seen a picture of him in Eranos. Do you think that he was a bit feminine?

DK: Feminine? Neumann? No, not at all. He was not only married, very married, but he also had his affairs. I am amazed that you asked me this . . .

LTP: I asked because of his appearance in that picture but also because in reading his work, he was also so feminine . . .

DK: I know why you asked me this. He was very understanding of the feminine soul. He was more of an artist than a psychologist. He wanted to be a writer. At age twenty-seven, he wrote an interpretation of Kafka. He didn't know Jung yet, but the interpretation is completely Jungian. He had the soul of an artist, where the Great Mother is always dominant. He was a very attractive man, and I had a terrible transference to him. Did you see his picture in the movie?

LTP: Yes, I did. You came into this world when your brother was three years old. Do you think that your parents made any distinctions between the two of you?

DK: Yes, very much so. That was the culture: the boy is the most important, after the father. I felt like this at his bar mitzvah. Do you know what a bar mitzvah is? It is a Jewish ritual which is important at the child's coming of age, at thirteen. The child gets many presents and goes up to the temple. My brother got a bicycle. I said to my parents, "I want a bicycle, too." They said, "You are only a girl, what do you want a bicycle for?" Only a girl! I got a present, a silver bracelet, very beautiful, but I wanted a bicycle. My father said, "A girl doesn't ride a bicycle. You get an outfit." So I got an outfit, but I didn't get a bicycle. But my father loved me very much. I know that I was very much loved by my father.

LTP: But you said that you had a better relationship with your father than with your mother. Why?

DK: Much better. I had a positive father complex and a negative mother complex. She beat me up and I didn't want to go to the kitchen. Because of fear. She was afraid that I would be good for nothing, dying from hunger, and wouldn't earn one penny and nobody will want to marry me.

LTP: Do you have pictures?

DK: (in a very slow voice) There are no pictures. Everything was gone, taken.

LTP: Nothing? Everything was taken?

DK: Yes, everything was taken. We left the flat as it was, and everything was taken.

LTP: So, you have everything only in your mind.

DK: Absolutely, absolutely.

LTP: What impressions do you have in your mind from your childhood?

DK: From the parents? My mother had red-brownish hair. She was a beautiful woman, with a strong temperament and will. I swore to myself when I was a girl of fifteen or sixteen, that if I have children, I'll never beat them. So, I had a son and a girl. At five years old, my son did everything he could to make me shout or something. Suddenly, I lost my patience. I gave him one slap on the tootsie. I've never seen a child so happy. He was so happy that I lost my cool! I learned something.

LTP: When you said, "It is not the ego, but the soul we should serve," how did you mean that?

DK: We are analyzing the person; their dreams and their characters. The aim of analysis is for the patient to achieve a working ego-Self axis. This is Neumann. Not only ego, a Self-ego axis. The ego is very important. Only in the second half of life, later in life, not in the fifties, but later, in the sixties or seventies, the Self is much more dominant, and the ego takes second place. But first, it is the ego-Self axis. This is the aim of the therapy, not that we should be happy.

LTP: Another question, you have been working as an analyst for . . . ?

DK: Sixty-three years and I hope that I'll work till my death. Because it is also my hobby.

LTP: I hope you do. The next question will be a very delicate one, what are the things that you dislike about yourself?

DK: About myself? That I am stubborn like my grandmother.

LTP: Like *babushka*?

DK: Yes, like *babushka*. I am jealous. I married at age twenty-nine. When my husband looked at another girl, and he looked a lot, I was jealous. Terribly jealous because my brother was preferred. So, I can't stand it when somebody else is preferred, I worked on this, this is for sure. This I don't like. I am also a manipulative person and I use it in my analyses, you know? In Theresienstadt, I called my girlfriend and told her to swear that she wouldn't say a word and I succeeded. I am manipulative, I am trying to use it for good. What more? Enough, it is terrible! (laughs)

LTP: Yes, okay.

DK: Ah, one more: I am afraid of my aggression. There was aggression after the Nazis, sure enough, but I am afraid of it.

LTP: Actually, you don't appear to act out this aggression?

DK: No, but I feel it inside. Sometimes, I feel that I have to say something to my patients, but I am afraid of my aggression. Marie-Louise von Franz, who

I believe was the best analyst there was. In reality, she is much clearer than Jung. She said, "You serve the patient in the best way if you point out his weak points and his shadow. You don't serve him if you are too nice to him."

LTP: Yes, but what if the patient cannot take it?

DK: Look, I try. If he can take it okay, if not, I go back. Then I wait. I wait until there is a good contact. I think that the analysis works well when you have a good transference and countertransference. Without the transference, you don't go far.

LTP: What would be your advice for the people who are now becoming analysts?

DK: They shouldn't hurry. All the new analysts enter their analysis, and some of them try to finish after two or three years. This is pure nonsense. To my mind, they are not okay.

LTP: Have you solved the problem with the supervision regarding sexuality?

DK: About sexuality?

LTP: Yes.

DK: Where was the problem?

LTP: Neumann said that you were not good at it.

DK: Oh, yes. Neumann said, "You don't even think about it." He tried to shock me. He used terrible language with me for instance when he said, "You are a stupid sheep." Now, at my age, I have solved it (laughs).

Chapter 13

The Father's Voice

Alfred Ribi
INTERVIEWED BY LAVINIA ȚÂNCULESCU-POPA
FEBRUARY 15, 2013 – ERLENBACH

Dr. Alfred Ribi is one of the first generation of Jungian analysts who trained and analyzed with Marie-Louise von Franz, one of C.G. Jung's closest colleagues. Dr. Ribi was born in 1931 in Zurich where he studied medicine, specializing in psychiatry and later psychotherapy. Since 1968 he has worked in private practice in Erlenbach, Switzerland. He studied at the C.G. Jung Institute – Zurich, where he was later head of studies, teaching analyst, lecturer, and examiner. He was the president of the Foundation for Jungian Psychology until 1992 and a past president of the Zurich Psychological Club. He is the author of eleven books in German and English: Demons of the Inner World, The Search for Roots, Turn of an Age, Die Dämonen des Hieronymus Bosch, Eros *and* Abdendland, Anthropos, Die feindlichen Brüder, Der Normal Kranke Mensch, Neurose und Lebenssinn, *and* Ein Leben Im Dienst Der Seele.

LTP: I am from Romania, a place where things related to Jungian analysis are just evolving now. Some of us are preparing to become Jungian analysts.

I have done interviews with several analysts to understand how their lives were at the beginning and what influenced them to become what they are today, apart from their certificates, names, and titles. Because I don't speak German, when I looked on the internet, the only pages that I could read about you were in English. But I saw that you are quite a well-known senior analyst who was also present at the early formation of Jungian studies in Küsnacht, and you were also president of the Analytical Psychology Club in Zurich.

AR: Yes, some years ago.

LTP: How are you handling this situation? Obviously, because you are a pre-eminent public figure, people like you are in danger because the demands of the persona associated with that role are very imposing. Under your persona, behind the social mask, I would like to know about the person. In other words, I'm interested in the personal side of your story. Therefore, please, tell us a little bit about you. You were born in 1931. Were you an only child?

DOI:10.4324/9781003148937-14

AR: No, I have a sister three years younger. But I need to tell you something about persona. Often, one doesn't quite understand what persona means. I was struck, in an interview, when Jung said, "Now I'm talking to you, the interviewer, of course I have a persona." But to me, he seemed absolutely natural. So, I was struck when he said, "I have a persona." And then, I asked myself, "What does it really mean?" Then, I understood he meant that we, in every situation, we adapt to the situation. When you are here, I adapt to you and the situation, which is a different situation than, for instance, when I speak to my children.

LTP: Obviously.

AR: Now, I can ask myself, "What is the real personality? Is it when I'm interviewed by you, or when I speak to my children?" There must be a big difference, here I put on the important persona, the mask. Persona comes from the Greek, but in Greece it was different. I said, "I'm Freddy Ribi," but now I'm playing the king and they took the mask. So, this is a very good expression of how Jung used it, which is the role which you play. When we speak together, I am in another role, and when I speak to my children, then I'm the father, but it is a persona too. My children are in the role of children and they are fifty. So you now can say, "I have no persona."

LTP: Sure, but you can say that persona forms somehow in certain stages in life. If you are two years old, you don't have a persona.

AR: No, a persona is our social adaptation, and it is something important. I always say that if you are going to a bank, to take money out of your account, with wild hair and a beard like that, they wouldn't give any money to this man. Only if he looks decent, then you trust him and you give him the money. So, the persona is something very important in the social contract. It is necessary. But, when you get identified with your persona, this is different. Identified means I'm taking over a role, whereas identical, being identical with the persona, it is occurring unconsciously. A lot of young people that admire others want to be the same with the ones they admire. That's identifying . . . an idol. But usually you are identical because you have certain tasks to do. Let's say, a policeman who is neglecting his clothes or is . . .

LTP: . . . naked?

AR: Or naked. Then, nobody would respect him and or obey him. You have to have a uniform, this is [a] typical persona; a uniform shows you are really a policeman. So, it makes you an authority and many people like to have authority. But it is not their own authority. It is the role of authority from the state assigned to the policeman. So, when I become identical with my persona, then I walk like that [he shows that he would walk proudly], "I'm so important as a policeman." I experienced this with my father! My father was the director of a bank and he had a perfect persona. My mother-in-law admired him because he was tall and he was handsome and he walked proudly down Banhofstrasse in Zurich on his way to the bank. He looked very important. For him, it was okay to have this persona, because his clients would consult with him, "What should I do with these millions of francs?" It was important because they trusted him to invest their millions of francs. He looked good and he was a decent man.

LTP: But in your home, was he the same?

AR: In the profession, he was okay. But at home, he was the same. When he said something, we had to obey. So, he was identical with his persona. He could not make a difference between his role in the bank and his role as a father. For instance, one day I said, "Look, my shoes are worn out. They have holes in them. I need new shoes." He was just putting his shoes down and he said, "You can have my shoes." I replied, "Oh, dear father, I would really like a new pair of shoes, not your shoes." You see? He had enough money to pay for new shoes, but he was a miser. In his profession too; he did not like to spend money. But when he invited us for his birthday, then he was very generous, "Do you want this wine? Do you want this menu?" He was not a miser in every respect, just in some. So, the question is very tricky, "What was his real character?"

LTP: Did you ever experience him differently? In moments when he could not hold onto his mask? When he was extremely old or ill?

AR: He did not think he had the mask on.

LTP: I know, this I know.

AR: It was always unconsciously.

LTP: Yes, definitely. But what about you? First as a son and then as a professional, could you recognize different things?

AR: No, I was a boy at this time, or an adolescent. I suffered, sometimes very much, because he was authoritarian and what he said had to be done. Sometimes when he was very angry, when something was not how he wanted, then he got mad and he said, "If I want something different, I will change it!" This was like Zeus with the lightning and the thunder. He was identical with the archetype of the father. I thought, "What is going to happen now?" I would wait and wait for days, but nothing happened. So, after some days when nothing had happened, I thought, "What is that?" He was basically a weak man because he was frightened, trembling in the air. So slowly I realized his emotion and his threats came from his background, because he was identical with Zeus, but it was not him. The archetype took over and for a moment he was Zeus, but then nothing happened. So, it is not his real character. He was a friendly, nice, benign man, but when he got angry, when things were not as he wanted it to be, then he became emotional and exploded; something from his unconscious, from his background, took over. So, then his persona was far away, he was outside his persona. This is the thing, when a man is identical with his persona, then he has no relationship with his *anima*.

LTP: Exactly.

AR: They exclude each other. Persona is adaptation to the world; *anima* is adaptation to the inner world.

LTP: Let's talk about that: Beyond persona is *anima*.

AR: As my father was identical with his persona, he had no relationship to his *anima*. This is a tricky, negative thing. Namely, each man has to have an *anima*, the *anima* is the soul. When he has no relationship to his soul, where is his soul? Then he starts to become his soul.

LTP: He starts to become his soul?

AR: This goes on unconsciously. He very much liked to talk with my sister, from the beginning when she was born, because she expressed the feminine, which he had no access to, because he came from a farming family. They had nine children and he was the youngest, but he was the most brilliant of the nine. His brothers were middle-class, good natured, nice uncles and aunts, but he reached the top. He was admired by everybody because he was so brilliant and rich. But because he lacked the feminine, sometimes his boyish part came out, for example, when we went to the village where he grew up, then he was very cheerful while preparing everything, running to the car. But he became angry when my mother was not ready. He disliked it when he said, "At 9 o'clock we start," and she was not ready. Then he got very angry and said, "Finally, you are coming?" Then, as he drove the car, he was singing a song, "Fly with Me to the Home Country." That was his boyish, natural attitude. There was no persona there. He would become like a farmer's boy again. When he arrived in the village, he was accepted and esteemed by everybody, because he was so famous. He was pleased and flattered to be so admired, this was nice for him. He was then an authority in the village and he liked to be with the peasants, he played cards with the peasants. He would become a peasant for the moment. There was no persona there.

LTP: What about you? Did you experience such a phase? Given your profession and your background, how did your persona form, and what do you remember before it was formed? How were you?

AR: I was very neurotic. In the family, the whole family was neurotic. As I said, he liked my sister very much. He took her instead of my mother on his business trips. When he had a business trip, my mother said, "Oh, I had so many times the opportunity to go," but he took his daughter and showed his daughter to his colleagues. I think this was not a good thing, not for my sister, or for him.

LTP: Or for you . . .

AR: My sister lived at home for a long time, until she was thirty. She met a boyfriend, later on, who was much younger than she was. She never married, that is also a typical sign. And my father cried. Can you imagine such a man? He was about sixty or seventy when she left. He was so affected because his soul was going away. It is so real, when you are identical. Then, when somebody takes over the projection of the *anima*, his daughter, it is very difficult. In a way, he destroyed my sister's whole life. She never married her boyfriend, whom she lived for, because he was fifteen years younger. When she died, her boyfriend was not yet sixty. He is still working. You know, when there is such a strong father complex, no other man can compete with the father. The father is so high up, so she cannot find a man who can compete because he can't be compared with the father. For me, this was not a problem. I suffered, of course, as you said, because she was always *The One*. For instance, when we played together, when we were little, and I sometimes forced her to play what I wanted. Then she would cry because she was smaller and our father would come and blame me, saying, "Why is she crying? You are a bad boy! She is crying because you hit her or did something wrong." The poor little girl cannot be the reason for crying. The boy, who is three years older, is the cause. Because they liked her so much, I was "*quantité négligeable*" and I suffered from that.

LTP: When did you leave home?

AR: I knew from the age of twelve that I wanted to become a medical doctor. I have no idea why I knew this, but I knew.

LTP: You needed to repair something or to heal something . . .

AR: So, this was my goal and I followed that goal. My parents said, "He was intelligent, he could go to the gymnasium. This is okay and you can become a medical doctor, this is okay too." So, they supported that. Then, in medical school, I had the chance to have a good professor who respected me very much. So, I was respected there. But not at home. They accepted what I made, because they thought, "He will become famous," or "He will earn a lot of money."

LTP: Your parents?

AR: Yes, my parents. This would be called achievement. But when I had this professor, he liked me very much, and we had a good relationship. I was his dear child, so to say, his follower.

LTP: What was the name of the professor?

AR: It was a professor of dermatology. My father basically wanted me to go into his steps; to become a banker. But I never thought to do this. I was not interested at all. He accepted it once I indicated that I wanted to become a medical doctor; then he had nothing against it.

I knew my wife, my later wife, during our studies. She qualified as a dentist and I as a medical doctor, so we were together for five years, during our studies together. But I wanted to marry only when I had my own money, not to be dependent on my parents. Eventually we married, on December 20. Nobody married on December 20 unless a child was on the way and they must marry. We did not have to, but I finished my exams in the fall and I had to go to the military service on January 3. So, we wanted to move together. This was the reason for December 20. The longest night.

LTP: Yes, the winter solstice.

AR: So, then I went my own way.

LTP: How old were you when this happened?

AR: Twenty-seven.

LTP: You told me about your father. But your mother?

AR: Yes, this is another case. For three years I was the only one, I had the impression that my father was still . . . how do you call in English the man before the marriage?

LTP: A bachelor.

AR: Yes, bachelor. Even after he was married, my father went out to meet his friends from before the marriage and often she was lonely. Then, fortunately, she had this little boy, and took him with her, when she felt the need. Only when she felt the need.

LTP: Not you?

AR: When she was doing the household chores, she put me into a cage because I was in the way. She had to vacuum, clean the house, and so on. So she didn't want me crawling around. So, it was not really love, it was her need. She felt the need for somebody to show her love, because my father did not.

LTP: Did not care much.

AR: Yes. I came two years after they married and she told me that after one year, my father said, "If you don't get a child, I will divorce!"

LTP: Oh, God!

AR: So, this was about persona too; one has to have a family and children. When you have a wife who doesn't have children, you do not have a family. This was very important in the banking business. It was important to show this, especially when we met other people from the bank, my father would say, "This is my son, he is studying medicine and this is my daughter, she is a teacher." She did not fulfil his expectations and she became just a teacher, but as he really liked her, this was okay.

LTP: "This is my son. He is a medical doctor. This is my daughter and she stays home with me."

AR: Yes. Everywhere persona is around. Even the family has to be a decent family, "Look at it, this is my wife. And this is my son, a medical doctor." My mother . . . later, when we would meet, she wanted to kiss me, so she would kiss me. I didn't like it. She would say, "Come, come. I will show my son to the neighbors." This is persona too, because she was identified with her son, "If I have a famous son, who became a medical doctor, then I'm a good mother. Look at him! I must be a very good mother to have such a wonderful son!"

LTP: But do you think they ever knew your inner *anima*? Your soul? Did it seem they ever grasped anything?

AR: No. When I got acquainted with Jungian psychology, they never understood why, "What is psychology?" They had no idea. But one cannot get famous with Jungian psychology! So everywhere, in every respect, you have a persona coming in.

LTP: But you had a famous environment. Everything was quite famous around you. For instance, not only your father but also your analyst; you worked with Marie Louise von Franz. How was this? It is important.

AR: But you know, a lot of people who worked with Marie Louise von Franz made a persona out of it. I experienced this when I was director of studies at the Jung Institute. A lot of people came and said, "I met Jung and he told me . . ." I hated it because it does not mean anything. Because they came with this idea, "When I met Jung he appreciated me very much, so I am a wonderful person, and he met with me." But this was not the case. I saw Marie Louise von Franz sometimes; she hated people who came to see her because of her renown and she didn't think much of that person. They used to say, "Jung once told me," and now people say, "von Franz once told me . . . I had a special relationship with von Franz." But nobody can prove these things, I could just pretend things that von Franz told me.

LTP: Did you met Doctor Jung?

AR: No. I came to analysis in 1963 and he died in 1961. Marie Louise always said, "Oh, it's a pity you didn't meet Jung." But I don't think it was a pity because I had many, many dreams about Jung. I once calculated the statistic; it was seventy-three dreams.

LTP: With him?

AR: Yes, with him in the dream.

LTP: But did you see him alive?

AR: Only in the dream.

LTP: No, no, in real life. You saw him lecturing?

AR: No, he died in 1961. I probably met him once because my sister, in her classroom, had one of Jung's grandchildren. She took me with this other schoolmate to Jung's Seestrasse.

LTP: To his house?

AR: In the house, I met her grandfather. I have no memory of that. I just remember that we once were there. So, probably I saw him, but, of course, I didn't know anything about him.

LTP: Apart from your professor of dermatology that held you in high esteem, did von Franz play a role in your development of the *anima*?

AR: Not only of the *anima*, of course, because she was a woman and my *anima* was developing, of course, but also we understood each other at an intellectual level. I am a scientist and she was a scientist too, investigating into different fields, and that was important for us building an adequate relationship. But people now worship *Holy Marie Louise*. For me she is not *Holy* which she became a noble person.

LTP: So, you downgraded her from the status of "holiness" to mortal human.

AR: Yes. This is a projection, *Holy Marie Louise*. For me she became a real woman as this projection fell off. Now I can see her good sides and her weaknesses. But for others, you could never say anything negative about Holy Marie Louise because she was considered perfect. Now, I see her as a gifted, very highly educated woman. It was very good because we could speak from a high level, and she respected me. That was important and I esteemed her for her work. I often said, "I like your work on alchemy very much." She told me, "No, this is the least esteemed." For the alchemical part, we could understand each other very well.

LTP: I saw when you lectured and talked about these pictures of Jung's *Red Book*. This impressed me very much because they are part of your soul.

AR: This is my soul.

LTP: When did you first have the consciousness of your soul?

AR: Like Jung, when he was eleven years old, he knew that, "I am that I am." I did not have such a consciousness. It struck me when von Franz told me, "Jung had to tell himself at a certain moment. I am not the little pastor's boy. I'm something of my own." Then I thought, "What?" The famous Jung had to tell himself that? Basically, I have to say to myself the same, "I am no longer the father's son, the little boy."

LTP: I am also myself.

AR: I worked something of my own. Perhaps this was such an important moment.

LTP: And this was around what age?

AR: I ended analysis in 1963 when I was thirty-two. At the beginning it was strange because von Franz told us she never had an analysand who had read the whole Jung when they came to analysis. I had read quite a lot, but not all, of Jung and this was when I was analyzing my dreams myself. I would say, "Oh, this is this archetype, this is the shadow, and so on." von Franz would accept it and say, "Perhaps one can look at it this way and in that way," and so on. I think that was very important that she took it this way. If she would have said, "No, no, you can't analyze your own dreams, it's stupid," with my feeling of inferiority I would have said, "Well, I'm not coming anymore." But she never said anything negative about my dream analysis. She corrected it a little bit and said, "Perhaps this, and this," until I finally realized my interpretations were absolutely theoretical and I didn't understand my own dreams. When I first went into my training analysis I thought, "Yes, I can understand Jung's idea, one has to undergo analysis, this is clear. But, I am normal, I have no problems." Slowly I came to realize, "Oh, I have lots of problems. Perhaps I am the most severe patient." But when you have such an inferiority complex, as I did, you cannot accept any criticism. So, she let it go, but slowly it dawned on me these were my problems, I had severe problems. Then I could accept it. Later on I thought, "Oh, why didn't von Franz tell me?" Then I would think she probably did tell me before, but I didn't understand it. Only now I see, when it became my own insight. When somebody from the outside tells you [that you] have certain problems, you have to work on that problem, this does not compel. This is so important with my clients. I came to my own realizations, so I cannot say to my patients, "Oh, you have a lot of problems." No, I must be tactful with those problems, just as Marie Louise von Franz was with me. Then my clients can accept. So this is how training analysis is working.

LTP: Exactly.

AR: It's an intersection of two psyches with each other. Because it happened sometimes that I had a dream that I could not tell because I was ashamed and then, when I opened up and told her the dream, she would laugh and say, "You too?"

LTP: You too?

AR: Yes, like other people. Apparently, I did not have the worst dreams. She accepted them. She didn't think they were so bad. Slowly, I could accept myself because she was not as shocked as I thought she would be if I told her. I thought she would be horrified, "What? You are a monster!" I am not a monster, I am a human being. It is not an intellectual thing. You can't say, "Read these twenty volumes of Jung and you will be individuated." No, it is a personal encounter.

LTP: The experience that you have.

AR: Yes, and therefore, you see, when an analyst has a persona of, "I am so important. I am so experienced. You know nothing about human psychology, but I qualified forty years ago." This doesn't work, this is nothing.

LTP: Modesty helps.

AR: The more I am a human being, who suffers too, who has his weakness, who knows about his weakness, the more he can understand the other, and the other trusts him and what he says. He has experienced himself.

LTP: Yes, and he is also a human being.

AR: He is a human being and could accept himself. This is what is going on in analysis and why the persona is not important. On the contrary, there should be no persona in analysis.

LTP: I really wanted to do this interview with you because I wanted to know more about your experience with the dark world and the "demons" of that world. How did you pick this subject? You have several books on this. We have a famous author in Romania, a philosopher, writing about angels, but you wrote about demons.

AR: (he laughs) I would never write about angels.

LTP: No? Why?

AR: There are not so many angels among human beings.

LTP: Are there a lot of demons?

AR: Yes. Because to look into my own abyss was important. In that book, I said that the complexes are our demons because we don't have a complex; the complex has us. We can't manage or repress the complexes and say. "No, I don't want you." They have us.

LTP: Can we still fight against them?

AR: Yes, this was also something which sticks in my mind. At a certain moment, von Franz said, "Jung had cleaned up his complexes." I thought, "Yes, this is possible. To make one's complexes conscious. Then we are no longer caught by the demons, we know them. Not that they don't exist anymore, but that we know about our demons." And this is important to know. I can't say, "I am perfect. I have no demons." No, no. Our weakness belongs to our personality. If somebody wants to have no weakness, this is ridiculous. Then he is inhuman.

LTP: Yes, but you can be better each day if you domesticate your . . .

AR: The more you know about your demons, then you can say, "Oh, today, if I am cruel or negative towards you, don't mind me, because I woke up with a negative dream or something got me." I know about it and this makes a difference. If I just get angry, because of nothing, then someone will wonder,

"What is happening to him?" But if I say, "I don't feel well today, don't mind me," then the other can accommodate to it and say, "Yes, he told me I shouldn't take it seriously."

LTP: "He's in a bad mood."

AR: Yes, yes.

LTP: So, can you fight with your demons by yourself?

AR: Yes, of course. But it is not fighting in this way that I want to kill the demon, but that I have to accept I am this way. I have to admit I have a dark shadow.

LTP: Yes. The demons are definitely extremely untouchable because they are not seen, as with the archetypes; you don't see the archetypes. That is, a pattern is not something that you really see. How can you really relate to it?

AR: This is also something important. As a Jungian, you live more consciously. When somebody has a reaction, then you might wonder, "What is happening? Did I offend the other person without being aware?" When there [is] an open relationship in analysis, and the other is telling me, "Last time I was so sad because you said so and so and so," and I ask, "What did I say?," it is an attitude from my side, to be more aware of the reaction of the other, because this is a much more honest way of being a mirror. The other is mirroring. I cannot see my own complexes, but with the mirror I see how weak I was.

LTP: Can God help you in this?

AR: Yes, of course, a lot. During an interview with Freeman, Jung was asked, "Do you believe in God?" Jung got stuck and repeated the question, "Do I believe in God?" Then he answers, "I don't need to believe. I know." His response triggered a lot of letters to Jung after the interview. In his responses, he explained what he meant. He meant that he doesn't know of a certain God, a Christian God, or Hindu God, or whatever, but he knew there exists something superior in us. For me, this fits exactly how I feel too.

LTP: So, you do believe in God?

AR: This is an experience. This is what explains. If I don't have an experience of something, I have to believe something, because I don't know. So I don't need to believe, unless I experience it; for instance, if there is a Trinity or not, unless I experience it.

LTP: You experienced it and you see it.

AR: For instance, I don't need to feel this pillow to see that it is green. I see it and I believe that it is green. I experience it as green. I think of belief, there a lot of pastors who say, "You must believe!" It is stupid, "Believe in God." Also, in the Bible, it is said one has to believe in God. If you bring a lady to me and say, "Love her," I would say, "Are you a fool? I can't love her. If there is something happening, then I love her. But not because you think [she] is such a nice lady and command me to love her."

LTP: I see . . . this is a good conclusion. It was very nice meeting you, Dr. Ribi. Thank you very much for your kindness, time, and generosity.

Chapter 14

The Performative Element

Andrew Samuels
INTERVIEWED BY LAVINIA ȚÂNCULESCU-POPA
(FEBRUARY 24, 2017 – KÜSNACHT, SWITZERLAND)

Andrew Samuels is a Jungian analyst, university professor, author, activist, and political consultant. He is well known for his work at the interface of psychotherapy and politics. His work on sexuality, relationships, spirituality, masculine psychology, and fathers has been widely influential. He is a former chair of the UK Council for Psychotherapy, co-founder of Psychotherapists and Counsellors for Social Responsibility and of the Alliance for Counselling and Psychotherapy. His books include Jung and the Post-Jungians *(1985),* The Father *(1986),* A Critical Dictionary of Jungian Analysis *(1986, with Bani Shorter and Alfred Plaut),* The Plural Psyche *(1989),* Psychopathology: Contemporary Jungian Perspectives *(1992),* The Political Psyche *(1993),* Politics on the Couch *(2001),* Passions, Persons, Psychotherapy, Politics: The Selected Works of Andrew Samuels *(2014), and* A New Therapy for Politics? *(2018). His books have been translated into nineteen languages. Additionally, he co-founded the master's program in Jungian and post-Jungian studies at the Centre for Psychoanalytic Studies at the University of Essex, UK.*

LTP: I believe we are living in a time in which old models are starting to fall apart or wear out. Not only because of how they work, but because they reflect how we have created them. I heard your lecture on politics and how important it is to step out and take action, not only think about it. You indicated that you have psychotherapy, politics, and spirituality as focal points in your life. The question that I ask most of my interviewees is, "Was there something in your childhood background that influenced you to become a Jungian? Was it entirely a choice?"

AS: I think I was born a rather aggressive person, so becoming a therapist was a way of organizing and making something creative out of this aggression by reacting to it. Now, I spend my life also involved in politics where the aggression is more obvious. I get a balanced experience: aggression in politics to the opposite of aggression – relationality, empathy and so on – in the therapy.

DOI:10.4324/9781003148937-15

But I have a third one, not just politics, not just therapy. I have a background in the theatre. In the deepest sense, everything is a performance. The reason I did this interview was because of the use of the word persona in it. I want to tell you that people who are deep, reflective, sincere, and spiritual are also personae in how they present themselves, how they perform, who they are. It doesn't mean being insincere, dishonest, or telling a lie, but it's also there: the performance, the context, the theatre you are in.

LTP: But is there anything else beyond persona, or before persona?

AS: I am sure there is. I am happy to talk about spirituality, about which I wrote a lot, but because you are a Jungian, a young woman, a student, and idealistic, I want to stress the personae, the performative element in relationships, including intimate relationships, because for the young, idealistic, spiritual, Jungian woman, she is not going to see it. So, that's why I want to stress it. Of course, there is something about, below, behind, and in front of performance, but unless you have performance in your *weltanschauung*, you're missing something.

LTP: Right! Of course! I don't want to dismiss the persona . . .

AS: Yes, . . . also, you want me only to say things that are boring that any fool can say!?

LTP: No! This is not boring!

AS: Right. This is not boring. But to say, "Oh, at the bottom, humanity is spiritual!" (grrr)

LTP: No! What I meant was that in my representation, persona starts to build later than our actual birth.

AS: We don't know actually! It is always a mixture about who you are and the environment. But this "performativity" [a concept from modern philosophy as introduced by Judith Butler], I think this word is very important. When it comes to psychoanalysis, it's even more important. Both people in the room are performing.

LTP: I agree! I must admit that this series of interviews, *Beyond Persona*, started with actors. So, I understand the importance of performance.

AS: Some people develop congruently with their family's values and their family's mores, some people go against it. I am absolutely against; I am against almost everything. I am a contrarian guy. Is this good, or bad? It is good and bad. But what I realized, and I talked about this in the lecture when I talked about "complementarity," the more you are a bad guy, the less you can be a good guy. The more you oppose, the less you can support the system or the status quo. That's the difficulty, people don't realize, they want to be both. They want to be the critic, the revolutionary, and they want to be sensible and strong and mature. You cannot!

LTP: Yes! You have to admit that you have one or the other! At one point I agree, but if you are against things, are you also deliberately "for" something?

AS: Certain political issues, but even there . . . I enter politics with the expectation of failure, but you have to do it, like you have to do in relationships, or you have to do in terms of sexuality, you cannot say no.

LTP: Because I am going to fail once.

AS: You are going to fail all the time. It is a question of how well you fail.

LTP: But don't these failures bring you enough pain to stop during life?

AS: Pain, sure! I am glad you asked this! It is obvious! See, I find this to be a very strange project. Who on Earth seriously thinks senior people in the professions don't have problems? You must ask yourself why this particular argument or this particular narrative. Sorry to turn your interview back but this is what I do.

LTP: It's ok. I am fine with it. I am not saying that people don't realize that other people have problems, whether they are senior or less senior. What I am saying is that sometimes you may not be aware, you may not be conscious enough. You were talking about the "Jung cult" and that there was an idea circulated that Jung had created a cult [Richard Noll, 1994, *The Jung Cult*]. I suppose that was because he was idealized.

AS: No question about that! He really was idealized and, of course, he was so clever. I wrote about this in the first chapter of *Jung and the Post-Jungians*.

(*after a short interruption*)

LTP: You were discussing how clever and idealized Jung was.

AS: Yes. If you are sixty-eight, one needs to remind you what you were talking about if you were interrupted and you didn't get to finish your idea.

LTP: You don't look sixty-eight!

AS: But I am glad this came in our discussion. In terms of the projections of the younger ones, or the junior ones under the senior ones, this question of appearance is very important. If I walked with a stick and I wore many woolen clothes and had white hair, you would have one reaction to me. Now, I am trying to look like a trendy guy, a *flâneur*, you have another reaction. Not just that I don't look sixty-eight, maybe I do look sixty-eight, but which kind of sixty-eight? Even in circles where there is no money, people think about how they look, how they communicate themselves, even in societies where they are not wearing Western clothes. It's the same thing. I am not saying life is only theatre or only an act. All I am asking is this be remembered.

LTP: Let's go back to you saying you were born aggressive. Why do you think that?

AS: Oh, no one knows the answer to this question.

LTP: But why do you say aggressive, and you don't say something else?

AS: Actually, I'll say I discovered it working backwards, exploring why I become a therapist to manage something in me, as everybody does. Some people become therapists because they were the therapists of their family, the so-called "parental child." I think a lot of men become therapists because they are identified with their mothers, and this too is a little paradoxical. I think a lot of women become therapists because they, too, are identified with their mothers.

LTP: In your case, was this a conscious choice?

AS: No, no! But I understand it now! I became a therapist, to some extent, by accident. I had a theatre company. It was a political theatre company, but this company also had a therapeutic job. So, we were working with young prisoners, with psychiatric patients, and community groups. In time, I realized I was employed for the therapeutic aspect more than the theatrical aspect. So, I asked someone about this. We had a consultant, a professor at [the] London School of Economics. He said, "Well, why don't you become a psychoanalyst?" and I said, "I don't know anything about it!" He replied, "Maybe, actually you'd better be a Jungian." And I said, "I don't know anything about that either." He said, "Listen, I just was looking at a book by Ira Progoff: *Jung Psychology and Its Social Meaning*." I got this book and I thought, "Oh, this is certainly an interesting therapist because he is interested in society, he is not always about problems." But this wasn't true. The book was a particular book. It wasn't by Jung; it wasn't even about Jung. It was a PhD by this guy who became very famous later. In the PhD you develop an argument, which I took literally. So, I thought this would be the best school of psychotherapy, but in terms of social meaning, it has such a struggle to be the best.

LTP: Now, I'm wondering why you became a person interested in theatre?

AS: It was always an accident. Somebody at my school said, "Do you want to act in this play?" As I got older, people would let me direct plays. What do I like about the theater? It's dangerous, it's teamwork; I like working in a team or a group. It's a dangerous art form because it can go wrong. I think, like anyone involved in the theater, I like to be looked at, so performativity is very deep in me, so the persona is no joke for me. By the way, in postmodern thinking – I am not a postmodernist – but in postmodern thinking we know that the surface is where the depth lies and people who struggle hard, consciously, to get in touch with depth, they never do it by working too hard to be deep. You get something like this happening in the Jungian world. They all write and think in this very deep way, it drives me crazy, I don't want to be deep like that.

LTP: But sometimes you don't have a choice.

AS: Of course you do. By the way, many senior Jungians are believers. It's like taking instructions in a church context if you train. By the way, it is also true in psychoanalysis, in person-centered psychotherapy, in Gestalt psychotherapy. They are believers, and people who rise to the top of the structures of the profession are believers.

LTP: Yes, I agree that you cannot do anything related to the human unless you are a believer.

AS: Yes.

LTP: Were you a beautiful child? Because, I think, you were a beautiful young man.

AS: No, I was not a beautiful child. When I was born, I was badly bruised.

LTP: Why?

AS: Because of a slightly difficult birth. But I think for my mother, I was a disappointment from the aesthetic point of view and the message, when I was a child, was always that there was something wrong with me, medically. It seems I was taken to a lot of doctors, but I don't think it was necessary.

LTP: But why?

AS: Because I think my mother had Munchausen's disease by proxy. So, I was put in the role of a performing child who needed medical attention. In fact, the doctors were not so stupid. They didn't do very much, but I was always seeing doctors. My mother wanted to be a doctor and gave it up after three years of study to get married. Why? Completely crazy. I wasn't born for another three years. I am the first. So, my mother could have finished. I think she was envious of me for having the freedom provided partly by her, of course, to do what I wanted. She didn't. She conformed to the middle-class Jewish standards of her time. If you got married, you built a house – excuse me, a home – for your husband. But it always makes me laugh. I once said it to her and she didn't look very happy: "If you got married in 1946 and you had completed three years of medical school, and I was born in 1949, so you could've finished." Now, it's possible they were trying to have a baby before. I don't know and I didn't ask.

LTP: Coming back to your appearance. Why were you a disappointment?

AS: Only physically. After that, I was an extremely gratifying child. Always at the top of school. But, in adolescence, I shat on it completely and I left home.

LTP: What age were you?

AS: About sixteen . . . I went to live with the alcoholic mother of a school friend of mine in London. He lived there. After his father committed suicide, his mother became an alcoholic, but she was rich. Also, they had a wonderful apartment in Kensington, and for the last two years of schooling I lived there.

LTP: What did your parents say?

AS: They were extremely bewildered, angry, and felt rejected . . .

LTP: I would imagine.

AS: Yes. I didn't like them. That's another reason – perhaps – I became a therapist. I really do not like my parents even now that they're dead. I do not like my parents. Didn't like them. And this is very important. It's very hard for people to admit it. But I never loved my parents. I have no idea whether they loved me or not, but I know for sure that I did not experience the love of my parents. They had some good features, and maybe there were good moments from time to time. But now, at sixty-eight, in the last twenty-five percent of life, I think it's important if you have a cynical experience in your background, to be honest about it. Is it a good thing? Absolutely not.

LTP: Did you like yourself?

AS: That's a ridiculous question. What's the next question?

LTP: The next question . . . let me rephrase.

AS: You just slipped into a journalistic mode. This is when you lost your intelligence.

LTP: What did you like about yourself? When I look at a man, I can envision how he looked when he was young. I look at you and I can see that you were a handsome man once.

AS: Did I like myself as a child for being handsome? No, because the message from my mother was always, "You are not." My mother was often very surprised that girls were interested in me. I know. . . . But I have spent my life making girls interested in me as a result.

LTP: Did you resemble your mother or father physically?

AS: Neither, but as I get older, I resemble my father more. My father was bald, lost his hair at nineteen, I was bald from thirty. But, when I look in the mirror, sometimes I see my dad's face. What do I feel about this? Ha . . . I feel. . . . Well, you spend your whole life trying not to be like your parents and now . . . failure. (he laughs)

LTP: You don't have a choice.

AS: I failed.

LTP: Yesterday you raised a very important point [during a seminar] when you gave us an example of a psychotherapist being amazed at a lady in a red dress in a therapy room. You were saying that he was lucky. Do you think – maybe [this] is another ridiculous question – do you think a therapist should be good looking as a man?

AS: No, because the traditional stereotype of the New York psychotherapist is one looking like Woody Allen. How he is, his clothes, his hair, everything is how the stereotypical American psychoanalyst is. In Britain, it depends. In the past, the great majority of psychoanalysts, even in Britain, were Jewish people. Now it is much more mixed. I'll tell you a story about this. Not about good looks, but it is connected. In the 1950s they organized the cricket match between the Jungians and the Freudians. There were many Freudians in Britain and very few Jungians. But the Jungians won the cricket match. Why? Because most of them were English, so they knew how to play cricket. Some of the Freudians were Germans, or Austrians, etc., and they didn't really know the game. That's a story about how people look. In Romania, I don't think there are many Jews.

LTP: As far as I know, there were situations in which Jews were persecuted in Romania, but also in which they were protected and created important communities in certain cities. I remember that in my city, Bacau, there was a Jewish community. Many emigrated to Israel in the 1960s.

AS: I'm not talking about the secondary immigration of Jews to Israel in the 1960s, or even in the 1970s, because under the communists there was another surge of anti-Semitism. But from the Jewish people's point of view, I think you'll find that Romania is not a very friendly place.

LTP: I would like to return to your childhood. Did you have a special toy?

AS: I once had a dream about toys, that I had a choice between an abacus – made for counting – and a little cuddly furry toy. I chose the abacus.

LTP: How old were you?

AS: Thirty-two or thirty-three when I had the dream. In the dream I was about eight.

LTP: But do you have a recollection of your memories from childhood?

AS: Of course, everybody does.

LTP: Not everybody does.

AS: Of course they do.

LTP: Some of them have a blank . . .

AS: Really? No memories at all? I have memories, they are not good.

LTP: Why?

AS: Well, I was sent in the English system to a boarding school at eight. It was a very bad experience. Very bad. I hated it. I was very unhappy. I worked like hell. I was top [of his class]. I developed my skills on the abacus. It was only when I began to get into analysis that I began to develop my attraction for the little teddy bear. I think as a child I didn't play very much. As an adult, I play all the time.

LTP: And your next brother or sister?

AS: Nineteen months younger, sister. I don't like her either.

LTP: Do you like anyone?

AS: Yeah, I always like the woman I'm with. I mean the woman I'm with that is upstairs, asleep. She's with me for a few days . . . I always like the woman I'm with until the relationship ends and then I don't like her.

LTP: How long was your longest relationship?

AS: Oh, fifteen years. How long was your longest relationship?

LTP: Five years . . . plus another ten that I always spent fancying about a guy. Anyway, are you married?

AS: I am not now.

LTP: But you were, weren't you? And your former wife died?

AS: It's more complicated than that. But yes, for the interview that will do. I was married once, and she died.

LTP: How did you choose her?

AS: How did I choose her? She chose me.

LTP: Did you choose anyone in your life?

AS: Actually, looking back, many years ago, I replied to a personal ad, you know, for a partner, and this woman I chose didn't last. It lasted, I think, eighteen months. It was after the death of the person you talked about, and I definitely chose her. But I can think of moments in the initial stages of all my relationships where, in essence, the woman chose me. . . . Maybe I made the first telephone call, or the first kiss, or something, but if I look at the whole thing, the woman did it. For example, with my current partner, we met at a conference, and after the conference she sent me an email with a selection of music that we'd been discussing in the break of the conference. That's the kind of thing. But of course, who called who and said, "Let's go to dinner"? I did. I am a man, it's traditional. But if she hadn't sent me this email, nothing would have happened. So, that's what I mean. By the way, if you talk to men, they think they choose. But often it's the woman who does.

LTP: Is it difficult for you to admit such things?

AS: No, why?

LTP: From your narcissistic point of view?

AS: Not at all. And the interview isn't difficult because you gave me permission to change anything. But I'm not so worried about that. What I'm more worried about is that you'll remember to look at that paper, to go back, because, as you said, it must be a shock to realize that quite recently I wrote about these things. Synchronicity . . .

LTP: What I mean is, this series of interviews is focused on understanding who a person was prior to establishing their persona. Of course, everything is acting . . . you want to please your parents, the others, to act, to perform . . .

AS: Here's the point. It's all performative, it doesn't necessarily mean you act to please or impress. But maybe one wants to rebel, one may want to shit on people. Maybe you haven't quite understood it, the full spectrum of performativity, it covers all things. You are talking – and this is probably from your own personal tendencies – you are talking about performing in the sense of pleasing parents; I absolutely didn't. Let me put it in the most extreme form. It's possible that at some level I really wanted to please my parents, but the act did not permit it, okay? But I think probably you more wanted to please yours.

LTP: Or I was trying to challenge you. Saying that yes, I didn't please them either . . .

AS: You were performing the role of an interviewer . . .

LTP: Yes . . . but I agree that somehow, I like your style. . . . In seven years of coming to this institute I have only picked maybe fifteen people to interview.

AS: But you picked me in part because I'm here.

LTP: No. I came because you are here.

AS: Oh, really?

LTP: Yes. I just came for three days . . . that's it. I'm leaving the day after tomorrow.

AS: You don't belong to this institute?

LTP: No, I don't. I came here several years in a row and study like a Further Education student.

AS: This is the Jungian world. I started this organization, and now I see some activism. There's a discussion list and a woman on it, Iulia, who writes about the Romanian situation. The only one who replies to her is me. I told about my history; about the absolute fascination I had in 1989 [during the Romanian Revolution] because I was watching on TV. I was trying to write *The Political Psyche* and I saw – not for the first time in my life (because I was a child of sixty-eight) – and I went on political demonstrations. But in the demonstrations in London or Paris you didn't die. Maybe they hit you, but if you died it was a mistake. But in Romania, especially in the beginning, the Securitate people, they shot into the crowd, hundreds of kids died. This sacrifice somehow awoke something in the military heart and slowly, because I read about the history, slowly the army began to change. . . . It was almost a miracle. Because the army were not nice guys, for God's sake, plus they were also Ceausescu's men, all of them, especially the senior ones. But they changed, they couldn't tolerate the shooting of the kids. That turned it. This is my version of the thing, but I don't think it's wrong. Plus, everybody secretly hated that guy and that woman, but they were frightened. Anyway, the point is I wrote to her, and I wrote on the list, and she was moved. Then another woman wrote about the Romanian situation and I asked her to please tell us, "Is the government sincere when they announced that they would withdraw the law?" She wrote back, "No, they're not sincere about this." I didn't think they were, I just wanted to know. I wrote to Iulia offering to come to Romania and she said she would write to the Romanian IAAP liaison officer. This amused me. She didn't write, "Yeah, we'd like to have you, because one of your books has just been translated into Romanian, there are two books in Romanian, people know you, they read all of your books in English, we'd love to have you in Romania." She wrote, "I need to ask the IAAP liaison." I thought, "Bye." I lost interest for that moment, because I thought, these are kids. They may be fifty years old, but they're children. If they want me to come, don't tell me when I offer myself to come that they're going to ask permission from somebody else. So, I thought this is what I talked about in the lecture about the Jungian missionaries. The IAAP liaison officer is a missionary, and you have to check what the head of the mission says about it.

LTP: That's because the IAAP gave us some funds.

AS: Sure, but that's exactly like Africa in the colonial days. . . . You people have to grow up, and you need to establish an Analytical Psychology for Romania. You know, I couldn't go to the [IAAP] Congress in Kyoto. I fell down and got badly injured.

LTP: Yes, I heard. Are you okay now?

AS: Yes, it's a miracle. You know, my personality didn't change. My attitude to life changed. I had a life-threatening accident, and it has developed my sense of humor, by which I mean that I don't take myself so seriously; in fact after my lectures, two or three of the old ladies of the institute who have known me all my career told me, "You're so relaxed now, you told so many stories and jokes, you don't give us so much theory, it's wonderful." Now, some of these old Jungian women are very smart, and they're right, I've relaxed.

LTP: Yes, but the cynicism that they say you are characterized by, I am not fooled by this. I can see you are very kind at heart – you suffered a turn. You are not that cynic any more . . .

AS: Since the accident?

LTP: You try to act cynical, but I don't see you this way.

AS: I don't know about cynical. I am skeptical about my project. I am a big enthusiast for therapy and politics, but I am also skeptical. Not cynical, skeptical . . . but the thing that I'm telling you is much more. Something just came to me. Since this accident, I've had more of a sense of humor. Do what you like with this idea, but make sure you write it down.

LTP: Of course. That means that you are relaxed in a way.

AS: Nothing matters. If you survive, nothing matters. Things mattered too much, my ideas, my books, my students, my children, my relationships. Now I can float more. I'm not on the ground so much. It's a paradox. A man who fell to the ground isn't on the ground.

LTP: He's fine now.

AS: A little bit more flying.

LTP: But why? Do you think that you are more ephemeral in a way?

AS: I'm not sure exactly why, but since nearly dying I laugh a lot more. There was a film in the 1960s. The star was an actor called Nick Williamson – a great actor, a drunk. Many great actors are drunks. The story doesn't matter very much except that it was set in Liverpool, and he was from Liverpool. He had moved to London, and he went back to Liverpool to settle some family problems after the death of his father or mother, I don't know . . . but you know when they are repairing the road, they put a temporary light so you can't go, you have to wait? He was arguing with his wife, and he didn't notice this. They had a choice – go back, stop, or increase speed and go on. He was driving a Jaguar and increased to maximum speed. He just escaped this huge lorry truck coming the other way and then he said, "If I can get away with that, I can get away with anything." A little bit ironic . . .

LTP: We have time for maybe one or two questions . . .

AS: And about Jung's trick? Remember? Jung's clever trick is in Chapter One of *Jung and the Post-Jungians*. He always said, "Thank God I'm Jung and not a Jungian. I don't have followers." This made all the followers feel great. We are not followers. He's told us we are not followers.

LTP: We are not followers. We are just beginners of our own journey.

AS: Yes. Bullshit . . .

LTP: Okay. Two more questions: Did you have any problems with addictions of any sort?

AS: No.

LTP: Not with the addiction of being praised?

AS: Oh, I thought you meant drugs or alcohol . . .

LTP: No, this is a drug as well . . .

AS: Oh, alright. I'll take you literally. Do I have any addictions? Yes, I was obsessed with my career for a long time. And then I had a friend – I don't want to say her name, but she became maybe the most famous psychotherapist in Britain, she had a bit of luck that made this happen – and I was not the number one anymore. I would never be the number one in Britain anymore. I am one of the most famous, but that doesn't mean a lot.

LTP: Oh, but it does. When I had to translate *The Handbook of Jungian Psychology* into Romanian, I was given a translation test. From which chapter in the book was the translation test taken from? From Andrew Samuels's chapter.

AS: Why did they give you mine?

LTP: Because it is very difficult to translate.

AS: No, it's not difficult at all.

LTP: It's very intricate. One paragraph is like this and then the next is written in another style. It was more difficult from the English point of view.

AS: Oh. Maybe my writing is bad.

LTP: No, your writing is very complex I would say.

AS: How many other chapters did you translate?

LTP: I translated seven in total, plus the index and the introduction.

AS: Anyway, I realized I had to get used to this. And now, there's another one. Very usually, they write popular books, both of them. I never tried to write a popular book, I never tried to start a school, it's stupid. How can we try, after one-hundred-fifty years of this profession, or whatever it is, one-hundred-twenty years, nobody is going to do anything completely new. You must be the rebel and the creator and the destroyer within the existing school. I am a Jungian analyst . . . but I had to accept that in British culture I am, now, number three. I don't think [in] Jungian [terms]. I am a Jungian, it's my base, my tribe. I used to talk about this with James Hillman: We were Jungians, this is our base, but we don't think of the world as a Jungian world. So, I go all over the world, mostly not to Jungian places.

LTP: But how do you rate number three? Based on what criteria?

AS: Oh, national recognition. I'm being a little playful in answer to your questions.

LTP: I can see. The last one, and I'll finish.

AS: You're very good. But you say you've been in this Jungian world for almost twenty years. You seem newer at this. It's very interesting. You must be older than you look.

LTP: How old do I look?

AS: It's difficult to know because your face is extremely without lines, maybe you had a lot of Botox, I don't know.

LTP: None.

AS: That's a joke. But your body is of an older woman. When you sat in the lecture, I watched you a lot because I'm very interested – I don't know why – in Romania. My partner upstairs, she taught in Romania a lot, but she doesn't want to go back because the European organizers of the degree are horrible. Romanians are not horrible, but the people outside Romania, organizing the degree program that she was involved with, and where she was the leader actually, she didn't like them. She doesn't want to go back to Romania. So, I was watching you. You have a very young face, girl face, but your . . .

LTP: My posture is . . .

AS: Really like a peasant's . . .

LTP: Thank you, I take this as a compliment. . . . How old do you think I am?

AS: No, no. You seem strong. A strong earthy woman . . .

LTP: So, how old am I, Andrew?

AS: Forty-five . . .

LTP: Forty . . .

AS: You're forty. Ok, I thought you were forty-five with a young face. I'm doing well at the popularity stakes . . . but I gave you an honest answer. I couldn't have said "Oh, you look thirty-eight."

LTP: If I were to put on other clothes, I might look thirty-two . . .

AS: You haven't asked me if I had any children.

LTP: You do have children. You said in your article. . . . You wrote that you started having children. That means you have at least two. How many do you have?

AS: Three.

LTP: The last question is, do you have anything from your personality that you want to get rid of but you can't? That you feel you'll die with?

AS: If I could lose something before I died?

LTP: Yes.

AS: Narcissism.

LTP: Tell me just something about your narcissism.

AS: You know, about me, like so many Jungians, it was a revelation when we discovered Kohut, ordinary healthy narcissism. My narcissism is between ordinary healthy narcissism and pathological narcissism, but it is not malignant, no way. My great love in my work is my therapy work. Really badly narcissistic people, they may do therapy, but they don't love it. I love it. I'll continue doing it after I stop being a professor and a political activist. I have almost stopped being a writer now after so many books. The thing I will do until I become senile is to be a therapist. I like it. I look forward every single day to going into my office and settling down to work with people. I work too hard because I have financial worries. So, after the sixth or seventh person, I get very tired and I go to drink four espressos, like I am doing now, and I feel better.

LTP: Excellent. Thank you very much.

AS: It's been great. You are really good. Seriously good. I am not flirting. She is upstairs, I cannot flirt. Why did you take your glasses off to do the interview?

LTP: I don't know.

AS: Because you're one of those women who looks very different without them.

LTP: Thank you. I have something for you – two albums with pictures from Romania.

AS: Perfect for the plane. Thank you.

LTP: I wrote something for you inside. I wanted to say, "For his unthinkable kindness."

AS: I accepted this interview, one, for Romania, and two, for persona. When you are inviting someone to give up their time for a project like this, first you have to make it clear it's a big project, which you did, and secondly you have to find an intellectual seduction. And somehow you got it with the idea of persona.

Chapter 15

The Wound of the Cultural Revolution

Heyong Shen
INTERVIEWED BY LAVINIA ȚÂNCULESCU-POPA
AUGUST 26, 2019 – IAAP CONGRESS, VIENNA

Heyong Shen, PhD, is a professor of psychology, a Jungian analyst (IAAP), and Sandplay Therapist (ISST)l founding president of the China Society of IAAP (CSAP); and chief editor for the Chinese translation of C.G. Jung's Collected Works. *He was the organizer of the International Conference of Analytical Psychology and Chinese Culture (1998–2018) and a speaker at the Eranos East and West Round Table Conferences and the Fay Lecture Series. Throughout his professional and personal life, Dr. Shen has promoted the "Psychology of the Heart."*

LTP: My interest is in understanding your early years, how this career became an option for you, and how your initial upbringing influenced that. I also curious about the context of you coming from another part of the world than the other people I have interviewed so far. Last, but not least, I hope, as a senior analyst and as the head of the Jungian analyst group from China, that you will share with us some of your ideas contrasting your culture with Western cultures.

SH: I began to consider your questions six years ago when we had a China-Jung peak project, which was supported by the Swiss government, here in Beijing and other cities. Some seven hundred people asked me similar questions – why did I choose to become an analyst, what was the reason behind that choice? My response was, "I think it is some kind of trauma laid on me which led me to becoming a Jungian analyst." During the Cultural Revolution [Ed. – a period of massive cultural, political, and social upheaval in China, initiated by Mao Zedong, from 1966 to 1977], I was about six years old. During the peak project, Luigi Zoja interviewed an elder about part of my family's story during the Cultural Revolution. Luigi and I visited the first museum of the Cultural Revolution. When I was six years old, I was wounded. For many years it was not only a personal wound but also it remains a wound of the culture, caused by the Cultural Revolution in China. Many years later I started in psychology and psychoanalysis. I received my PhD and then became a professor. That was in 1993. There was a professor there who introduced

DOI:10.4324/9781003148937-16

Sigmund Freud in China. I studied with him for seven years, for my master's degree and PhD and became his assistant.

After that, I went to the United States. Initially, I spent several months in self-analysis, in the middle of a forest, apart from people, just alone by myself. I worked on my dreams and in the reality of the campus of Southern Illinois University, which was surrounded by forests. I kept a record of my dreams from 1982 on, so in 1993 I had ten years of dream diaries. So, I just walked through the dreams.

Several months after that I took a train from St. Louis to Los Angeles. I had a dream on the train that I detached my head from my neck. I set my head on a table and had a dialogue with my head. It was very interesting because my eye was on my head and my head was on the table, but I could see my head very clearly. That was me seeing the Jungian heart. You can see from your eye, and you can see also from your heart. That was an amazing dream, but in one part of the dream I tried to remove a mask from my face, a very heavy iron mask. Since that dream, for many years I have tried to carefully rip the mask off my face. When I removed the mask, it was still bloody, reflecting the wound I experienced during the Cultural Revolution. It has remained a very interesting dream for thirty years. My body was wounded during the Cultural Revolution, and the wound remained fixed there.

A second significant dream I had when I was in Küsnacht. I stayed across from Jung's family house and there I had another dream; a dream in which I was wounded in my feet by a black nail. In the dream I tried to pull the nail out, but the nail was buried very deeply. When I tried to pull it out, it was [dark] with blood. It was in the same place where I was wounded at six years old during the Cultural Revolution. It is like the story of Oedipus; the complex was nailed into me when I was a boy. These two dreams were related to a personal trauma wound, but they also symbolize the cultural wound perpetrated by the Cultural Revolution. It is not only personal but also a cultural wound. This became a significant thread.

LTP: So, during the Cultural Revolution, when you were six years old, how was the wound inflicted on you? What happened?

SH: My father was a leader in the city and my mother too. So, the radicals took over the office. . . . It was my father's office. I tried to get the toys that belonged to me, so they hit me on the head.

LTP: You were hit by . . . ?

SH: The Red Guards. Like in Germany, the party guard. It's very interesting because Jung, together with Richard Wilhelm, published a book in 1928 called, *The Secret of the Golden Flower*. I studied Freud and psychoanalysis when I was with the professor who introduced Sigmund Freud in China. When I was doing my self-analysis in the forest, I brought one book with me, *The Secret of the Golden Flower*, but the reason I chose that book was not because of the title or the authors, but due to the subtitle of the book, *A Chinese Book of Life*. I had borrowed the book from the library of Southern

Illinois University because I was attracted by the subtitle. When I read the book, I realized that C.G. Jung and Richard Wilhelm found the key thread: the key for Jungian psychology is the relationship with Chinese culture. This is a very important thread. Secondly, I realized that if I learned Jungian psychology, it would be like a key to open the door to the original resources of Chinese culture, through the instrumentality of depth psychology. The principle is working both ways because Jungian psychology is like a key, opening the door to Chinese culture, and Chinese culture, in turn, opens a path to Jungian psychology. That is quite another story related to my personal process with Jungian psychology.

After that, after several months of self-analysis, dreams, and wounded stories, I arrived in Los Angeles. There I met Murray Stein, Thomas Kirsch, the president of the International Association for Analytical Psychology, and his wife, Jean Kirsch, president of the C.G. Jung Institute of San Francisco. I contacted them and visited the C.G. Jung Institute in 1993. I even encountered Sandplay. I established very good relationships, especially with Murray Stein and the Kirsches, and I invited them to China. They came for an official visit to China in 1994. In the next year, in 1995, they invited me back to Zurich to deliver a presentation there. After that I started the personal analytic process and feel grateful for that process. It took a lot of time, ten years. I trained in Küsnacht and worked with Mario Jacoby. I love him for that. I was also acquainted with Robert Bosnak. I also did a two-year internship at the San Francisco C.G. Jung Institute. After that I got my psychotherapist's certification.

LTP: What year were you born in?

SH: In 1959.

LTP: What was happening in China back then?

SH: This was a very difficult time. I was born in December of that year and soon followed three years of disasters in China. First came starvation because there was not enough food. This was a critical moment before the Cultural Revolution. It was very difficult in China. My parents lived in the city, but because of the famine, when I was three years old, they moved me to the countryside. I came back from the countryside when I grew up, but when I was about six years old, the Cultural Revolution began. There were no schools anymore, they closed the schools, pretending it was necessary because we were in a critical moment of the Cultural Revolution.

LTP: You were sent to the countryside to stay with your grandparents?

SH: Yes.

LTP: Are you the only child?

SH: No, we are five brothers and sisters. I have two brothers, one older sister, and my twin sister.

LTP: Oh . . . so, you two were the youngest ones?

SH: Yes, the youngest.

LTP: As the youngest, how were you treated by your other siblings?

SH: It is very interesting because that is also related to Jung's psychology. My parents were also from large families; their parents each had six children. The 8-symbol is a basic element in the I-Ching. In Chinese tradition, my father has an animal symbol as a zodiac sign. My father was born during a dragon year, and my mother is a horse sign, so they almost corresponded to the I-Ching. My oldest brother is a tiger, another sign belonging to the I-Ching system, and my second oldest brother is a fire symbol [*li*]. My second brother, I think he is a *kăn*, which is the twenty-ninth hexagram [Ed – "abysmal water"], my sister, who [is] two years younger than my second brother, is also a fire. The youngest daughter is a mountain (*gèn*) native, like me; I am a mountain, and my twin sister is a lake. The thirty-first hexagram [Ed – *xián*] of the I-Ching is the most important principle for the heart-to-heart connection. I think that symbol is the first principle of Chinese cultural psychology, which Jung appreciated very much. Only the youngest daughter has this kind of sincere heart-to-heart influence. Richard Wilhelm also developed a beautiful work on this hexagram. Although we were five siblings, my mother lost a child between my first and the second brothers, a sister probably. If she was meant to be a sister, she would have belonged to the wind [Ed – hexagram 37 – *jiā rén*]. The wind and the wood would be associated with the first woman of the family, the first daughter. As the youngest, I appreciated my brothers very much, they can protect you. I appreciated my older sister for helping me, washing our clothes. I was very lucky to be the youngest one.

LTP: I want to make sure that I understand the chronology of the children in your family. In the Chinese calendar, what years were all five of you born?

SH: The first one was born in the Year of the Tiger in 1950. My second brother, in 1955, the Year of the Sheep. We lost a sister in between. The second sister was born in 1957. That is the Year of the Rooster. My twin sister and I were born in 1959 in the Year of the Pig. C.G. Jung was also born in the Year of the Pig. My mother is a horse, but my father is a dragon. If my first-born sister would have lived, we, the siblings, would have made a complete hexagram.

LTP: All five of you were sent to the countryside?

SH: No, when I was two years old, only my twin sister and I left for the countryside. In the meantime, my brothers remained in school in the city. But as we grew up, in 1976, when I was sixteen years old, families in the city could keep only one child, the others had to move to the countryside.

LTP: Who was picked?

SH: My two elder brothers were selected for the Army, so we remained only three children in the family. My older sister and I had to go to the countryside. My twin sister stayed in the city.

LTP: So, the youngest daughter.

SH: That was the situation in the seventies.

LTP: How did you feel being picked to go away again – to not live with your parents?

SH: That was a certain political moment in the country. For me personally, during that period of two years in the countryside, I made friends there and learned how to be a farmer in a farmer's state. I took books with me and kept reading. This was one part, when I was sixteen, I spent two years exercising by running in the morning, learning Chinese kung-fu, and learning how to be a farmer. In fact, on one side, it was fine. On the other hand, I lost the opportunity for formal education. I lost that chance at sixteen. But I had the opportunity to have experiences close to life, to the country, to the land, to the people, and to get close to the poor people. It was good for my becoming a Jungian analyst, but I lost two years of my formal university study. Even if I lost those years, I gained something else on the other hand.

LTP: What happened after these two years? Did you feel that something was changing in the political climate?

SH: The policy changed; they stopped the policy of sending young people to the countryside. So, we had the chance to come back to the city but there were not enough jobs for so many young people. So, I decided to join the Army for eight years.

LTP: Did you kill someone?

SH: No, it was a time of peace for China. I played basketball in the Army. At eighteen I was promoted from a simple soldier to an officer. That was not very important for me, but I still learned some things from the Army. In the meantime, I kept reading. Reading is very important to me. While I was in the Army, I read a small book by Spinoza. That led me to psychology. Not to Jungian psychology, but it was still psychology. After Spinoza I read *The Interpretation of Dreams* by Sigmund Freud, I started to keep a diary of dreams in 1982, which prepared me for Jungian analysis. As I mentioned, I had ten years of dreams when I arrived at Southern Illinois University in 1993. Prior to that, while still in the Army in 1984, I had taken and passed a national examination to become a graduate student in the field of psychology and was accepted as a student by one of the best Chinese psychologists, the one who introduced Sigmund Freud in China; his name is Goji Fu. I started a master's degree with him and then a PhD. When I graduated, I became his assistant. After that I spent two years interviewing the senior Chinese psychologists, opening an avenue for research prepared by Chinese psychologists. I interviewed twenty-six different professors, the best teachers in the country. They were in their eighties and nineties. My focus in Jungian psychology is based around the Cultural Revolution, life in China, and Christian psychology. I had the mission to dialogue with the senior Chinese psychologists trying to find out the history of the making of Chinese psychology.

LTP: Does your name bear a special meaning?

SH: Shen is a family name, signifying "to be a teacher." It is related to the word for the divine; divine means that the God Shen, in Chinese, is associated with spirit, spirituality, soul, or God. All these terms are written with the same character and linked to the family name of Shen. These attributes belong to all the families bearing that name. It is thousands of years old, coming from a meadow in my home city. My city is on the oldest lake in China, originating in prehistory, where the surface of the dry lake means "land." The water underground, that is the unseen eternity. That is how the eternity is continuing to expand, the land being only the visible part of eternity. There is an [inclusivity] to "land," measuring the full extent of Chinese culture, *Heyong*. The "He" is originally the name of the land and "Yong" is eternity.

LTP: Do you think the hidden symbolism of your name has created part of your identity?

SH: Somehow, some part. When you get the right meaning of your name, it is related to your destiny or to your faith. One philosophical principle emphasized by Confucius requires the necessity of the right understanding of your name, so that fact is very important. For instance, if we define an object as "table," we name it so, it really becomes a table [laughing]. Determining the true name, the *numen*, is part of the approach of Jungian analysis, playing an active role in the incarnation of experience. We learned that from Confucian philosophy.

LTP: So, are you a Confucianist?

SH: Or Taoist. I appreciate Confucianism, Taoism, Buddhism, and Chinese culture.

LTP: Are you a religious person?

SH: Not really. The country is my religion. It's not that kind of typical Christian religion. Chinese culture is my religion. So, I take my religion from Chinese culture and make a psychology of the heart from it. In the *Red Book*, Jung tried to discover the spirit of the times, the spirit of depths, and said that true depth lies in the knowledge of the heart. What he tried to seek is the knowledge of the heart. Who can teach something like that? That led Jung to Chinese culture. For instance, *The Secret of the Golden Flower* and his dialogue with Chief Mountain Lake at the Taos Pueblo in New Mexico in 1924, these were both about thinking with the heart. This touched Jung very much. Chinese culture is the culture of the heart. For Confucius, of greatest importance was the hygiene of the heart, the image or archetype of the heart. So, I learned from Chinese culture, which I combined with my Jungian analysis and analytical psychology, to arrive at my idea of a psychology of the heart. I delivered a lecture on the subject, which I finished last year. I gave that lecture twice at the Eranos roundtables. The lecture was a series of presentations given across three days during which I talked about this psychology of the heart.

LTP: The heart has knowledge, or it has emotions?

SH: Both. It's like the image of the Self. Only the Self contains both conscious and unconscious, both reason and emotion. C.G. Jung appreciated Pascal's saying, "The heart has its reasons, which reason does not know." I quoted this sentence seven times in my lecture.

LTP: We say also in Christian Orthodoxy that the heart is the place of God. It's over there. It is where it lies.

SH: That is very close to our saying, "Only if you have a pure heart you can go to heaven."

LTP: Yes. I would like to resume the discussion about your childhood, because it seems to me to be an important theme. What's the name of your sister?

SH: My twin sister's name? Her name is "Beauty," *Li*. Only the second character has a meaning.

LTP: Do you still have a special connection to her?

SH: We have several common stories, that's for sure. We have lived several stories together, but we are not the kind of twins that are overly close. But we have a kind of influence with each other. I used to feel her, and she can feel me even from a long distance. It's true. When something happens to her, I don't know, but my body has some reactions. For instance, through dreams we have an amazing connection. I have written several books, like one about Sandplay therapy in which I outline a concept of Chinese culture. In that book, I wrote about a personal dream. The dream is amazing. The unconscious aspect of the Self can express itself in our dreams or emerge in our lives not only as a dream but embedded in imagery reflecting symbols of life. For me and my twin sister there is a mutual influence, a connection from heart to heart. Robert Bosnak sent me an email just one week ago. He is in Santa Barbara, in the mountains, where he has lived alone for the past seven years . . . but just one week ago, he wrote to me that he was touched thinking about my sister.

LTP: Are there other significant influences from your family in shaping your choice to become a Jungian analyst?

SH: Yes, from my father's side. I have a grandfather and uncle who are Chinese doctors – probably they influenced me. Myself, my wife, and my son stayed for many years in the United States and in Switzerland, so I could pursue my studies in Jungian psychology. When we decided to return to China, I packed our bags to send them home. At that time, my son was young, and he wanted to put his toys in the bags. Because of all the books I had acquired, we left his toys in the United States and he complained. I tried to explain to him that we can buy new toys for him when we arrive in China, but the books cannot be found there. After our negotiations he agreed to abandon the toys, not having enough space for them in the luggage. This illustrates how, for someone who is Chinese, the process of being a Jungian analyst is a difficult one. When I started analysis with Jacoby, financially it was rather difficult at that time because of the situation in China during the 1990s. It was difficult for a Chinese person to earn a living, and it was so expensive living abroad while also saving money for my Jungian studies. I have some stories related to this matter, how I became a Jungian analyst. One of these is a very interesting story about how I lived for a period with Jacoby and then with Robert Bosnak. Later I will write to you about these periods.

LTP: How would you describe your mother?

SH: She was great, and I love her very much. I dedicated one book to my mother. Just one story about her, my mother developed cancer and eventually died of it. She was very ill, but she insisted on stopping the treatment. I asked her, "What's your reason for stopping the treatment?" She answered, "It is very expensive." She was a leader in society and the government was providing her medical support, but she didn't want to use too much money, feeling that she was taking too much from other people's medical treatment.

LTP: This is love and altruism.

SH: This is not a reason to stop the medication. We could have borrowed money, and we have a medical system to which we had contributed. As her first reason my mother indicated, "We cannot use the government money for ourselves!" Secondly, she told me, "I came to this city from far away, from my home city. I went a long time without working and I should go back there." I interrupted all this, "Sorry, but you are my mother. It's my duty towards you. We are three brothers who are responsible for you. So, this is not a good reason to stop the treatment." One thing is certain, my mother was very beautiful. At last, she said, as the most important point, that she wanted to remain in the mind of her children as an image untouched by disease. If she had continued the treatment with that medication, she would have lost her hair and developed side effects she could not control. She wanted to remain beautiful in the memory of her children. We, the children, could not agree with that. One day she had a dream about the goddess from the mountain. She dreamt that the goddess asked her to come along with her. She woke up in the middle of the night. My older and younger sisters also received this dream. All three of them had the same dream, to be prepared for the departure to the mountains. My mother asked to be washed and her clothes to be changed. She passed away the same day. My sister, who is a doctor, said, like Freud, that it was a matter of premonition.

LTP: Your twin sister is a doctor?

SH: My other sister is a doctor.

LTP: And your twin sister?

SH: She has written some books and she is a teacher.

LTP: What about your father?

SH: My father was in the Army for many years and was wounded during the Civil War. He became an officer and held an important position in the city, but during the Cultural Revolution he twice attempted to commit suicide. It was a very hard life for him, and after the Cultural Revolution he had difficulties. He passed away at the age of sixty. So, he was wounded in the war, he tried to commit suicide twice during the Cultural Revolution, and had poor health. He was traumatized both in his body and inside. When he passed away, the cycle of the Dragon Years was complete.

LTP: What qualities did you take from your parents and use later in your career as a psychotherapist?

SH: Sometimes I tell two stories about why I initially chose the same career as my father, translating somehow his destiny. I took care of several plantations, gardens, and followed the theme of the missing women in China [Ed – a long-term distortion of the population sex ratio in China in which the number of male births far outweighed the number of female births that reflected cultural valuing of male children over female children and compounded by the Chinese government's "one child" policy implemented in 1979]. However, from my mother's side and from my father's side, through the contact with my parents, I did not extract specific features of my father or mother. But I understood the cultural meaning or image of the fatherly and motherly condition, which went far beyond my personal experience of my parents. I think that the ancient I-Ching hexagram provides the quality to be a father and a mother. I think I have learned that from the personal connection to my individual father and mother, but behind this there is another thread that leads to the cultural meaning of the parental figures.

LTP: Thank you so much for this interview. It was quite enriching.

Chapter 16

Careful Elegance

Murray Stein
INTERVIEWED BY LAVINIA ȚÂNCULESCU-POPA
(FEBRUARY 24, 2017 – ZÜRICH)

Murray Stein, PhD is a training and supervising analyst at the International School of Analytical Psychology Zurich (ISAP-ZURICH). He was president of the International Association for Analytical Psychology (IAAP) from 2001 to 2004 and president of ISAP-ZURICH from 2008 to 2012. He has lectured internationally and is the editor of Jungian Psychoanalysis *and the author of* Jung's Treatment of Christianity, In MidLife, Jung's Map of the Soul, Minding the Self, Outside Inside and All Around, The Bible as Dream*, and* Men Under Construction. *The first two volumes of his* Collected Writings – Individuation and Myth and Psychology – *have been published and several more are in preparation. He lives in Switzerland and has a private practice in Zurich.*

LTP: For these interviews, I don't have a preset list of questions. The main thing I want to understand from the people that I am interviewing is what were the influences in their lives that led them to choose Jungian analysis as a profession. Perhaps a toy from your childhood, a historical event or a family context, your parents, your typology, or anything that led to your choice? I would like to start by asking you to tell me about your earliest memory.

MS: My earliest memory is from when I was around two years old. I was with my father in a small country store. This was in the town where we lived at the time in the province of Manitoba, Canada. It was an old-fashioned country general store with many kinds of things sold in it; groceries, dry goods, and things people need for everyday life. I can just remember a scene. My father is playing hide and seek with me. I am laughing and so is he. I remember his laughter vividly. We were having a lot of fun.

LTP: Were you an only child?

MS: Yes, until the age of twelve. When my mother gave birth to me, I was very big. I was over eleven pounds in weight, and it was a very difficult birth with forceps used to deliver me from her womb. The doctors advised her not to have more children at least for a time. So, my parents refrained from having

DOI:10.4324/9781003148937-17

more children for quite a long time, until ten years later when my mother became pregnant and had my sister, who was of normal size. Her birth was easy, and everything went well that time. But I was a big problem at the beginning! I have a mark to this day on my forehead from the forceps. This was in Yorkton, Saskatchewan, near the tiny village of Ebenezer where my parents lived at the time. My father was always very appreciative of this fine Jewish doctor and would praise him whenever I had a birthday. I remember his name well, Dr. Portnoff.

LTP: Do you remember the birth of your sister?

MS: Yes, of course. I was ten years old. I remember my parents bringing her home from the hospital. We lived in a small town in South Dakota in the United States at the time. It was a summer day in June. I was allowed to carry her in a blanket. Because I was so much older, I had some responsibility for helping to take care of her, as a babysitter. There was once a very traumatic experience when I was supposed to be watching her. My mother was in the basement doing laundry, and I was upstairs and supposed to be keeping an eye on her. But I was reading a comic book and not paying much attention to her. She was a toddler, two years old, and she was able to make her way to the top of the stairs. She wanted to go to my mother and went tumbling down the stairs. Oh my God, it was a disaster! She wasn't hurt, fortunately, but I felt so bad and so guilty that I took all my comic books and burned them.

LTP: You did that?

MS: Yes, I felt so bad!

LTP: You punished yourself!

MS: I punished myself, yes! My parents didn't punish me in any harsh way for this. Of course, they were very upset that I wasn't watching her properly, but they didn't punish me physically. I punished myself. But I must say that this was not only a story of "crime and punishment"; it was also a discovery of what I can only call "responsibility." One is responsible for others. "I [am] my sister's keeper," is what I discovered, to put the lesson into a biblical context. This was the message I received from the Self in that experience. Years later I read a book by a famous American theologian, *The Responsible Self*. He had been the leading scholar at Yale Divinity School, where I studied from 1965 to 1969. That is the perfect phrase for what I discovered in this experience: the responsible self. And I have never forgotten this moment of coming to consciousness. I was around twelve at that time.

LTP: Maybe that's why you currently have a very careful attitude. With me, at least, you are very careful!

MS: Yes, everything in one's life is connected. I wrote my thesis at the C.G. Jung Institute in Zurich on the topic of conscience, the inner voice that calls one to responsibility for others and for oneself. Freud talks about this as a "super-ego." But this type of oversight of one's actions and overhearing of one's speech is not only punishing as Freud would have it. It is a locus of consciousness about responsibility. The word "conscience" means "to know" (from "*scire*") "together" ("*com*"). Conscience speaks for justice to self and others. Jung writes about this type of conscience as the voice of the self. It is much greater than social conformity. It is a sense for what is fundamentally just and right.

LTP: Responsible for others?

MS: Yes, absolutely.

LTP: But what about you, did you take care of yourself? How would you take care of yourself?

MS: It is also about responsibility for oneself. "I am my sister's keeper" also refers to the *anima*. As an only child, I developed a quite independent attitude early in life, and this is a prerequisite for taking care of oneself. This attitude of independence was also embedded in my family's culture. My father was a Protestant pastor. In the denomination that he served, it was standard practice for ministers and their families to move every few years to another congregation in a different location. As my father climbed the professional ladder to bigger and more important congregations, we would move to larger and more important towns and cities. That was the typical story of the pastors' families in this denomination. Because we moved quite frequently, our family became very tight and self-reliant. We had to regularly uproot ourselves, go to another place, make new friends, adapt to a new school system, and so forth. In some respects, this is painful, but on the other hand, one develops the ability to make new friends while remaining somewhat detached and independent. In a way, that capacity for independence has served me quite well, although it has its drawbacks. I also became independent from my family quite early.

LTP: When?

MS: When I was an adolescent and started developing intellectual interests that went outside their interests. My father had a decent education in his field and a well-stocked professional library that we took with us wherever we moved, and my mother was educated as a teacher and later earned a master's degree. She loved teaching. But their interests were quite narrow and largely focused on their religious beliefs. My interests began to reach out to other subjects as I advanced in school.

LTP: What did your mother teach?

MS: Mathematics. She loved this subject, and she taught math at the middle school level. She was an introverted thinking type with extroverted sensation as a secondary function. My father was an extroverted feeling type with intuition as his secondary function. They were quite opposite typologically, as often happens in couples. My father had some intellectual interests too, but he was not an intellectual type. I had those inclinations. I started reading early, mostly thick books after the comic books incident, among others Freud's *The Interpretation of Dreams*, when I was a teenager, and I also started reading philosophy and history at that time. That wonderful book by Will Durant, *The Story of Philosophy*, entertained me for an entire summer vacation when I was a teenager. I also loved imaginative literature like the great novels. This opened my eyes to a much wider world than was offered in the home of my parents. Also, I had very good teachers in high school, and they encouraged this type of interest. In a sense, I outgrew my parents intellectually. That separated me from them as I gravitated in the directions suggested by my reading and my teachers. I took care of myself with books, and early on I started building a library. I saved the money earned from jobs I had and bought books. My parents didn't object because they liked to see me reading and studying instead of getting into trouble with questionable friends. I always had good grades in school, and they let me read and study as I wished. I had a lot of freedom in this area.

LTP: But didn't you also miss something as a boy: spending time just being with other boys, outside and doing nothing serious?

MS: I did a little of that too, but it was always very restricted because of the church. We had very strict rules – you couldn't do this; you couldn't do that. There were a lot of limitations placed on outside involvements. We were not to be too "worldly" and that meant staying away from enjoying sensual pleasures too much.

LTP: You were the son of the minister!

MS: Yes, and I had to be a model for the others. I had a friend when I was a teenager who was also in the church, but he was a bit of a shadow figure for me. He was much better with girls than I was, more relaxed and able to dance and joke around with them. He would introduce me to girls as a kind of go-between and secretly introduced me to smoking cigarettes when we were fifteen years old. We would go down into the woods by the river and smoke cigarettes and look at girlie magazines. So, he got me a little involved with those forbidden pleasures.

LTP: Mercurius!

MS: Yes! We also learned about sex together. It was a deep secret, of course.

LTP: But what about your father, didn't he take any initiative in teaching you about sexuality?

MS: No, not at all. We never touched the subject. I think he was afraid of the topic of sexuality because of his own repression of it. He loved pretty women, that was clear, and my mother kept a careful eye on him. But it was a topic not discussed in our home by anyone. Also, there was no sex education in the schools in those days. But I was a reader so I could read about all these forbidden topics. My friend would get girlie magazines, like *Playboy*, and we looked at the pictures together and dream of such pleasures.

LTP: You were educating yourselves together!

MS: Together and through reading and later through films.

LTP: From these initial experiences what did you keep later on?

MS: I think I got what I call a "missionary impulse" and a "service orientation" from my family. When you grow up in this kind of church atmosphere where they want to bring other people in and want to spread the word and "the good news" to everyone, it is infectious at an unconscious level. When I became a

Jungian analyst many years later and started traveling and lecturing around the country and the world, I started to think this was an extension of that early conditioning, "I'm a Jungian missionary, spreading the word around the world," I thought! This feeling that there are good ideas that are valuable and should be shared with others was an extension of experiencing the missionary spirit in the church. There are values and ideas that people should hear about, and they should have the opportunity to learn about them too. That perspective was very much in my family. I remember my mother once, when we were traveling, giving me these little tracts to hand out to people we met in restaurants and gas stations. There were two or three pages of information about the Bible. I hated to do that, being a bit shy, but I did it to please her. About spreading Jungian ideas, I have not been so shy.

LTP: You were a missionary!

MS: Missionary activities, yes! One other thing that stayed with me from family life is the value of "the Book." Like the Jews who are a people of the Book, namely the Bible, we carried the Book with us wherever we went. Years later I gave a series of lectures on the Bible, which have now been published as *The Bible as Dream*. Following the example of Jung's famous *Answer to Job*, which is his testament to the biblical narrative's meaning, I reworked my understanding of the Bible based on analytical psychology. You can read the Bible as a great literary text, or as a divinely inspired theological text, or as a psychological text. I took the third approach and considered the book as the story of the emergence and incarnation of an archetype.

LTP: Like the Jews, you have lived with the Book!

MS: Yes. The Jews carried the Book with them wherever they went. It was a constant presence in all their wanderings. The same was true in my family. The Bible was at the center of our family culture. We changed places, we moved here and there, and always the Bible came with us. It was a constant thread, and it gave us spiritual orientation no matter where we were. I became more at home in the geography of the Bible than in the geography we lived in. When I was in Israel for the first time, I thought, "Wow, I lived here as a child! Here is Jerusalem, there is Bethlehem, these are the places of my childhood." My parents met in Canada, and I was born there. The family moved to the United States when I was two years old, and I spent the rest of my childhood and youth there; but the spiritual landscape wherever we went was biblical.

LTP: Do you consider yourself a German, Canadian, American or . . . ?

MS: This is a good question. We lived as immigrants in the United States, but I never thought about it. I am an American citizen. My parents became American citizens, and in America everybody's family is immigrant if you go back in the generations, so you don't think twice about it. You are an American. Recently, though, with all the migration going on in the world and Trump being elected president, I've started reflecting much more about it, and now I think of myself as an immigrant and descended from immigrants. I am living as a resident in Switzerland nowadays. I am not a citizen here, only a permanent resident, an "ex-pat" as we are called, although I claim it in a way as my "mother country." On my mother's side of the family, her ancestors originally came from Switzerland, as I have put the pieces together. They were descended from the Anabaptists who originated in Zollikon, just outside of Zurich. They were persecuted by the Zwingli Protestants of Zürich, and some of their leaders were put to death in the River Limmat because they wouldn't baptize infants. So, they left and went north into Germany. From there they migrated to Canada in the late 19th century. It is a story of immigration.

LTP: Are you baptized?

MS: Yes, of course. How could I not be? My father baptized me when I was eight years old. I was immersed, it was that kind of total baptism.

LTP: Immersed into the water of life, into death, and getting out from death to life again!

MS: Yes, that's right. It's about getting over into a new life. That experience has stayed with me.

LTP: Were you a believer from your childhood?

MS: Oh, very strongly in my childhood. Later, the beliefs were, of course, challenged by philosophy and the study of history and reading world literature, but I have always maintained a strong connection to the Christian faith, if not so much the practice. After college I chose to study at Yale Divinity School, a famous preparation ground for Protestant ministers in the United States. I didn't know quite why I was doing that except I didn't see another path I wanted to follow. The ministry was in my family, and I thought, "Well, maybe it's a possibility for me." I was interested mostly in the intellectual side of religion and not so much in the practical. Then I discovered Jung while still at the Divinity School. And that really changed my life's direction dramatically.

LTP: Yes, but as far as I know, reading Jung is a form of spirituality as well. Had you been considering other career possibilities as well?

MS: My major area of study at Yale University was English literature. I had some wonderful teachers, among them the great literary scholar and critic, Harold Bloom, and he encouraged me to go on in that field. I considered it, and I think I would have enjoyed becoming a scholar of literature, but for me there was something missing as I imagined academic life. My image was that the air is too thin in the academic world. It's too far away from life, too much in books, and I didn't feel it was grounded enough in life for me. I also thought about going to law school. But, again, it didn't appeal to my heart. It would be just a way of making a living.

LTP: It was not enough "in your family". . . . But Jungian analysis was not in your family either, so?

MS: When I read Jung's autobiography, I found I could identify with him. He too was the son of a pastor, and I could understand his struggles with his father, which were different from mine somewhat, but there were parallels. What

I was looking for without knowing it at the time was a profession that could combine the spiritual and the psychological in working with people individually. In the church, as a minister, you are talking above everybody, preaching to them from on high, but you have very little to do with most areas of their life. You don't engage with them deeply, individually. That's what appealed to me so much about Jungian analysis when I discovered it. Here you can engage with individuals on a personal level, and to me that really opened a whole new avenue. I still looked on it as a form of ministry, and I was eventually ordained as a minister in the Presbyterian Church. The church authorities said I could work as a Jungian analyst in what they called an "alternative ministry."

LTP: So, in a way, you are a minister but also the shepherd for a lot of "sheep" in the Jungian world?

MS: I didn't intend it to be the way it turned out. I thought I'd have a practice as a Jungian analyst when I returned to the United States from Zurich after training at the Jung Institute, and that would be that. But when I came back home to the United States, a whole new and unexpected area of activity presented itself: teaching, lecturing, and training other people to become Jungian analysts. Suddenly, I was exposed to all the institutional aspects of the Jungian world. I had no preparation for this. At the time when I returned to America, the interest in Jung was just beginning to appeal to many people. This was 1973. I came in at the beginning of a movement to set up new training institutes, and I became a founding member of the Interregional Society of Jungian Analysts in 1976 and of the Chicago Society of Jungian Analysts in 1980. I became very involved in all this institutional business, and this led into the IAAP when Thomas Kirsch invited me to join the Program Committee for the IAAP Congress in Berlin in 1986. That was my introduction to the IAAP. Tom Kirsch became a close friend, and we worked together on many projects. I cherish memories of him deeply.

LTP: When were you a president?

MS: First at the Jung Institute in Chicago (1980–1985), then with the IAAP (2001–2004), and finally at ISAP-ZURICH (2010–2014). All were interesting positions, and rewarding in their own way, but the IAAP presidency was special. The IAAP is a very complex international organization with many societies and analysts from a wide variety of cultures, each holding different views about the practice of analysis and having been trained by mentors and teachers other than the ones I knew in Zurich or the United States. As the leader in that organization, you must take great care to hold all these strong personalities together. This was very interesting for me and a challenge.

LTP: You must take care of others. Talking about taking care of others, can you describe to me a normal day from your childhood, a time when someone else took care of you? You woke up and what did you do next?

MS: Well, we all got up early and had breakfast together: my mother, father, and I, and later my sister. The day always began with the Bible. My mother read a chapter from a large children's version of the Bible that had colorful pictures and was written in a language suited to youngsters. After that we would say a prayer of thanks, and we always had a good breakfast cooked by my mother. My mother baked the bread we ate, and she made delicious jams and jellies from the fruit in our garden. My father was a gardener, and we had big gardens behind the houses we lived in, usually spacious parsonages near the church he was serving. After breakfast, if it was a school day, I'd go to school. I could walk to school or take my bike. We lived mostly in small towns. When I got older, I bought a car. I was thirteen years old at the time.

LTP: At thirteen years old you bought a car?

MS: At thirteen, yes.

LTP: Was this legal?

MS: Where I lived it was legal because it was an agricultural area, and they allowed the young boys . . .

LTP: To drive tractors? (laughs)

MS: (laughs) Exactly! And to drive cars. I could get a driver's license at thirteen, and I had saved enough money from my newspaper delivery job to buy a used car. My father also helped me to get it.

LTP: What brand was your first car?

MS: It was a Studebaker, and then later I bought a Ford.

LTP: Were you tall for your age?

MS: Fairly tall and pretty strong and healthy. I wasn't a great athlete, but I could do well enough.

LTP: Were you well-groomed as a child? Did you take special care in picking your clothes, for instance?

MS: When I was very young, my mother made my clothes. She had a strong sensation function and was good at making things with her hands.

LTP: A tailor?

MS: A tailor, yes! She sewed clothes for me and my sister and for herself. Her mother did the same thing. Her parents were children of pioneers in Canada and had to make everything for themselves. The men worked outdoors on the land, and the women worked indoors and in the gardens. They raised animals and lived off the land granted to them by the Canadian government. They developed extraordinary skills at handwork, and my mother learned that from her mother. She made me little suits and shirts. Later, of course, we wore store-bought clothes. As a minister's family, we had to dress well.

LTP: Little suits. . . . That's why you wear suits all the time?

MS: I guess it's a habit. My father wore a suit every day. I became habituated to this type of dressing early in life. When I went to college in the 1960s, we had to wear coats and ties to all our meals. We couldn't enter the dining room without a tie. Sometimes they were very dirty ties, but everybody had to wear a tie and a jacket. That was a part of the training to become a gentleman in that time. Now it's very different.

LTP: Now it is very different, indeed, but could we say that this comes from your family?

MS: We had to dress well. My father was of the professional class in our community, and we had to show that when we went out in public.

LTP: How large was your wardrobe when you were young?

MS: From the time that I can remember, I always had a suit and a tie. Of course, I also had blue jeans and school clothes. One time when I was a teenager, in a moment of madness I bought a black motorcycle jacket. I thought, "How cool to have one of those." But when I wore it out of the store and onto the street, people looked at me in such a strange way that I became afraid of the impression I was creating, and I couldn't bring myself to wear it again. I wore it once and that was it! I couldn't fit into that juvenile delinquent persona, so I put it away in the closet and it just stayed there. It was too shadowy for me, it scared me.

LTP: You never wore this leather jacket again?

MS: No, never. I guess it was too early for me to integrate the shadow. I had some friends who were into that and lived on the other side of the tracks, as we say, and we had a kind of shadow brother relationship. I remember one kid who started smoking regularly, out in the open, when he was twelve years old and wore a black leather jacket. I thought he was quite cool. But this image was really beyond my capacity to integrate. When I started reading in Jung about the shadow years later, I immediately could locate this feature of personality in my past. I was very much identified with the light side, and the other side, associated with motorcycles, open sexuality, smoking, and drinking alcohol, was strictly taboo. Later I stepped into these areas somewhat, but even then, they remained of "the underworld."

LTP: Aha! Until later . . . I was about to ask you if you didn't miss these things?

MS: When I went to college, my parents drove me there. They were very proud to take me to Yale, a famous Ivy League university. This was way beyond their social status and economic means, but since I received a scholarship, I could go there. When they dropped me off at the college, I waved goodbye and they drove away, and the first thing I did was go to the tobacco shop and buy a pipe. That was the beginning of my life of freedom. Living at college offered much more room for exploration and experimentation.

LTP: That's a nice memory! So, later you learned to combine the opposites.

MS: Yes, to a degree. Smoking, drinking beer, that sort of thing. I got drunk a few times and got sick, so I was put off. Drugs didn't really come in until later, in the 1970s.

LTP: Were you part of any group, gang, brotherhood when you were young?

MS: Where I grew up, we didn't really have gangs, but we had something more like a club. When I was in high school, my parents moved to Detroit, and it was the first time we lived in a big city. The high school I attended had, I think, 5,000 students altogether. But they had special classes for the brighter, more gifted students who were college bound. I was placed into a small, very good class with about fifteen students, and we took all our classes together. Some of us in the class formed an informal club. We would listen to operas together, go to the art museum in Detroit, attend theater performances, and then endlessly discuss the meaning of what we were taking in. It was sort of an intellectual club, so nothing like a gang.

LTP: I thought your ring maybe, had something to do with belonging to some group. What does your ring represent?

MS: This one? I found it by chance in a shop in Zürich around the time I was writing *In MidLife*. It's copied from a Greek medallion and is the image of a man riding a swiftly running horse. I think of it as a Hermes ring. I became fascinated by the Greek god Hermes when I translated Karl Kerényi's classic study, *Hermes, Guide of Souls*, into English. That came together with my studies at the University of Chicago where I was introduced to Victor Turner's work on liminality and liminal communities. Also, the "midlife crisis" was a topic of the day, and I knew about Jung's famous midlife experience as he described it in *Memories, Dreams, Reflections*. All of this, plus my own midlife experiences, came together in these lectures. I felt the spirit of Hermes was with me in the writing, and it was like riding a high-spirited horse. The energy just carries you along. I feel the horse and rider on the ring represent that kind of experience.

LTP: Writing at night is also somehow part of the shadow?

MS: Yes, nighttime, when the whole world is in the shadows.

LTP: Apparently carrying the shadow was a part of your life since the very first beginning: you "broke" your mother's body when you were born.

MS: Yes. I felt terrible about that when I found out that I could have killed my mother. She went through a physical and emotional crisis because of me. When I was six months old, she suffered from depression, not really a serious clinical depression, but I think I was too much for her. I was a difficult baby, with colic and crying a lot in my first months. So, for a brief time she handed me over to her mother, my grandmother, and for a couple of months my grandmother took care of me. I loved my grandmother! My mother was more introverted and a thinking type. My grandmother was warm and cheerful, loved flowers and colorful clothes, and was much more outgoing and related. Hers was a feeling personality, and I became very attached to her. As a child I always cried when we left her house in the village and drove back home so far away.

LTP: So, apart from your mother and grandmother, tell me about your first love.

MS: I was four years old when I met her. I had gotten a hernia from jumping down some stairs and had to be taken to the hospital in a nearby city for an operation. My parents came with me and were present throughout, but while I was in the hospital a nurse also took care of me. I don't remember exactly what she looked like, but I absolutely thought she was beautiful as she leaned lovingly over my bed. I would reach out to touch her, and she would smile. It was love at first sight, and I think she responded as well. I remember that she wore those little badges that nurses have on their uniforms. She was really lovely, and I adored her. That was the first love of my life, aside from my mother and grandmother. It was an intense experience that I remember vividly to this day. This was my first experience of the power of the *anima*.

LTP: What about the first experience of falling into love with someone the same age as you?

MS: The next that I can recall was a girl named "M." We were in junior high school, so about thirteen years old. She was a cute girl with long blond hair, and when we had dances at school – called "sock hops," because we took our shoes off to preserve the floor of the gymnasium where they were held – we always paired up. We were a "couple." It was all very innocent, and I don't think I ever even kissed her. It was an experience of what we call "puppy love." Then when I was about sixteen, I had a powerful experience of infatuation at the movies. The film was titled *A Summer Place* and starred a young actress named Sandra Dee. She was a teen idol, and I really fell for her character in this movie. It's a story of a teenage girl going on a summer holiday with her parents and falling in love with a boy on the beach. They are eighteen years old and have a romantic relationship that includes sex, and when she gets pregnant, they want to marry but are underage. Eventually they succeed, so the story has a happy ending. I was so moved by this story and the characters portrayed that it took me a good week to get over it. I couldn't stop thinking about and swooning over this girl.

LTP: You wanted this kind of love story?

MS: Absolutely! I was drawn to it so powerfully. It was super intense and quite frightening as well. Love can lead to great crises in life. When I grew up, there was no effective birth control – the "pill" came later and brought with it the sexual revolution – so with girlfriends there was a strict prohibition on sexual intercourse. If occasionally a girl got pregnant, they would have to get married. To me this looked like a catastrophe. Often, it was an embarrassment for the families.

LTP: It was not in your case!

MS: No. I was very careful. I didn't want to go there, and I had an eye on preserving the freedom to pursue a meaningful career. I didn't want to complicate life too soon.

LTP: For Eros!

MS: (laughs): No, not even for Eros!

LTP: Who would mess up the Logos for Eros? (laughs)

MS: (laughs): Indeed!

LTP: Did it come from the family?

MS: I think my father was quite a sexual person but very restricted, and I don't think he ever acted out.

LTP: So, in a way, that was your father's shadow.

MS: Yes. He was severely restricted by his job, his vocation, his marriage, so the road he walked on was very narrow in that sense.

LTP: Did the differences between you and your sister increase over the years?

MS: We were never close to begin with because of the age difference. I went away to college when she was six years old and was just entering elementary school. We didn't have much in common. She became a teacher like my mother. She has lived a more conventional life than I have, becoming a mother of three children and now a grandmother of ten. She stayed on the path of the family. She still regularly goes to the same kind of church, married a man who is also a member of that church, and their family is very committed to the type of religious belief we grew up with in our family.

LTP: Can you re-create for us the journey of your life and the cities?

MS: I was born in Yorkton, Saskatchewan, Canada, and brought home to a tiny village nearby named Ebenezer. This is in the middle of the vast country of Canada and relatively uninhabited, with lots of trees and animals but few humans. When I was six months old, we moved to a small town in the neighboring province of Manitoba, called Minitonas, where we lived until I was two years old. Then we moved across the border into the United States to a small town, Ashley, North Dakota, and five years later we moved again, this time to a town in South Dakota named Tyndall, where we lived until I was in the sixth grade, so until I was twelve years old. During the crucial period of my early adolescence, junior high school and the first half of high school, we lived in Grand Forks, North Dakota, a university town. Here the general cultural level was quite high because of the university, and the public schools were first rate. I was in the middle of high school when we moved to Detroit, Michigan, for the rest of my high school education. This was a major city and at the time offered great cultural resources. From there I went to New Haven, Connecticut, to study at Yale University. I lived there for eight years but in that time spent a year out of school, working in Washington, D.C. At the age of twenty-four, I came to Zürich and lived here for four years while studying at the Jung Institute, and from there I moved to Houston, Texas, where I lived for three years, and then moved to Evanston, Illinois, just outside of Chicago. I lived there for twenty-five years and then moved back to Zürich and Goldiwil, Switzerland. I left Zürich when I was thirty, and I came back when I was sixty. I love the symmetry of that.

LTP: Do you think that this journey helped you also formulate "the map of your soul" and the book?

MS: Perhaps all this moving from [one] place to another instilled in me the value of maps. They help one orient oneself to new landscapes. In my family, the Bible was our spiritual map. For writing the book, *Jung's Map of the Soul*, however, I got the idea from something Jung said about himself. Jung often claimed that he was a pioneer. Pioneers are mapmakers. They must map the territory they have entered and are attempting to inhabit. America was populated by pioneers moving ever farther westward. My grandparents were pioneers in Canada. They came from Prussia, from a small village in what is now Poland, when my grandfather was six years old. They moved because they didn't want their sons to be drafted into the Prussian army. They were

Anabaptists and didn't believe in war. They were rather pacifistic in their philosophy of life. They made the courageous decision to move to Canada, and they arrived in the fall of the year in the early 1890s. Government agents took them out into the wilderness and said, "This is your land!" They had to make their home there in the great unexplored forests of Canada. At the beginning, they dug a hole in the ground and covered it with [a] tarp, and they lived there through the first winter. Miraculously they all survived! They had to survey the land and establish boundaries. Then they started clearing the land. It was all wooded, so they had to cut down the trees to create land where they could grow food for themselves and crops for sale. My mother was born in a log cabin. So, when Jung said he was a pioneer, I thought, "Oh, like people going into the wilderness and discovering what's in the unknown territory and making it habitable!" That's where the idea of mapping comes from. Jung ventured into the unknown territory he calls the unconscious, and he mapped it like an explorer. Pioneering is also about naming places and making them familiar and a part of consciousness and culture. Pioneers like my grandparents created villages and towns and named them, often after biblical places. The first town I lived in was named Ebenezer, a place name from the Old Testament.

LTP: But do you feel you were acting like a pioneer at some moment in your life?

MS: It wasn't so much pioneering as planting the flag. That idea is embedded in the *MidLife* book, where I write about Odysseus being given the mission to carry the oar from his ship inland so far that people don't recognize what it is and think it's a winnowing fan. There he is supposed to plant the oar in honor of Poseidon, the Lord of the Deep. This is how I think about my work following the years of training in Zurich. Jungian psychology was still unknown in many parts of America, especially inland between the coasts. My teaching and analytic work in Houston and Chicago was pioneering in a way, but when I would go out into other areas of the country where word of Jung was absolutely a new thing and give lectures to audiences who were puzzled about it all but eager to know more, I felt like Odysseus planting the oar. There is a funny story about a Jungian teacher going to a city to give a lecture about Jung to the women's club, and afterwards one lady was overheard saying to her neighbor, "That was so interesting! I thought Jung was the name of that new hotel in New Orleans! I'm so glad I came to this lecture." In America, in those days, it was definitely a kind of pioneering work to be a Jungian analyst. Then, when I became involved in the IAAP, I traveled to a lot of countries as one of the first Jungian analysts to visit there. When Tom Kirsch and I went to China in 1994, we were the first representatives of the IAAP ever to visit mainland China. We were pioneering and planting the oar. It was similar in Russia and Eastern Europe in the 1990s, also in parts of South America. I was very involved in creating what is now called the "Router Program" in the IAAP, which is an IAAP-sponsored training program for people who want to become Jungian analysts but live in countries where there is no training available.

LTP: That is very impressive! So, you still have the courage to live the next thirty years?

MS: Thirty years? Wow! Maybe! So far, I am healthy, I don't have any serious illnesses to my knowledge, and I take pretty good care of myself. I enjoy life, and I enjoy what I am doing.

LTP: We can see that you're taking care of yourself! I think you are going to live long, because I feel you have a sense of self-preservation, I can see that.

MS: Yes, I learned about pacing oneself from a much-loved senior American Jungian analyst named Joseph Henderson. He once told me that he had an awakening experience when he was in his fifties in the form of a serious health scare. The doctors thought that he had suffered a heart attack, and he was hospitalized. After that, he started to pace himself. He didn't overwork. He took a week off every month to study, write, and recover his energy. I picked up the idea of pacing from him. If you want to run a long race, you must find a pace that will allow you to make it to the finish line.

LTP: The last question if you agree to answer. You are healthy enough, but are you wealthy enough?

MS: As is well known, no one is ever wealthy enough. There is always anxiety about having enough money. I live comfortably, and I think that if I am careful this will continue for the rest of my life. But who knows? Economies collapse, people lose their jobs, children get sick. Many things can happen that wipe out one's wealth. My father taught me to save. He took me to a local bank when I was five years old, and we opened a bank account in my own name, to save money. From a very early age I became a saver. I saved for a purpose so I could have something I wanted. I could deny myself buying a chocolate bar or a Coca Cola because I wanted to buy a car. I learned to think like that. I still do. I am the opposite of a gambler like Leo Tolstoy. That kind of risk taking with money is beyond my capacity. It frightens me. I think this is embedded in my family culture. My parents and grandparents never borrowed money because they saw what happened in the Great Depression when banks foreclosed on debt and people lost their homes and their property.

LTP: So, you had a target!

MS: Yes, I saved for a purpose and then I would spend what I had to get what I wanted. I have done the same with my time. I spend enough, even generously, but not too much.

LTP: And without being stingy.

MS: I hope, yes, without being stingy. I'm not a miser, but I am careful. It's an aspect of my heritage.

LTP: Thank you very much! This was a good interview!

Chapter 17

Collecting Memories

Luigi Zoja
INTERVIEWED BY LAVINIA ȚÂNCULESCU-POPA
NOVEMBER 30, 2018 – MILAN, ITALY

Luigi Zoja, PhD, is a senior Jungian analyst who obtained his diploma from C.G. Jung Institute – Zürich (1974). He is a former president of IAAP (1998–2001). He had a clinical practice in Zurich (1975–1979), in New York (2000–2002), and also in several periods in Milan, where he currently maintains his private practice. He has lectured in Italy and abroad and has been a visiting professor of Beijing Normal University. Dr. Zoja is the author of papers and books pub-lished in fifteen languages, including Growth and Guilt *(Routledge, 1995),* Ethics and Analysis *(Texas A&M University Press, 2007),* Paranoia *(Bollati Boringhieri, 2011),* Drugs, Addiction and Initiation *(Daimon, 2012), and* The Father *(Taylor & Francis, 2018).*

LTP: Most of the people I interviewed I met while I was attending courses and seminars as a continuing education student in the C.G. Jung Institute in Zurich.

LZ: So I am the only Italian?

LTP: Yes, you are the only Italian, but you are not Italian anymore because you are very international. You lived places and you trained in various places, you taught in various places.

LZ: Sure. Multiculturalism is very important in Jungian psychology and also sometimes contested. I was referring to it now with this concept because I've been part of this group called *Jung and Political Activism*, although I am not an activist. I am a pacifist, but I'm interested in socio-political issues. I think they are important. And I think that to have Trump as president in America, although it is another country, it influences all of us.

LTP: All of us, of course. So, this is the same group with Andrew Samuels?

LZ: Yes, Andrew is one of my first friends and he is almost six years younger than me, although I was pretty young for them. He started even younger. So, we have been friends for an eternity (he smiles).

DOI:10.4324/9781003148937-18

LTP: I am very interested in the antecedent experiences people have in their lives, whether it is the history of the times or in one's personal history; the experiences that led them to choose the path of Jungian analysis. Over time, I'm sure that people have asked you a lot of questions related to your work and about Jungian concepts. But I am very interested in knowing what your favorite toy was or your favorite form of play. What do you remember about your early life, your family life?

LZ: My first reaction when reading about this in your email was that I will disappoint you because I had very little life before making that choice.

LTP: When did you make the choice?

LZ: The choice was very clear because of a dividing line, 1968. In Italy it is not even a number, it is a concept. In Italy and France, 1968 was the year of the big student movement and when everything officially started. Through my desire, from the gods, or the Self, or whatever; give me enough life and enough energy, because it will take some years. There will be a book about Italy, about the concept of Italy, the archetype of Italy, and so on. So, I am . . . collecting memories, particularly of what is more than just Italy; addressing World War II and in the decades following World War II. In reality, having been part of this movement and being a bit interested in social historical reality, I could say that 1968 did not start in 1968. It started a bit earlier. For instance, very clearly in Germany the movement started in 1967. In Germany, this movement was important because that led to the founding of the RAF (*Rote Armee Fraktion/Red Army Faction*). In Italy, the Red Brigades started a little later. The movement in France, which began in May 1968, is the most well-known. But then in France, only a few months later, there was an important national vote and de Gaulle won the majority. I think the Gaullists got more than half of the parliament. So there was a big reaction in my family.

LTP: Charles de Gaulle?

LZ: Charles de Gaulle, yes. In Italy, the movement of 1968 was influenced by France in the beginning. France is the country in Europe which most influenced Italy. In 1968, I decided to go to Zurich. In those times, studying in Zurich was much more difficult because you had to live there. Transportation was more difficult, and there was also the problem of the exchange rate: we had the Italian lira, which kept devaluating. In one year you could find that the exchange rate had nearly doubled. Very difficult. But anyhow, I went to Zurich in 1968. I don't know if it makes sense that I go on with this.

LTP: Please, go on!

LZ: So, in 1968, a big change happened and somehow I realized I was embedded in the collective and very repressed, and my life before was not a life. I had finished university.

My psychological birth is somehow linked with the big change in 1968. In 1968, I left Milan and moved to Zurich. Although I kept moving because for the following ten years, I was traveling every week between Milan and Zurich. Actually transportation has changed a lot in the world, but that has not changed so much. I would do it by train in five hours. Now it is down to three and a half hours because there is this big tunnel, but somehow it's not such a big change. In 1968, when I arrived in Zurich, I learned practical English and German, because I had a very traditional education with a lot of Latin and Greek, but very little foreign languages.

LTP: How many languages do you speak?

LZ: Several somewhat badly, because when you learn them as a grownup, the accent and the pronunciation are bad. But yes, I learned English, German, and French, and also Spanish by going to South America. So yes, I now sort of speak five languages.

LTP: Excellent!

LZ: In 1969, I had a meeting with the daughter of Jung who was an astrologist.

LTP: Gret Jung?

LZ: Yes, she made me a chart, so I have her chart of my birth and the interpretation. For a few years, I was sort of involved with esoteric knowledge, then I left it. During my first year in Zurich I was doing a lot of I-Ching readings, but I think you have to respect these things. I saw horrible things; people who did it all the time. I think you have to use it once every five or ten years, only when there is a very important question. I did not have a good impression of people who used these quasi-esoteric practices too much; in a way that corresponded to giving up the responsibility we have as moral beings. I also have doubts about the Catholic teaching of free will and free choice because, as an analyst, I assume we have many unconscious components to our behavior. I believe rather in Erich Neumann's position regarding ethics and the unconscious. So are we responsible for our unconscious? Yes and no. If it is unconscious, by definition, no. If we are particularly somehow involved in psychology, we have the responsibility to try to do our best in order to know a little more. So, the point is that our will is not so free; certainly there is not a narrow path, but not full freedom. So in this path, we have to use all our human moral responsibility.

LTP: What do you remember from what she said?

LZ: Frau Jung said to me, "Remember there are cycles in Saturn." Saturn, it's an important planet and typically responsible for melancholia. My father was a very melancholy person; I was influenced by that as a child. Anyway, she said Saturn has a cycle of seven years. I have noticed that every fourteen years, so twice seven, I have experienced big changes because approximately fourteen years after 1968, I had a very difficult divorce. But since then, I have stayed with and even married Eva. Then fourteen years later, again, I was trying to move to America. I was somewhat superstitiously thinking that that was my new next big change; a geographic one. That did not really work. I did not settle down in America, as I did in Zurich. Zurich became my city; New York did not. Unlike stereotypes, Switzerland is small and conservative, so it was okay to take roots there. Unlike the stereotypes of America, like the country of immigration, it was too difficult. So, I thought about changes and did not choose a geographical immigration, but rather an inner immigration, in that I dedicated more and more time to studying and writing.

LTP: But when you moved to Zurich, you are sure that you wanted to pursue . . . this career of studying Jung?

LZ: I had put my life on that, but I didn't know anything about Jung. I just didn't want to go on with my previous life. It was a rather negative choice, but I did it.

LTP: But why Jung?

LZ: You know, in retrospect, it's easy to say, "Oh, Jung!" In reality it was a series of coincidences. I had read some Freud, but practically nothing of Jung, but I had the minimal conditions to apply to the institute and they accepted me, I was very surprised. I had the minimum age, the minimum conditions – three letters of recommendation. I got the three letters of recommendation from analysts here in Italy, but who didn't know me. I had done no analysis at all. So I don't know why they accepted me, but it worked.

LTP: Was it also an oral exam or only an application?

LZ: No, you had to submit papers. An application is self-presentation, very vaguely, and these three letters. Then, yes, you had to have a personal interview with each member of the Curatorium [the committee responsible for organizing and running the institute].

LTP: After that, they accepted you?

LZ: Yes. I think there were five members of the Curatorium then. I think one was Adolf Guggenbühl and one was Franz Riklin. I think one was Pope, an Englishman. One was probably Hilde Binswanger, who I eventually had for supervision, a very nice person. The fifth, I don't remember. Anyhow, they accepted me.

LTP: Three men and two women?

LZ: No, maybe just one woman; Jolande Jacobi was there and she had been the person who had decided to create the institute. I had always heard this and then, a couple of years ago, I heard it again because my daughter did the translation of the Jung–Neumann correspondence.

LTP: Which daughter, Sara?

LZ: No, no, the other one, the youngest daughter who is bilingual, Italian-German. Anyhow, in the correspondence is the story of Jolande Jacobi which corresponded with what I heard. But that was the admission process. You had these interviews and they went well, although I was so shy and so nonarrogant that they decided there was no risk.

LTP: But were you handsome?

LZ: I don't know, I felt very, very shy with women. I didn't have . . . it was also another time, so no . . .

LTP: No, but tall, brunette . . .

LZ: I was tall, but that was it. I didn't consider myself . . . I didn't have a persona in this way. Let's say I had a lot of insecurity with girls. I had good potential for heterosexual relationships because it was easy to have girls who were interested in me, but I didn't notice that. I later noticed in analysis that this happened, but I didn't notice at the time. I was very shy and I grew up in a Catholic school where there were only boys.

LTP: So, you were born in 1943? What years were you at that school?

LZ: 1943, yes. I went from the first elementary class to the last exam, always to that school. My two brothers went to the same school. I only had brothers; only boys in my life around.

LTP: You were three boys?

LZ: Three, yes.

LTP: And which one are you?

LZ: I am the eldest. I was born during the war, in August 1943, and my brothers were born after the war. My family was living in Milan, but then they left Milan because of the bombings. In July 1943, the Council of Fascism dismissed Mussolini. It's something you might not know outside Italy, but on July 25, even the fascists turned against Mussolini, because of the idiotic war which was very destructive and on the side of Hitler. So Italy was left, from August until the beginning of September, almost without any government and in a state of chaos. Then, of course, on the part of the Germans, they felt betrayed by Italy, which was a repetition of World War I, because Italy was in an alliance with Austria and Germany when they entered World War I. So we had Nazi troops entering Italy to rescue Mussolini. From then on, for two years, we had civil war between the partisans and the king in the south with the Allies. The king announced that he was switching sides and staying with the Allies. The Allied bombing was mostly in Germany because that was their biggest enemy; the most industrialized. But they eventually also focused the bombing on Italy because it still was a pretty big country and the Allies wanted to push Italy totally out of the picture. That is also the point, at the end of July 1943 when the Allies disembarked in Sicily. It made things much easier for the Allies. They bombed Italy but declared Rome an open city, no bombing, because of the Pope. The bombing was concentrated on Milan, which is the second largest city, but by far the main economic center with all the factories. So my family moved away. My grandfather moved his pharmaceutical factory outside Milan. There were maybe fifty workers.

LTP: Your grandfather was a . . . ?

LZ: He was a pharmacist, but at the end of the 19th century, he was one of the first to transform a pharmacy into a factory manufacturing medicine. I still have some of their advertising. It was very nice. Initially, the factory and the family were in Venice. My grandfather said, and I agree, "Venice was the most unbelievable, the most beautiful city in the world," but it is not really a place for creating a factory. So, he moved to Milan. He opened a second pharmacy and then moved the factory here. In 1943, they moved the factory to Lago Maggiore, on the lake where he had a summer villa . . . a beautiful house where I have my first memories. So, being a pharmaceutical factory, it was also one of the few in Italy at that time where the workers were women.

So they were not drafted into the war, and they were very happy because my grandfather also provided housing for them, as well as relocating the factory where it wouldn't be bombed.

LTP: That is very protective . . .

LZ: Very patriarchal, but my grandfather was patriarchal in a good sense, yes.

LTP: Your grandfather from your mother's side?

LZ: From my father's side. It was Zoja, which is a name from Venice, or some even say it is Slavic name. It is not Italian because it has a "J," which is not in the Italian alphabet. It could be Slavic because in Venice, over the centuries, the population was very mixed, there were Greeks, Croats . . .

LTP: And you were born on Lago Maggiore?

LTP: Yes, in Varese, which is the main city there. My mother was a medical doctor, one of the first in fascist Italy. Very few women had a diploma. She was a very exact person, but not psychologically exact. She joked, "In my textbooks of gynecology, there was no case of a child born so late after the due date." I think I was due at the beginning of August and I was born more than fifteen days late. So I stayed inside her much longer, and she said it was unbelievable.

LTP: Almost ten months.

LZ: Let's say nine and a half months. She said, "Evidently, psychologically you didn't like the world outside because you were there in the bombing."

LTP: Was this something that repeated later in life? Namely, did you adapt easily in responding to the outside world?

LZ: In a way, yes. I am quite introverted, for an Italian at least. In the other sense, yes, interested in history, in the war, and things like this. Varese was the next big city with hospital and gynecologic services. My mother went there on her due date but I didn't arrive, so she stayed in the hospital for a long time. Nearby there was one of the few Italian factories for airplanes, so the Allies were bombing near the hospital. She was in the hospital, but she said she was, "Sitting in the garden all the time, because there were alarms." For the first two years I lived in the villa on the lake, but I don't remember anything. I have photos of myself, there was a lot of snow in the winter of 1944–1945 when I was one and a half years. They said that the Allies had planned to liberate the north of Italy earlier, but it was a very cold winter, and the Nazis and the Fascists had made a line on the Apennine. Everything was collapsing, but nevertheless, they were fanatics and they would resist. Then, of course, there were partisans, particularly where we lived. I still remember partisans being hung beside the lake; there were photos of this. I remember my parents speaking about this.

LTP: Seeing that would be very shocking for a child, even if they didn't understand it.

LZ: Yes. It was a difficult time, although my family was safe; my grandfather was a wealthy person. They, of course, had to give up cars and so on. My father followed [in his] footsteps and started the factory with his father. He was Giorgio Luigi, also the same name.

LTP: Your father was also a pharmacist?

LZ: Yes, he studied pharmacy at the university and worked in the factory. Yes, like the father of my grandfather . . .

LTP: Your great-grandfather?

LZ: Great-grandfather, yes. He was also Giorgio, Luigi Giorgio. So, I was supposed to be the next in the line.

LTP: But you are the first Luigi?

LZ: No, Luigi was also my grandfather's name. They would go by bicycle to the factory, which was a few kilometers away. I vaguely remember that after the war my father had one of the first Vespa motor scooters.

LTP: Oh my God, so pioneering!

LZ: All these things, yes. But it's uphill and it's very difficult to do by bike.

LTP: You just mentioned that the only vehicle that you have now is a bicycle.

LZ: Yes, I try. I also have a car, but I always forget about it because I never use it. Sometimes in the summer I have to buy a new battery to start it.

LTP: What type of car?

LZ: I think it's a Citroen. . . . It's about fifteen years old because I never use it.

LTP: What was your first car?

LZ: When Italy had few cars, my family had one Lancia and possibly an Alfa Romeo. They had a big Alfa Romeo in the war, but kept it hidden, because it was compulsory to give it to the state. I heard that they had the little truck, a lorry, for the factory that they used during the war. The villa was relatively high, one of the last beautiful houses on the lake, and behind it there is a mountain. Beyond that, there was the border with Switzerland. It is still one of the most wild parts of Italy with the park and the trees. Then it was full of partisans. The partisans even made that zone an independent republic for a while. The partisans sometimes came to the villa through the garden at night and knocked at the back door to ask for food. It was not weapons, but food that they needed.

LTP: How old were you?

LZ: In my first two years. Once they asked for the truck from the factory. So the factory was left without the truck because the partisans were there with the guns. My family was also pretty antifascist, but bourgeois antifascist, not aligning with the guerillas, many of which were Communists. They had to give them the truck and then the partisans got into a fight with the Fascists and ran away, leaving the truck. There was a big discussion in the family about whether to recover the truck, and they decided not to, because that would imply that they had some arrangement with the partisans, which would mean being killed by the Fascists. So the truck was left there. I heard these stories later. Of course, there was no form of entertainment. It was difficult, often impossible, to obtain newspapers and the newspapers that existed had Fascist censorship. So they would listen to Radio London, the Allied propaganda, but in secret. I also had an aunt who influenced me a lot. She was the elder sister of my father, who was not married. She was also very sick. She had poliomyelitis when there was not yet a vaccine for that. So she lived at home with my grandparents, who luckily could provide her with medical assistance and so on. But she was an intellectual; she was friends with professors of literature, painters, intellectuals, and Jews, which was, of course, forbidden. They did dangerous things like offering help and hiding antifascists and Jews, although it was risky. And my aunt was reading to my mother and to her sister; my father had two elder sisters. My aunt would read every day something from the *Song of the Divine Comedy* of Dante, which is very beautiful and refined, to pass the time. Because my aunt was literate, she could also explain it.

LTP: But what about your first memories? Your first personal memories.

LZ: My first memories are of probably being on vacation in summer, always at some beach. We went to the seaside first and then to this villa . . .

LTP: You still have the villa? The family?

LZ: It went to a cousin of mine who is the daughter of that sister of my father, the other sister who married a count, an aristocrat, and they lived in Rome. Anyhow, the first memories are of the seaside and boats in some part of Italy.

LTP: How old were you?

LZ: It could be the summer of 1947 when I was four, or it could be the summer of 1946. I don't know, it runs together. There are pictures of this big Alfa Romeo of my grandfather, which my father would borrow from him. In some pictures I have long hair. I know my mother wanted a girl. After me, she had two boys. Then my brother and I started having boys and she was always disappointed. So, she was very happy when Sara arrived because finally there was a girl. In these photographs, you can see we were sort of a happy family even during the war because of my grandfather's efforts. They even bought a cow!

LTP: They bought a cow?

LZ: Yes, and the cow had a calf so we had milk all the time. We had produce because there was a big garden with fruits, so we had no food shortage. When the war ended, my grandfather calculated that he had enough rice and tomato paste for another war. Because he was very patriarchal in . . .

LTP: He arranged for provisions.

LZ: Yes. An enormous amount of provisions. This is what I remember about how we survived the war. My first real memory is of boats on the shore during a summer vacation. Probably me and my cousins entered some of the boats, just to see how they were, and the watchman scolded us. So I have the memory of being scolded for doing something forbidden, because the boats were not ours. We were just . . .

LTP: Sneaking?

LZ: Yes, as children do. I didn't begin kindergarten at that time.

LTP: Why not?

LZ: I think my parents were sort of overprotective. I remember very well the first day of school that I was extremely scared. Because we had to wear a uniform and there was discipline. All the other children had gone to kindergarten before, so they knew something about discipline in the school. But I was scared. Also, they had promised me I would be with my friend who was living in the apartment below ours, so he would be going to the same school. He was born on the same day as I was. Our mothers joked that they met in a bomb shelter when they were both pregnant and full. Then they learned that they had both delivered on the same day. This friend and I were sort united by the bombing.

LTP: He was like a brother?

LZ: Somehow. . . . In reality he has lived a totally bourgeois life here in Milan, and we have lost the friendship. But in those times he was my friend, and my parents had promised me I would be with him in school. But he was not in the same class. So the first day of school was a nightmare.

LTP: Were you called Luigi?

LZ: No, I was called either Gigi or Ligi. Sort of short names, which I dropped because there are too many short names in Italy. Anyhow, my entrance to school was not happy. The teacher was relatively rigid, a nonfeeling one, and the school system was like this until the end. I had only one relatively good teacher during middle school who appreciated me, particularly because he was the primary teacher of literature and Italian. He appreciated my way of writing. I liked to write, but other teachers, for instance, in high school, my Italian professor always gave me bad grades on my Italian, because he said I would put in too much fantasy and I should stick to the topic he had indicated.

So the school years were not quite good. I was good at school, but mostly ranked the second in the class, not the first. The first one was a guy with whom I was friends and then I sort of came to hate. He is still part of the business elite in Milan, sort of a well-known family, but too cynical for me.

LTP: When you say cynical, what do you refer to? Arrogant?

LZ: We were at school and we were only boys and we started studying together how to start meeting with girls, but I saw that he had a very male chauvinist way of behaving.

LTP: Machista?

LZ: Machista, very machista, but the families would still say at a certain point that "Boys, don't touch a good girl, if you really don't . . . "

LTP: Intend to marry her . . .

LZ: Yes, "Don't touch, but if you really cannot hold yourself, we'll give you some money and you can go with prostitutes." This occurred in a certain milieu of bourgeois families, despite the fact that it was a Catholic school with Catholic education. I am not so critical of all the Catholic education; as I said, I had cousins in Rome and my cousins were also in a private Catholic school, but they were with Jesuits. I envied them because the Jesuit education was very good. They would teach sexual education, they would teach cultural problems. They would, in my opinion, teach responsibility.

LTP: You just mentioned sexual education. What age would that begin?

LZ: It's difficult to go back and remember. Everything changes so quickly. Theoretically, it should start in middle school or even in high school. But nowadays with the smartphones, you have a new generation coming of age that is reaching puberty having been consumers of pornography from primary school. So there is an enormous mis-education and it's worse in wealthy families, because all the children have smartphones and the families are not capable of setting limits. I am no expert, but I am worried. For my children, I think it was okay. I have one boy and two girls, and there have been quite difficult moments, but I am happy with how they have grown up.

LTP: Yes. Coming back to your school, was it a daily school or a boarding school?

LZ: No, no, it was daily school. My parents had put me there because it was on the next corner.

LTP: From you to your next brother, how much time between?

LZ: Three years to the next, the one who has died, and four to the other one. So they were born in 1946 and 1947, close together. They had an education after the war which was much more free. I think mine was more rigid. But I had privileges . . . I always had one of the family cars. There was always a second car for my mother, but [she] used it very little and she was very protective, so I could use it all the time.

LTP: But you said that you experienced a more rigid education. How did this affect you, your true nature?

LZ: I think it was affecting me. Yes, because, for instance, my brothers, particularly the last one, were more open with girls. I mean they had friends with sisters. They were allowed to go out in the evening. I think it was more liberal. For instance, I was denied a motorcycle although I wanted one, because my parents were afraid of the risk. I think they were right. I was given a Lambretta, but just in my last year of school, and then as soon as I had the driver's license, I was given the keys to a car. But by then my brothers could then buy a motor scooter, if they wanted that.

LTP: What do you think you received from your mother?

LZ: How important it is to be serious. She was a serious person and consistent.

LTP: And from your father?

LZ: It was the other way around for my father . . . the importance of feeling. How important it is to be warm and accepting.

LTP: Do you find this inversion interesting?

LZ: I don't know. I think this inversion has affected me and because of this I have been interested in the theme of the father. They told me as a child up to five years, I was more extroverted prior to going to school. I was more easy going and very spontaneous, very creative. Also, I was drawing and writing in spite of not having gone to school, like I would copy some text and I would start to write from the right to left, like Leonardo. But I was being particularly noisy one day and my mother kept telling me, "Behave, behave, behave." At a certain point she told me, "You have so misbehaved today that I will tell your father when he comes home after work. You will see!" That was a traditional way of saying this warning, although I knew in my family, my father was not a very angry person. So my father comes back. I was in front of the elevator with my parents. Immediately she tells him, "He has very badly misbehaved today and I have told him, Luigi, that I will tell you and you will take care of that." And I vaguely remember my father bending down and saying, "Oh, did you misbehave?" and I said, "I think so." My father replied, "But you promise that you will not do that again?," and I answered, "No, no, no, no. . . . Okay then it's okay?" He hugged me and it was over. But it was not over because a few minutes passed and I was so happy after my fear that I very stupidly went to my mother and said, "Mama, have you seen, you have told him, but he has hugged me?" She said, "So what? Aha, you are joking? Okay, next time I will punish you!"

LTP: Ohhh, . . . so, she was upset . . .

LZ: Of course, I offended her and her authority by saying something like, "He is the authority but he is more sweet than you." That was my reproach. Of course, she didn't laugh at this.

LTP: Right! Did she cook for you?

LZ: Yes, she cooked. She was more traditional. Of course, she never worked. She was a medical doctor but she married and then she had three children. They had two servants after the war. Maybe during the war we were in this villa, and there were a couple of servants, but more for my grandparents. After the war, my parents had two maids, one who was the cook and the other one who was the cleaning woman. So my mother would cook, but not so much. She organized things, like the shopping. She was very careful. The house was perfect, absolutely. They had guests, but not many because they were introverts. My father and my mother were introverts. The only thing they did outside the house was music. . . . My mother liked music and they had a subscription to *La Scala*.

LTP: Have you seen Maria Callas?

LZ: Probably, yes. They brought me a few times, but I would fall asleep because it was too late in the evening. I would fall asleep and very often my mother would say to my father, "Do you want to go?" It was once a month. It was very selective and expensive. But often my father, who was rather depressive, melancholic, and introverted, would say, "I am too tired, mama, I am too tired." I think the subscription was shared with the parents of my friend Alberto, and so my father would say, "Do you want to go with them?" My mother would say, "No, I won't." She wanted to go with my father but often my father said no. They had the possibility of being sociable, but they were not so sociable.

LTP: What about the grandfathers from your mother's side?

LZ: I knew them less. My grandfather was simply a self-made man. I think the family had a small laundry. He didn't go to university, but he started on his own abilities and he entered the insurance business at the beginning of the century. He brought Zurich Insurance to Italy, which was already one of the biggest insurance companies in the world. He started a branch in Italy and became the director of Zurich Insurance for Italy. He had a good position, but nothing of his own property, just a self-made man. He told me that during the war it was forbidden to send documents to Switzerland, so he went to the border and made an appointment with the director of the foreign departments of Zurich who came to the border from Zurich by train. They could not exchange documents, but they could speak, so they would shout in front of the Fascist watch guards at the border, "This year we had so many things and so many new clients, we closed at . . . and so on!" Very funny. They were carrying on their business transactions because they had to put the figures into the books at the headquarters in Switzerland.

LTP: Quite an atmosphere in those times!

LZ: During the war, when the Nazis entered Italy and the Fascists were recruiting everybody for the last fight against the Allies, of course my father went into hiding. He was hiding in the villa but then he went with my uncle, the aristocrat count from Rome, and a friend who was a Jewish lawyer. They crossed over the mountains into Switzerland. But in Switzerland they were caught and sent back.

LTP: Oh, my God!

LZ: Yes, there is more to this story. I once had a tape recorder when they were all together; my mother and father describing those times, and my father told us that he said to the Swiss policemen, "Please, please don't send us back, no. I am a deserter from the Fascists," and his friend said, "I am a Jew. I would be sent to the work camp! It's very dangerous for us to reenter Italy." And the Swiss policeman said, "Listen, I cannot allow you here. But what I will do is, I have an agreement with the Nazi over there . . . that typically those they sent to Italy, they were more elderly people who didn't want to fight. Let's wait until he lights a cigarette. We have an agreement that when he lights a cigarette, he will never turn on this side. He will pretend he is smoking and will only look at that side. So you can cross, as long as the cigarette is lit." So they reentered Italy safely with the Nazi smoking. So there are . . . all these little things.

LTP: Little things but quite important because somehow . . .

LZ: Because they saved their lives, yes. Theoretically, they should have been put against a wall and shot, but . . . .. then everybody found ways of surviving, particularly during those two last years of the war.

LTP: Don't you find it interesting that both you and Andrew Samuels have written about the father?

LZ: Yes.

LTP: How did you choose to write about this subject?

LZ: Because the subject of the father is clearly missing in our literature, much more than the mother, but we need both. In my family, somehow I had this feeling that I needed a father in the sense that my father was a very good, loving person, but not "the father," if you speak of father as a psychological principle, as I did in my book.

LTP: Yes. Today, how do you think the presence of the father, or the absence of the father, will impact the younger generations in terms of interacting with law, or order or rules, or . . . ?

LZ: Almost everything. . . . In my book there is a primary parental function, which in a patriarchal society, is a patriarchal tradition, that now acts absolutely independently whether we like it or not, as I said about 1968, and so on. I also belong to those who criticize that although I was not in favor of too much extroversion, violence, violent changes, and so on. In the patriarchal tradition, the primary function is that of the mother of fulfilling the desires of the child, and then there is a secondary function, which is entrusted to the father, of teaching the child about limitations. Not fulfilling the desire, but setting limits to the desire. We all see that there are too few limitations, for instance, in the use of the internet and cell phone. Or just the fact that children get obese. Now, there is a second edition of my book on the father, an updated version. In Italy we have an expression which is "*il mammo*" that is "the father-mother." So, there is some compensation occurring, more attention being paid to it. Young fathers are more present, but they are not fulfilling the psychological principle of the missing father. They are good helpers of the mother, they are "good enough mothers" in Winnicottian terms. Now I have addressed that, of course, also with Andrew [Samuels], but it does not yet fill this big hole. Another role is typically more of the containing, particularly with male adolescent children. Traditionally, there was a father there placing limits. For instance, researchers have found that the south of Italy is the decisive recruiting region for the Mafia. When you don't have enough of the father, then the Mafia will go and recruit its soldiers from there because it is very easy to recruit them from families where there is no father.

LTP: And what do you think is the impact in the case of gay marriages?

LZ: It's another issue to address. For me, it's just like this. I can certainly insert that in my ideas about the father, because I am speaking of a *father principle*, a psychological principle. In the book, I put in a footnote, a terrible, impressive sentence from a patient of mine who said, "The traditional father of the family [she was thinking about her grandfather] was a tyrant, but he was a father. The average worker or middle-class father is an idiot sitting in front of television." That is, the absent father does not necessarily have to do with the divorced father or runaway fathers. It has to do with their . . .

LTP: Lack of energy?

LZ: About the rejection of the role of father, giving up your responsibility because you don't want to enter into trouble with your children. You don't want to quarrel with the children and it's not a solution to have the "*mammo*." It's very good to have the "*mammo*." I have done the changing of the diapers because nowadays very often both parents have to work and then you alternate. But that does not fill up the vacuum, the empty, problematic space of these secondary functions of the typical father. So, once again, this father principle can be present in a gay couple, although it's difficult. But if you look clearly, it is sometimes there with a gay couple but not present in a heterosexual couple, where the father is just giving up his role because he wants to be quiet and . . .

LTP: Buy time . . .

LZ: Yes. You have seen those people.

LTP: Yes.

LZ: Is very typical in Italy. But coming back to your question, it varies greatly because it's one thing for a gay couple with an adopted child in San Francisco, where there is a significant proportion of gay intellectuals, and the atmosphere in a Sicilian village, in the south of Italy, where the mentality is still quite traditional. So, the family can be relatively complete if you have a maternal principle and a paternal principle, but the problem arises when the child goes to school; there can be quite a bit of bullying from the other children. I think very often parents are egocentric. They want the child because it's a prosthesis, the child is an extension of their identity, and very often that is frankly quite egocentric. Also for women; sometimes she wants a child at any price because having the child becomes her identity. For instance, once I refused to take a woman into analysis who was a lesbian. She was single and said, "I now am trying to go to bed with, to make love with, this guy who is a good friend in order to become pregnant, because then I will have a child." I said, "Look, I have written about the father. I studied the subject so much, I am afraid of my own countertransference in this case." I liked her as a person. She was a nice person. She came to me because of something we had in common. I said, "This is a risk because I might project something negative, because I am sort of convinced on this issue. Sorry, but this is part of my life. It has been a long part of my life also because of my personal life, the study of the father. The fact that you dismissed from the very beginning, the presence of a father in the life of this child, to me, there is something wrong with this. So, I invite you to reconsider for a moment this decision, or to go into analysis with some colleague who accepts this. I am afraid of my own reactions."

LTP: Thank you for sharing this experience. Do you think that the father subject is connected, in any way, with another favorite subject of yours – paranoia?

LZ: Apparently paranoia could be considered more masculine because what I consider is paranoia in conflicts, in politics and in war. But in reality it is also feminine. For instance, in families, in jealousy, there is a lot of paranoia, a lot of projection onto other woman, for instance. It is universal.

LTP: What contributed to your interest in paranoia?

LZ: I say it's the fact that I was living in New York during the attacks of September 11th [2001]. It was not specifically the events of September 11th, but the reaction on September 12th, the paranoia among people. The fact is, I was always engaged a bit in politics, as a subject. I am not politically active. I don't like political fights. I don't like politics in Italy. I was never part of a political party, but I don't think the solution is to remain at home and not care, because there are then disasters.

However, I should complete the story that I started to tell you. After the Catholic school, where I was quite unhappy, and I was telling you I was good at school until the first year of high school, when I was sixteen. Then I met the sister of a school comrade and I fell in love the first time, and then, in school, I fell from the best to the worst, because I was . . .

LTP: Madly in love?

LZ: Yes, for a short while. It was very serious for me. But later, she didn't notice me. Much later, I was not interested anymore. But this girl persecuted me, following me the rest of her life. But I understood how serious the problem was, and I never completely forgave the school for only admitting boys. But also for never mentioning dating, we had no education in this. Also, my parents for never talking about the subject, as if this enormous part of life did not exist.

LTP: So, until you were sixteen.

LZ: Well, we started having parties and getting to know girls. Then I saw that it was easier if girls were also interested in me. It was not usual to have a premarital sexual relationship, but I had some flirtations. The same at university. At university, I chose economics because of the family factory, and because of my father. I was the first son and I felt the expectations. Nobody obligated me to that choice; theoretically I was free to choose myself, but I had introjected that idea. Also, most of my colleagues, my school comrades, went into the same university, Bacconi University, which is actually the only Italian university ranked in the top one hundred universities of the world.

LTP: When did you graduate?

LZ: I graduated university in 1967. I finished school in 1962 and there I had an episode which might interest you because it's very similar to something that Jung tells in his *Face to Face* interview. . . . It's a bit ridiculous, being a private school, the commission examining us for the state exam was . . ..

LTP: External?

LZ: Yes, an external state commission. The professor of Italian literature was, of course, an outsider and a very difficult, very neurotic man. He was a retired professor and a veteran of World War I, where he had been wounded. He was very clearly one of those veterans who was from the army of Mussolini. They all became very fascist. . . . The veterans of World War I were practically the backbone of the Fascist party.

But as I said, I liked to write and I usually always had good grades. They would give you a theme to write on, typically it had a rather rigid focus. I would prefer more open themes, but I was also good at that . . .

LTP: Composition?

LZ: Composition, yes. Usually they gave us the whole morning and, unlike the mathematics test, the professor did not check on us or even went away. So we simply had to leave him the test when we finished. I was among the last, but I would only write in the last hour, if four or five hours were allotted over the morning. I would only start at the end when there was almost nobody left anymore. It was silent and I could concentrate on writing and not correcting. I did not do what was usual then, to make a draft and then the final version. I would write directly because I was concentrating and writing, knowing the sentence beforehand and not correcting my writing after it was on the page. But when we had the state exam, it was compulsory to give the commission both the official copy and my draft with the corrections. I thought, "Oh my God, what do I do?" because I was used to working in a different manner. So I did the reverse. I did the official one and then recopied it into a draft, and the professor saw that they were identical. He said, this would deserve the best note, but evidently it was not mine, because there were no corrections. Which is exactly what Jung said about a fight he had with a professor who would not believe a completed assignment was his work, although for Jung it was not in the final exam at the school. I think I had to repeat an exam in the autumn session but then I passed. That was very frustrating and I remember my aunt, the intellectual writer, said, "That's the first injustice of your life. But to become a grown-up, an adult, one has to go through some injustices. You have to learn." Somehow she understood that I was too protected by my parents, and she said, "You will overcome."

LTP: Coming back to the graduation from university . . .

LZ: Yes . . . I had gone to study economics. Because of the business of my father and most of my comrades that were in the milieu of my school went there. I've lost contact with all of them now, because it was this bourgeois milieu in business, which I was not interested in. In the end, I did a dissertation in sociology, not in economics. There was a new professor there, and they had added sociology as a subject, although I had already taken all the exams. So it was not possible for me to pass an exam in sociology, but they had introduced it as a discipline. So I could choose a dissertation in this field. This was a very different professor because, coming from sociology, he was more leftist in comparison to what was Italy in those times, rather like those times in 1967, less rigid. He gave me Charles Wright Mills to study, who was then the chief ideologist of the American students movement, sort of an American Marxist, although today to speak of an American Marxist that does not make sense. Herbert Marcuse and Charles Wright Mills were the focus of the dissertation. Then the professor asked me to enter an institute of sociology. Sociology was starting in Italy and psychology as well. They didn't exist before. Otherwise, I would have studied sociology or psychology, but they didn't exist when I entered. It was the year between 1967 and 1968 and all the other assistants, instead of staying in the institute, were often in the streets and clashing with the police. I shared some of my ideas. I came from a privileged family, I thought it was right to re-examine society and share more of the economic power. But I was not an extrovert, I could not go and throw stones.

LTP: Maybe you also had sins and you cannot raise the stone and [throw it].

LZ: Sure, I had seen it and I didn't like it. I saw blood in the streets. I didn't see killing, but I saw the blood from somebody who had been killed by a grenade from the police, because then the police answered with tear gas. But then, of course, in the students movement, some started saying, "Oh, it's a plot." Then I started being interested in paranoia and the associated delusions.

LTP: No, but I'm saying not seen, like s-e-e-n, but you have sin, like Jesus said, "He who is without sin cast the first stone."

LZ: For me, it wasn't amusing. . . . In one of the protest movements, maybe the only one I had really participated in, we were supposed to shout certain slogans. The slogan, they were usually actually quite stupid, because they would speak of "*Coscienza*" [Consciousness] and actually with slogans you become more unconscious, you belong to the mass. But anyhow, the slogans were very simple, like one said: "*Padroni*" [Master].

LTP: Padrone?

LZ: Padrone, yeah, but *padre et padrone* [father and master] there was another slogan, "*padroni, borghesi, ancora pochi mesi*" [Capitalists and bourgeois, you are left with only a few months]. When the movement merged with the armed Red Brigades, it wasn't play anymore. They also started killing.

LTP: But you were a bourgeois.

LZ: I said, "First my father, my grandfather, they are 'padrone' and they are nice people, like I don't want it . . . but I, myself, I should have only a few months of life and they should be killed? Are you nuts? I cannot shout that. I cannot shout that."

LTP: *Padroni, borghesi, ancora pochi mesi!* [Capitalists and bourgeois, you are left with only a few months].

LZ: Yes. You will have only a few months and then you are over, which implies . . . we will kill you . . . destroy you.

LTP: This is a slogan that you would not say?

LZ: Yes, a slogan of 1968!

LTP: A powerful statement of your attitude! To be aligned with yourself, with whom you really were. You did not say that, but what did you say to your kids? What is one of the lessons that you taught them?

LZ: Oh, I didn't give lessons. I hate it. Let's say from the Catholic church and then from the communists, which for me are too widespread in Italy because it's another monolithic institution, you know, a mono-party. Mono-parties that are quite similar to, frankly, the structure of the Catholic church, both hold with one truth above all else. That is the opposite of individuation. So, I never gave my children principles, but I tried to give them, to share with them, some interests I had. So, for instance, I would read to all three of them, although two are from my first marriage and because it was a difficult divorce, it was difficult to keep . . .

LTP: Contact?

LZ: But I was very present as a father. I manage to have more and more time with them.

LTP: What were their ages when you divorced?

LZ: Stefano was six and Sarah was not even in kindergarten, she was one and half years old. They were very young. But in terms of the relationship with Eva, she accepted them and they accepted her. There was a lot of interrelationship.

LTP: And the next one . . . the third one is with Eva?

LZ: Yes, her name is Elisabeth. With all of them, I read *The Iliad*, *The Odyssey*, and *The Aeneid* and a lot of classic literature and mythology. Not just because I am a Jungian, but because I like them. These works are among the infrequent good memories of my school years; we studied them a lot in high school. We studied a lot of Latin and Greek and classical myths. So I read a lot of these with my children and even when they wanted to watch something, but I didn't let them watch television. Instead, we rented specific movies on VHS cassettes with historical themes. Then we could discuss them and make a bit of a home cinema club.

LTP: Are you also a grandfather now?

LZ: No. Although Stephano, the first one I had, now has bought an apartment and he will live with a girl and he's turning forty. So . . .

LTP: It is time.

LZ: Yes, I think it will happen . . .

LTP: Who was your analyst, if you can say?

LZ: Sure. His name was Rudolf Michel. He died long ago, although he was relatively young when he died. He was an analysand of Jolande Jacobi, and he was responsible for the archives, for the drawings, paintings, which he inherited from Jolande Jacobi. So, as a man it's compulsory to also do some analysis with a woman analyst. So, I tried analyzing with Jacobi because he had analyzed with her, but I didn't have a good relationship. She was too much of an *animus* for me. And then, I analyzed with Liliane Frey-Rohn, who is also well-known.

LTP: And how did you come to arrive in psychoanalysis, mostly Jungian analysis?

LZ: When I was studying economics, in sociology I started becoming curious about political movements. Then, when I was in the institute of sociology, I began reading psychoanalysis. But I didn't want to go and throw stones at the police. Do you know the name Pier Paolo Pasolini?

LTP: No.

LZ: He was one of the most famous Italians of that time and also a movie director and a poet. He was a very funny mix because he was Catholic, a leftist, and, I think, a member of the Communist party, although he was always quarreling with the Communist party. He wrote a long poem, criticizing the students movement. Then I felt understood. He said, "You young people throwing stones at the police, but look at their background"; that is what I felt. There were poor people among the police, very often illiterate, coming from peasant families from the south of Italy. And we in Milan and Rome were from the bourgeoisie, intellectuals, you know, hurting those poor policemen who in the end, all turned into fascists somehow, because they hate these intellectual leftists. So it was interesting reading Pasolini . . . he had immense authority because he was respected and expressed what I felt, that is, that we were spoiled and had no right to be so anti-establishment and so violent.

LTP: As a Jungian analyst, we need to be both father and mother to our patients. What would you say to people who are now training or trying to make a career out of being a Jungian analyst? What impaired or helped you from your childhood, or your upbringing, to become what you are today?

LZ: What helped me was to be a bit of a fish out of water.

LTP: A fish out of water . . . ?

LZ: Yes. An introvert or an isolated black sheep, although I never was a black sheep in that sense of being a rebel. For my parents, for everybody, I was not rebellious, but a bit isolated, a bit different, a bit of a dreamer. That helped me. Those qualities made me suffer earlier. . . . But I must say, I discovered Jungian analysis by chance. If I am sincere, I went to Zurich because I wanted to go away and find something else. I had read Freud, not much Jung. Just *Psychology and Religion* without understanding much. But I agreed with Jung's idea that religion is not, like in Freud, an overstructure. For Freud, religion is an overstructure, like for Marx it is an overstructure. The reality for Marx is the economy; for Freud it is the sexual instinct and that is over everything. No, religion is, in reality, itself very important. This I got from Jung but only very vaguely. I cannot say I understood. What also helped me was relatively good economic conditions. The fact is that my parents were very scared by my choice, but they said, "Okay, we will pay for those studies," but I said, "No Papa, I don't want you to give me lots of money every month." Because I have brothers, I also said, "I don't want to use the money that is for them. You give me, like in the gospels, in anticipation of my inheritance, just the part enough to finish the studies in Zurich. I want you to deduct that." In the end he accepted. I wanted more responsibility. My parents did not understand. I saw this as a basic principle of individuation. Also, because I went to Zurich when I was very young. I was twenty-five and had never worked, never being independent. So, I thought it was a very important step towards becoming independent.

LTP: And you worked in Zurich?

LZ: No. Later I came back to Zurich and I worked for years at the clinic in Zurich, because I wanted more involvement in the medical world coming from a background with health. My mother was a medical doctor, and my father was in medicine, so I worked four years in the clinic in Zurich. This was after the diploma, I went back to Zurich in 1975 and there was a position. I had finished my studies at the institute in 1974.

LTP: What was your final paper on?

LZ: It was a comparison between Freud and Jung. The idea of the self being more balanced, instead of the ego . . . frankly I don't remember clearly. What I remember is that after I took the propedeuticum examinations, I had already begun to see patients. So that was only after one and a half years. I was twenty-six, because then it was three semesters, not four semesters. Later it became two years. So, I started taking on patients, and I immediately had a lot of patients in both Milan and Zurich. So, every week I was commuting back and forth and seeing patients. So I went back to my father and said, "I still have more than half of the money you gave me."

LTP: You were a good accountant.

LZ: Because I was already independent.

LTP: Were you married by then?

LZ: No, no, I was twenty-six. I married one and a half years later. That was quite a disaster because it was a marriage into a very bourgeois family.

LTP: It was arranged?

LZ: No, no. I met this girl and I chose her, but she was very linked to her family, and it immediately went wrong. Immediately she went into analysis to try to recover the marriage and she studied at the Jung Institute. That was my first wife. So, somehow, it was also a conversion for her, but she was from a more quiet family.

LTP: She was an analyst?

LZ: She died. She became an analyst and was the mother of my first two children. But she used to smoke intensely and sadly she developed lung cancer. Anyhow, I was telling you this example because I was only twenty-six and the studies were expensive. But having patients, I could pay for the studies and live in both in Zurich and Milan without problem. So I offered to my father back more than half of the money, which I still had.

LTP: He accepted?

LZ: No, he was very moved and said, "I am very happy to leave it."

LTP: A lot of young men don't take on this level of responsibility. How did you become so responsible?

LZ: I don't know if I am so responsible . . .

LTP: You were!

LZ: You must ask the little one, Elisabeth, she was born in 1989. She has a critical sense and she's half-Italian and half-German. When I was writing about the father, she once famously said, "This one (pointing her finger at my door when I was in the office; not with patients, but writing), this one who, instead of being here, helping me with my homework, he is there writing about the good father." She was a small child, but with a very good sense of criticism and a sense of humor. That's the sense of humor she used to tell me that I am not so responsible; I was speaking and writing about responsibility and the good father, but I was doing what interested me.

LTP: What career did she pursue?

LZ: She is still switching between many types of studies. She will probably become a teacher. She studied literature for five years in Germany with very good results, both literature and translation. But then she saw that it's too difficult to make a living just doing translation, because they are very badly paid and you are isolated as a professional, so she wants to become a teacher.

LTP: Thank you very much for your time and generosity of sharing all these things with us. I am really glad that you believed in this project.

LZ: This is a historical work and it will remain.

Chapter 18

Coming Into Being

AN INTERVIEW WITH MARK WINBORN, PHD

LTP: As we arrive at the end of our work on this book, what are your thoughts and feelings now?

MW: I am struck by how the development of this book parallels the individuation process. The life of this volume began twelve years ago when you were captivated by the urge to conduct interviews with the analysts you were encountering during your training as a candidate in the IAAP Router program and while participating in classes at the C.G. Jung Institute in Zurich/Küsnacht.

LTP: Do you remember how we met?

MW: Yes, very well. You attended some of my classes at the Institute around 2014. We maintained intermittent email contact after that, and I was delighted to be present when you were certified as a diplomate Jungian analyst in 2016 at the IAAP International Congress in Kyoto, Japan.

LTP: That was a very important moment of my life, indeed! And also a very important moment for me was when we started our work editing this book . . .

MW: It was 2019 when you contacted me with this proposal to collaborate with you in editing a book containing the interviews you had collected. At the time I thought it would be a relatively quick and simple process. As with many experiences in life, the project did not unfold quite as I expected. I initially thought we would easily complete the book within a year; an assumption that was much too optimistic.

LTP: We had our "pains" in the process . . .

MW: Yes, we had to work through disagreements over how various elements of the book and interactions with the interviewees should be handled. However, working through these disagreements led to greater trust and mutual appreciation in our relationship. At other times, reaching the interviewees for final approval of their text was difficult and, in some instances, they had changed their minds about their interviews being published.

LTP: Also, the COVID-19 pandemic erupted . . .

MW: . . . and threw the world into uncertainty and chaos just as we were entering the main process of compiling and editing the interviews. But in many

DOI:10.4324/9781003148937-19

respects, such a circuitous path mirrors the path of individuation. But, as the stories in this book attest, we rarely end up where our conscious attitude anticipates or plans for. We are pulled off course in one direction or another, thinking it is the "right" direction, only to find that the path did not lead us where we thought it would. The circumstances of life – such as war, social standing, financial hardship, cultural traditions, and opportunities lost and gained – all shape our individuation paths, much like the unpredictable experiences of the main character Santiago in Paulo Coelho's *The Alchemist*.

LTP: In your view, what is the backbone of this book?

MW: Co-editing your interviews renewed and deepened my appreciation of Jung's concept of individuation and my recognition that there is a uniquely personal path that drew each of these individuals into relationship with Jung, analytical psychology, and analysis. It prompted me to reflect on my own path into this world, a path that has shaped my entire adult life.

LTP: Did you find anything in common with the other interviewees?

MW: Like many of the interviewees, I had no conscious plan to become a Jungian psychoanalyst, yet when I look back at the unfolding of my life, I can see all the subtle (and not-so-subtle) influences which guided me towards this path.

LTP: Could you expand on this, starting with your beginnings?

MW: I grew up in a household of readers – we all read widely and voraciously – which naturally opened worlds I would never have imagined on my own. My father was a university professor and a man of curiosity. He had doctoral students from a wide variety of countries who often visited us at our house, exposing me to cultures I would not otherwise have encountered. My parents also valued traveling to other parts of the world, and I was fortunate to spend an academic year, when I was fifteen, living in other countries and cultures: an experience which shaped me in ways I wouldn't recognize until much later. Despite these experiences, as an adolescent and young adult I had little idea about who I wanted to "become" in life. When I went to university, I had no sense of what I wanted to study. I choose "general business administration" as a major area of study simply by default, assuming that there would be employment of some kind following my studies. During my first year at university, I "accidently" stumbled into the Army Reserve Officers Training Corps and was immediately captivated by the sense of adventure, physical demands, and structure of the program. At the same time, I changed my university major to criminal justice because several of my new friends in Army ROTC indicated it was an "easy" major that would allow me more time for ROTC training activities. During this period, I aspired to become an infantry officer in the Army, and I excelled in that environment. In the summers, I attended the Army Airborne and Air Assault Schools, learning to parachute out of airplanes and jets and performing combat rappelling from helicopters from two hundred feet [sixty meters] above the ground. It was all very exciting to me, and I was fully identified with and emotionally invested in the archetype of the warrior.

LTP: As often happens in the individuation process, psyche had other plans for you . . .

MW: Indeed. Midway through my third year at university I fell into a serious depression, and I began neglecting my ROTC activities and the studies for my criminal justice major. At twenty-one years old, the only thing that seemed obvious to me was that I needed to change my major at the university.

LTP: And you did . . .

MW: After a frantic search to identify a new major, it turned out that psychology was the only major in the entire university that I could transfer into and still graduate on time. My father was a psychologist, so naturally I didn't want to follow in his footsteps!

LTP: Naturally . . . and still . . . ?

MW: Despite my reservations, I did transfer into psychology and immediately fell in love with the material in those classes. Quickly, I realized I needed, and wanted, to go to graduate school to obtain my PhD in psychology. Despite having a late start in the study of psychology, I was accepted into several programs, and the Army permitted me to take a four-year delay, to complete the PhD following my university graduation, prior to entering active military service.

LTP: What happened after completing your PhD?

MW: I knew I wanted to be a psychologist, but I had no idea what kind of psychologist I wanted to be or what kind of psychology I wanted to practice. Again, psyche provided a guiding hand. I needed to complete a one-year clinical psychology internship following the PhD. There were four internship sites available to me in the Army medical system, and I carefully screened each of them, ultimately deciding upon William Beaumont Army Medical Center in El Paso, Texas. The internship faculty, all Army psychologists, were incredibly warm and supportive. During the first day of orientation there, the faculty asked the interns, "Who do you want to be as a psychologist?" I panicked momentarily because I did not know how to answer the question, even though it seemed like I should have an answer. The faculty said to all of us, "Don't worry. You don't need to know today. But by the end of this internship, we want you to have an idea of who you want to be as a psychologist. And we will do everything in our power to help you discover what that is for you."

LTP: So, they kept their word!

MW: Incredibly, they held true to their word and supported every reasonable request the interns made of them. Through one of the faculty members, I became exposed to Jung's writing.

LTP: And what were your first impressions related to Jung's writings?

MW: Almost immediately I knew this was what I needed and wanted to do. Soon after, I entered my first psychotherapy with the psychologist who had exposed me to Jung's writing.

LTP: And how did life unfold for you from that point on?

MW: Upon completion of my clinical internship, the subtle hand of psyche again guided my next transition when I received my first Army duty assignment to become the staff psychologist at the US Army Military Academy at West Point, New York. For the next three years I lived and worked about forty-five minutes north of New York City. While at West Point, the staff officers I worked with at the mental health center were also very supportive of my interest in analytical psychology and psychoanalysis – always being flexible with scheduling when I needed to be away for analytic training activities. The proximity to New York City allowed me to enter my first analysis with a Jungian analyst, and I was able to begin taking classes in analytical psychology at the New York Jung Foundation and begin a year-long period of study with Don Kalsched at the Institute for Depth Psychology in Rye, New York. I greatly value the experiences I had in the Army, experiences which laid a valuable foundation of self-experience that I still draw from daily. After fulfilling my obligation as an Army officer, I returned to Memphis, Tennessee, in 1990 to enter private practice.

LTP: And your formal journey as a Jungian, how did it start and, afterwards, developed?

MW: I was formally accepted as a candidate to train as a Jungian analyst in 1993, and I graduated in 1999. There have been many other synchronicities and developments since then that have shaped who I've become as a person and as a Jungian psychoanalyst. I have had many more opportunities to teach, publish, present, travel, and form relationships than I could have ever imagined. The journey has carried me further than I thought was possible. Along the way, individuals of generous spirit saw potential in me that I hadn't yet seen in myself. Almost daily, I am deeply surprised by and grateful for the turns my journey has taken (and continues to take). All these experiences have reinforced for me the deep reality of the individuation process; a process that we are privileged to live into but cannot "know" in advance.

LTP: I am grateful that you accepted my invitation to co-edit this book. Even if both of us experienced working on this book as a wonderful, fulfilling experience, would you say that there was a special feeling or discovery you had while editing the interviews?

MW: One of the most moving and memorable images in this book appears in the interview with Dvora Kutzinski. As a young woman she was interred in a Nazi concentration camp during WWII. She shares a memory of being marched across the train tracks to the crematorium with her friend Magda. On the way to the crematorium Magda spotted a sewing needle lying on the ground and bent to pick it up. Dvora said, "Magda, where we are going, you won't need it. Throw it away!" Magda said, "You never know!" When Dvora and her friend Magda arrived at the crematorium, they were told the crematorium had too many people to process and they were sent back to their barracks. The next day they, without further explanation, were placed on a train and transported to another concentration camp. Dvora concluded the story saying, "The needle served us until the end." This small vignette from Dvora's astonishing story illustrates so beautifully the idiosyncratic, nuanced, tumultuous, synchronistic turns that mark each individuation process. Most importantly, the story illustrates the prospective aspect of the psyche that sees beyond the limits of our conscious perceptions.

LTP: It was, indeed, very moving for me too.

MW: Still, each of the stories in this volume illustrate the curious task of attempting to discern and follow one's individuation process. Each story also underscores the deeply practical utility of Jung's concept of individuation – our "coming into being."

LTP: A closing statement from you, Mark?

MW: I am grateful to you, Lavinia, for having the foresight to capture these stories and for your invitation to participate in crafting of this book. The journey continues.

Chapter 19

Beyond Conclusions

A Bridge Over Time

Lavinia Țânculescu-Popa

The idea of this book came to me after meeting so many fascinating people and feeling unable to keep these encounters just to myself. This is a collection of precious meetings that I deeply wanted to share with other people. I believe strongly in the existence of eternal time, sacred time. I think that we are all part of that *illo tempore*, even if the reality of it is sometimes blurred by our ordinary vision. However, if we close our eyes for a second, the innocence of childhood can resurface inside us, just as morning comes when the sun resumes its daily journey across the sky. In that time, we are all children again, and the sound of it echoes within us. We taste grandmother's desserts, hear the birds chirping in the grove or some occasional scolding from grown-ups, we feel blood trickling down our leg after grazing a knee, or bruise an elbow during a fall as we run through the woods while playing hide-and-seek. It is a time before we learn to reproach ourselves for shortcoming, when we still feel the vibrations of the universe at our core. Everything seems amplified and incomprehensible, yet memorable, leaving an indelible mark on our being.

Beyond the persona, it can be quiet and peaceful, a quiet that makes our ears ring if we listen to it patiently. Or there is darkness; a darkness across which there can be budding light if we wait long enough. This is similar to the feeling of childhood. It is like the smile of children, the clinking of bells, unadulterated joy, yet easily disrupted if interrupted by a slap on the face: from home, from school, from life, an alcoholic parent, war, inflated egos, poverty, neglect, racism, bullying, disease, death – all slaps. . . . Slaps that contribute to the growth of another layer of skin over the sensitive skin we already possess, "a second skin" that steels us, prepares us to face reality, injustice, betrayal, and the bittersweet taste that is also part of life.

We close our eyes and we are children again. We see familiar landmarks, ones that have guided us all our lives. If we reach within ourselves, we realize that this guidance is intended for us and has been inside us for a long time already. This inner wisdom is where direction and potential security are available. With this connection we can create, dream, and become a part of those dreams. As we grow, especially from within, we have the possibility of becoming a landmark for others, forming an axis of the world. And on this axis, there is all that we are. That is how this book came to be. These figures, these axes of the world that we look up to, it is from their stories of becoming that this book emerged.

DOI:10.4324/9781003148937-20

These pages are a record of lives. We don't know when we begin the Great Journey, we are not really aware when our "lives" begin: whether it is inside our mother's womb, or inside our parents' thoughts, or during adolescence. Our parents are our creators, at least in part. God notwithstanding, we are the children of our time, we bear the weight of it. These are moments and memories that could have been caught on film, whether silent, black-and-white, or color, but their stories poignantly document their world, both inner and outer. This book is a collection of frames or snapshots from inner worlds. The narrative camera is rolling for the readers, showing part of home movies from their lives before professional personas emerged, showing what was never reported before. Capturing in text pictures that might otherwise be lost in time.

"Tell me a snapshot, a glimpse from your childhood that has stayed with you forever," this is what I usually ask my patients in our preliminary sessions as well as the interviewees in this book. Sometimes it is a dream of what might have been, what they might have become, a dream they have had, or perhaps a dream from the caregivers at their side. Perhaps they carry a dream of their ancestors, which moved into their psyche outside their awareness. I also ask these wonderful people I have interviewed to provide the reader a journey through time, reaching back to the beginnings of their lives: a whiff of perfume; the warmth of sunshine; a toy; the joy or cry of a child; the arms of a mother; the sound of a car; the attention, presence, or absence of a father; the way in which a love for the people around them was born. These memories have a way of coming together . . . and forming a story. What a great privilege I experienced in hearing about the creation of their lives in these interviews; people who have been assisting at the psychological birth of others for decades!

It is a gift to hear about the birth of "the psychological *individual*" (Jung 1971, para. 757),[1] how they navigated different directions as they moved away from family and cultural norms that did not adequately define them. Also, hearing about the beginnings of the ongoing process of individuation by which they came to know and define their own inner norm, their voice, their path that guided them along avenues that were truer and closer to their own selves. This birth is clearly not possible outside "more intense and broader collective relationships and not in isolation" (CW6, §758). I spoke with my interviewees about all these connections with as much open-mindedness and understanding and with as much of a lack of prejudice as I could manage. Some of these secrets or private moments chose not to be told, while some were only hinted at, only being partially revealed in the glint of an eye or a meaningful glance.

Other things were the topic of longer talks. While touching upon these subjects, the atmosphere of past times was resurrected. I had forgotten how long I could talk about queuing up for bread or milk as I used to when I was a child – standing in a line for four or five hours at 4 or 5 in the morning – until I heard stories about unspeakable atrocities in the Nazi concentration camps, about the horrors of racist segregation in the United States of the 1940s, about the echoes of World War II in an as yet undecided Italy or in a defeated Germany, the impact of colonialist power such as the UK, or a still warring Israel. All of these world events were hidden from me against the background of my childhood in gray communist Romania. Yet my life was also marked by children's smiles, clear and crisp as the ringing of a bell, sometimes occasioned by a first suit of clothes, a first hat, a first set of paint brushes, a first fishing trip, a first collection of books, so much so that I again realized how rich one's childhood is, with all its small joys readily evolving into important landmarks in one's life. Do you know what I mean?

Truth be told, I have listened to many more life stories than those included in this collection that were also impressive to me. Apart from the stories that were not available for public reading, there are other overlapping stories of those that paved the road so that the stories included in this volume could be conveyed to the readers: whether they were parents, educators, important figures in the lives of my analysts, or of my parents, my teachers (my deepest thanks go to my three very important professors in my high school and university training as a psychologist: Professor Lucica Dandu, Professor Mihaela Minulescu, PhD, and Professor Horia Pitariu, PhD), the people around me who have inspired me to become what I have become, and therefore able to ask these questions. The stories told are as authentic as could be, however indirect they might turn out to be. I wonder how long it will be until we all realize that we are all in the same field of experience, that there is only *Unus Mundus*, that suffering and joy felt by one are felt by all? I hope that there will come a time when this will be as easy as it is to look upon blooming trees and realize that spring has returned. Perhaps when we realize that our inner territories are eternally connected, we will see that our individuality, the need to be special individuals, unique and separated, will not seem as important as our shared, interconnected experience. Then we can begin clearing the paths within ourselves to see and experience our connections with others, for seeing those paths is a first step in seeing what step to take to avoid choosing the end of the world.

I would like to express my heartfelt thanks and deep appreciation to all those persons included in the volume for having accepted to reminisce with me so we could forge a unique story, yet a collective narrative that deserves to be told. I would like to express my thanks and appreciation for the translation of the Introduction and Conclusion chapters, which I found easier and more natural to write in my mother tongue, but which were masterfully translated into English by University Professor Nadina Vişan, PhD. I would also like to express my thanks to Narcis Pintilie, the DTP designer, who generously, patiently, and extremely skillful helped us to obtain the graphic layout of the photos included in the book and all the people who have helped me transcribe some of the audio recordings over the years. My sincere thanks go to Mark Winborn, the co-editor of this volume, for having provided invaluable help in publishing this volume. Without you, Mark, maybe none of us would read these lines published today. My thanks also to the staff at Routledge for believing in this project!

Note

1 Jung, C.G. (1971). Psychological Types. Collected Works, Vol. 6. Princeton, NJ: Princeton University Press.

Index

For Product Safety Concerns and Information please contact our EU
representative GPSR@taylorandfrancis.com
Taylor & Francis Verlag GmbH, Kaufingerstraße 24, 80331 München, Germany